A. Sutzkever

A. Sutzkever

Selected Poetry and Prose

TRANSLATED FROM THE YIDDISH BY

Barbara and Benjamin Harshav

WITH AN INTRODUCTION BY BENJAMIN HARSHAV

UNIVERSITY OF CALIFORNIA PRESS
BERKELEY, LOS ANGELES, OXFORD

University of California Press
Berkeley and Los Angeles, California

University of California Press
Oxford, England

Copyright © 1991 by The Regents of the University of California

Library of Congress Cataloging-in-Publication Data
Sutzkever, Abraham, 1913–
    [Selections. English. 1991]
    A. Sutzkever : selected prose and poetry / translated from the Yiddish by Barbara and
    Benjamin Harshav ; with an introduction by Benjamin Harshav.
        p.   cm.
    ISBN 0-520-06539-5
    1. Sutzkever, Abraham, 1913–   —Translations, English.
I. Harshav, Barbara, 1940–   . II. Harshav, Benjamin, 1928–   . III. Title.
PJ5129.S86A24   1991
839'.0913—dc20   90-29174
                                                                                      CIP

Printed in the United States of America

1   2   3   4   5   6   7   8   9

Contents

Sutzkever: Life and Poetry

Poems from My Diary (1974–1985)

Twin Brother

PART ONE: POETRY

Blond Dawn (1934–1937)

Siberia (1936)

From the Forest (1937–1939)

from **Ecstasies**

Epilogue to the Forest (1939–1940)

Faces in Swamps (June–July 1941)

Written in Vilna Ghetto (1941–1943)

Three Roses

Partisan Forest (1943–1944)

Clandestine City (1945–1947)
(Episodes from the Epic Poem)

Resurrection (1945–1947)

In The Chariot of Fire (1947–1951)

Elephants at Night (1950–1954)
A Trip Through Africa, 1950

Blind Milton (1954–1962)

Square Letters and Miracles (1964–1967)

Zeykher Le-Ghetto

The Shard Hunters

Ripe Faces *(1968–1970)*

From Old and Young Manuscripts *(1935–1981)*

New Poems *(1987–1990)*

PART TWO: PROSE

Green Aquarium *(1953–1974)*

Where the Stars Spend the Night *(1975–1989)*

Postscript (1990)

Sutzkever: Life and Poetry

By Benjamin Harshav

I. Poetry and Its Contexts

Sutzkever is one of the great poets of the twentieth century. I do not say this lightly. He is not a philosophical poet; there was no sophisticated philosophy in Jewish culture. Nor is he a descriptive poet; the language of Modernism was opposed to description, and the fictional worlds of Sutzkever's poetry are presented through evocation and allusion rather than direct statement. But the language of his poetry—the profound sound orchestration and the metaphorical and mythopoeic imagery—is as dense, unmediated, and suggestive as that in the poetry of Mandelstam or Rilke. And his responses to historical reality are as sharp as any in the verse of Brecht. The paradoxical amalgam of these two extremes of twentieth-century poetry— self-focused poetic language and ideological *engagement*—is successful in Sutzkever's work because both are presented through the events of the poet's own biography. As he himself observed dryly, in a retrospective poem written at the age of seventy-five:

> Inside me, a twig of sounds sways toward me, as before.
> Inside me, rivers of blood are not a metaphor.
>
> ("Inside Me")

The twig of sounds is as tangible as the rivers of blood, both are swaying inside him as a budding branch in the spring; there is no ambivalence, but one, entwined, double source of poetic energy.

Three magic circles enclose Sutzkever's poetry, making it difficult for the contemporary reader to see his greatness: (1) the all but obscured, rich, literary Yiddish language; (2) the misleadingly private Jewish Holocaust;

and (3) his terrifying and exhilarating biography. I shall try briefly to evoke all three.

Sutzkever came to Yiddish literature in a moment of populist excitement with the earthy, idiomatic, folksy, often coarse, spoken Yiddish language, idealized in literature at the turn of the century by the satirical realist Mendele and the tragicomic imitator Sholem Aleichem, and reborn in the Expressionist poetry and fiction of the 1920s and in the social realism of the thirties. In this context, he strove to create exquisite aesthetic objects, as refined as music, as colorful and unreal as Expressionist nature painting, as rich and precise as the language of the Vilna Yiddish Scientific Institute. Sutzkever is an incomparable virtuoso of meter, rhyme, strophic forms, and ever-changing dynamic rhythmical patterns, forms that may seem obsolete to the contemporary English ear, but are nevertheless essential to much of Russian or German modern poetry. His is a "Neo-Classical Modernism," which combines the emphasis on well-designed strophic forms with a Modernist metaphorical poetic language and "unreal," mythopoeic fictional worlds.

Mallarmé said that a poet is not one who invents new words but one who invents new places for words. Sutzkever both invented words and found new places for them, new word-and-sound combinations. But the unmistakable precision and freshness of Sutzkever's Yiddish verse require a reader who would both know the rich, multilingual, and multilayered context of "juicy" Yiddish and could, at the same time, savor the effects of Modernist poetry. This great poet is only great as a poet can be: in the context of his own language. This is especially true for Modernist poetry, intensely invested in language innovation, rhythm, and sound orchestration.

The Holocaust seems to erect a barrier between Jewish writers and many non-Jewish readers, as if it were a private business of the Jews. But actually, in Sutzkever's poetry, it can be read as a focused close-up, a parable of the unbelievable times of this century, of human nature and dignity, of the inexplicable puzzles of existence and the palpable reality of extinction, and — through all this — of the beauty of observation, consciousness, and language.

The Holocaust dyes all of Sutzkever's writings but by no means does it absorb him entirely. From his very beginnings, the poet was marked by a curiosity about nature, a wish to merge with the vis-à-vis, as only a truly narcissist poet may have. His eye and ear for the colors and sounds of the icy blue roads of his childhood Siberia, the forests and swamps engraved by glaciers in the Lithuanian north, and the sand dunes and craters of the Israeli Negev, never let go.

Sutzkever wrote obsessively throughout the darkest times, hiding in a chimney or fighting in the swamps. Yet, his Holocaust theme gained depth with time, precisely because he was able to confront it from the base of another alternative of Jewish existence. Sutzkever is, at the same time, one of the great poets of Israel, of its nature and revival. Writing in Yiddish rather than Hebrew, he perceives the Israeli landscape as an intimate outsider, through the discourse of biblical scenes from his childhood imagination. A similar historical perspective marks his perception of the Holocaust, indeed of the totality of annihilation of a millennium-old European Jewry, as symbolized in the demise of its northern capital, Vilna, the "Jerusalem of Lithuania." In his world, the Holocaust is part of personal memory, steeped in those two years of hell, but it is never cut off from the larger view of Jewish past and future, as it is with some assimilated writers. The omnipresent, explicit or tacit, coexistence in his poetry of the alternative domains of Jewish history—Vilna, the Bible, Israel, the Destruction, and rebirth— places each theme in a multiple perspective. They seem to be mirrored in one another. And then, all are reflected again in the other, intimate mirroring between his lyrical I and his imaginary "Twin Brother" (see the poem by this name), his slaughtered self over there and his unbelievably surviving writing self now.

II. Jerusalem of Lithuania

The myths and meanings of Jewish culture and beliefs are not embodied in godlike persons but are anchored in space. The moral and narrative story of the Bible focuses on the relationship between a people and their God, as dramatized in the recurrent loss of and return to their promised land. The prophets predict and mourn the downfall of Jerusalem, the "Faithful City" that became like a "whore." And the most family-oriented holiday, the Passover Seder, produces a narrative performance symbolizing the myth of exile and return to the land as the very essence of Jewish existence. It concludes with the wish to be "Next year in Jerusalem." Jerusalem became the spatial metonymy for the ethical, cultural, and spiritual being of the people and their link to an abstract, all-encompassing God. By calling a city in Northeastern Europe "Jerusalem of Lithuania," they assigned to it the symbolic locus, the spatial base for a transformed Diaspora culture and consciousness.

Jews appeared in central Europe at the beginning of the Christian Era. Others moved up from the Byzantine Empire to Eastern Europe and apparently spoke Slavic languages. We do not know when individual Jews migrated to or through Lithuania but their settlements there are documented from the fourteenth century on. In the sixteeenth century, an influx of Jews from Germany enlarged the Jewish population and spread the Yiddish language.

Lithuania, the last pagan country in Europe, was a grand duchy ruling over a vast area of forests, rivers, and swamps, stretching from Prussia to the periphery of Moscow and from the Baltic almost to the Black Sea, including what are today Lithuania proper, all of Byelorussia, southern Latvia, parts of Russia and Poland, and the Ukraine (later ceded to Poland). In 1322, Grand Duke Gediminas (in Polish, Giedymin) built his new capital Vilnius (in Polish, Wilno) on the banks of the river Vilya. In 1386, Giedymin's grandson married the Queen of Poland and merged the two dynasties. Lithuania accepted Christianity and eventually entered into a formal union with Poland in 1569. Lithuanian aristocrats and intellectuals assimilated to Polish culture and a Polish language university was founded in Vilna in 1803. The great Polish Romantic poet, Adam Mickiewicz, and the Nobel Prize Laureate, Czeslaw Milosz, both "Lithuanians" by origin, were connected with the city and the area (see Milosz's memoirs *Native Realm*). Vilna became both a Polish and a Jewish cultural center.

The Jews of Poland and Lithuania created an autonomous state within a state. The "Council of the State of Lithuania" was a kind of Jewish autonomous parliament. The four "Principal Cities" of Jewish Lithuania, Vilna among them, had jurisdiction over dozens of smaller towns, and those, in turn, ruled over Jews scattered in many villages. They dominated the entire Jewish population, imposed religious rules, and collected taxes for the Jewish communities and for the king. A network of social, cultural, and religious institutions—schools, synagogues, printing houses, books, professional synagogues or unions, hospitals, and philanthropies—covered all aspects of life (except for power and territory). The Jews were the only ethnic group in Europe not divided into official classes, or castes. The social and linguistic gaps between Byelorussian peasants, Polish magnates, and the German- or Polish-speaking citizens, and between all of them and Western Europe, did not exist among the Jews. They belonged to one extraterritorial network, speaking and writing their private two languages — Hebrew of the texts and Yiddish for daily life. It was a network reinforced by a private universe of discourse with an intensive code of beliefs, behavior, and texts, dominated by the totality of a separate religion. Hence it was natural for the Jews to move between those tightly closed classes and nationalities — from the countryside to the small towns, to the cities, and overseas, and vice versa — facilitating trade and spreading crafts and artifacts. It was a network with no boundaries and the ties of Vilna to all corners of the empire as well as to Western European communities were manifold.

Vilna became a famous center of learning, first rabbinical, then secular. "Lithuanian" rabbis and teachers spread throughout the Jewish world. In the eighteenth century, this central role was symbolized by the towering figure of the Vilna Gaon ("genius") (1720–1797). He dominated all of Lithuania and stopped the spread of the Hassidic movement in the name of the "Misnagdim," who based their Jewishness on learning. Religious academies ("Yeshivas") were founded in small Lithuanian towns, such as Volozhin, Mir, Slobodka, and Navaredok. In 1795, after the second partition of Poland, Vilna was incorporated into Russia. When only two rabbinical seminars were allowed in all of Russia, one was established in Vilna and later became a teacher's seminar. Of the two permitted Jewish printing houses, one was in Vilna, the famous house of Rom, which executed the formidable task of printing the whole Babylonian Talmud (in highly complex page designs) as well as hundreds of books in Hebrew and Yiddish.

We must remember that the population numbers throughout the period were small. It is estimated that in 1650, about 350,000 Jews lived in all of Eastern Europe. In 1765, 3,887 Jews were counted in Vilna proper. At the outbreak of World War II, in 1939, only 60,000 Jews lived in the city (in a general population of 200,000). With the refugees coming in from Poland at the beginning of the war, they amounted to 80,000. To the contemporary reader, this may seem a small city. But the point is that the structure of the population was different from what we know in modern urban societies. Jewish Vilna was small, but the area it dominated was immense. It was, as it were, the "shopping center" and learning campus of a huge hinterland, which in the twentieth century reached several million. People would come from surrounding towns and villages to trade or study and return to their hometowns or move to the West, and still be proud of their "Vilna" origins. The parents of the Vilna Gaon; the Haskalah historian of Vilna, Rashi Fin;

the founders of the YIVO (Yiddish Scientific Institute), Max Weinreich and Zelig Kalmanovich; the Yiddish poet Sutzkever and the Hebrew poet Abba Kovner; and the Polish poets Mickiewicz and Milosz were not born in Vilna itself, though their names are linked with that cultural center. Jerusalem of Lithuania was the symbolic focus and aristocratic pride of a vast, extraterritorial Jewish empire.

Ironically, it is the Jews who preserved the boundaries of the Grand Duchy of Lithuania, which was six times the size of the present-day Lithuanian state (though they did not speak Lithuanian, which never was the common language of that empire). *Líte* (pronounced *Leé-tah*), as the area is called in Yiddish, and its Jews, the *Litvaks*, are marked by a separate Yiddish dialect, cooking traditions, typical mentality, and the passion for learning. In the mid-nineteenth century, *Líte* became the center of modern Hebrew literature: works of fiction and poetry, historical scholarship, and translations of world literature were written and published in Hebrew. And in the twentieth century it became a center of Yiddish education, publishing, and scholarship.

The Jewish secular movement in the nineteenth and twentieth centuries revolted against traditional orthodox society and tried to create a Jewish culture and society molded upon European models. But it, too, adapted the glory of Vilna—"the city of the Vilna Gaon"—as a center of learning and culture. The modern Jewish myth of "Jerusalem of Lithuania" took over the vacant seat of the long-abandoned Lithuanian capital and combined it with the biblical discourse of Jerusalem, which, like Vilna, had "hills all around her." In 1897, the Jewish Socialist party of Russia and Lithuania, the "Bund," which became a major supporter of Yiddish culture, was founded here. In the twentieth century, the city became a microcosm reflecting all the Jewish ideologies and cultural trends of the time. Between the two World Wars, the city belonged to Poland (1920–1939). At that time, there were in Vilna: a Hebrew, a Yiddish, and a Polish-Hebrew teachers' college, each supplying teachers for the vast hinterland of Eastern Europe and for Eretz Israel; secular schools in Yiddish, in Ashkenazi Hebrew, and in Sephardi Hebrew; religious schools in traditional Yiddish for teaching Hebrew texts, or in Polish for "modern" Jews observing the Sabbath; Yiddish theater; several Yiddish newspapers; major publishers; Yiddish journals for linguistics, economics, and children's journals; the Union of Female Glovemakers and other trade unions; health organizations; youth movements; and political parties of all shades. In the privately endowed Strashun Library, young and old, gymnasium students and scholars, read the Talmud along with the writings of Herzl, Moyshe-Leyb Halpern, and

Karl Marx. Young Jews went to the Polish University, to the universities in the West, or snuck across the nearby border to the Communist paradise. All those cultural and political options lived in constant dialogue with each other; they conducted a multidirectional argument on one stage. It was the epitome of a new Jewish secular culture as a galaxy of interrelated and competing possibilities.

Like Prague, located between the empires—between Russia and Poland and close to the cultural and trading roots with Germany—Vilna remained a strong Jewish center, where both intellectuals and the masses spoke Yiddish. At the same time, the links with the outside world were open: Vilna émigrés lived in South Africa and America; one could encounter Vilna students and tailors in Paris, Liège, and Berlin; there were intimate cultural ties with Eretz Israel and all major Jewish centers in the world; and Sigmund Freud was a member of the YIVO Board.

Vilna was proud of its literary tradition. Zalman Reyzen, a prolific translator and author, who single-handedly wrote an eight-volume *Lexicon of Yiddish Literature*, published and edited the daily newspaper *Vilner Tog*, in which he promoted Yiddish literature and published budding writers, including the first poems of Abraham Sutzkever. (Reyzen perished in a Soviet prison.) Russian, Polish, German, and world literature were read and translated. The Jews were powerless, poverty was rampant, but Culture was everything. And above all, "Jerusalem of Lithuania" was a symbol of the Second Jerusalem, the Jewish national and cultural life that subsisted in Europe for a millennium. This is the atmosphere in which Sutzkever grew up.

III. Childhood in Siberia

Abraham Sutzkever was born in 1913 in Smorgoń, then a middle-sized industrial city southwest of Vilna. In 1915, during World War I, the Russian high command expelled a million and a half Jews from their hometowns, as potential "spies" for the Germans. All Jews of Smorgoń were ordered to leave within twenty-four hours and the city was plundered and burned. Today the Holocaust has overshadowed the events of World War I, but then too a large Jewish population was uprooted from places were they had lived

The poet's parents, Herz and Reine Sutzkever.

for centuries. The two Vilna Holocaust poets, Sutzkever and Abba Kovner, were among them; exile was their childhood experience.

On the roads, the Sutzkevers met a rich merchant, who helped them move to his town, Omsk, a central city of western Siberia on the Irtysh River, far from the Jewish Pale of Settlement. Sutzkever lived there until he was seven years old. In Omsk, his father died of heart failure at the age of thirty; typhus and civil war ravaged the city; but the enchanted world of Siberia, as perceived in a child's imagination, became the first fictional space of his poetry. The symbol of Russian oppression and exile, the haunting name itself, became inverted in his classical poem "Siberia" (which attracted Marc Chagall to illustrate it from his own childhood imagination). The beauty of the white expanses, the power of the ice breaking on the Irtysh, the music of father's violin, all merged in images of the palpable, lasting nature of the nonmaterial world: "wonder-woods sway wide on window-panes," "snow-sounds falling on my head" when father played his violin — and a wolf peeping in the window "to sniff the music's flesh."

The world of his Siberian childhood is unattainable, beyond the boundaries of normal reality, hence eternally beautiful as evoked in imagination and poetry. A key image of the poem is the snowman, left behind in the Siberian winter: enclosed "in a hut of sounds," it can never melt. The snowman is a monument to his childhood, but the poet himself is a "snowman in a cloak of skin," an unreal, imaginary being, and the sounds of his masterful strophes will remain a monument to him. The poetic topos of human images preserved in a sculpture (as in poems by Pushkin or Keats), which are endowed with eternal life precisely because they are dead, frozen in the spring, and remain forever young—this poetic paradox is enhanced here in a manifold additional unreality. In Sutzkever's poem, the spring is a winter, and only winter can keep the young snowman intact; the sculpture is made not of bronze but of melting snow, and only freezing time can keep it alive; it is not a sculpture present to the eyes of a meditating poet but placed in a distant space, present only in memory; and, in its unmelted form, it lives only in the magic sounds of poetry. And today, a new dimension is added: to most readers, the sounds of Sutzkever's Yiddish words themselves are as inaccessible as the Siberian snowman.

All this is relevant because the same pattern, formed in Sutzkever's childhood imagination, became a key to his post-Holocaust poetry. The poet's belief in the *real* existence of the nonexistent—or their *subsistence* (as Bertrand Russell would say) in some distant, unattainable world—is transformed later into Sutzkever's evocation of the no-longer-existent Vilna from the landscapes of Israel. The dead who disappeared in the Holocaust must be alive in some realm because they are vividly present in imagination and recalled in poetry. The power of a child's fantasy becomes the poetic myth of the mature Sutzkever.

Among his Siberian recollections, he tells that once, when the Tsar and his family were killed in the Urals (not far from Omsk), a soldier brought a huge stolen diamond that had belonged to the Tsar and sold it to the watchmaker Berger. Berger was afraid to keep it in town and brought it to Herz Sutzkever who hid it in his house. The father, ill and frail, showed the treasure, the mysterious emperor's diamond, glimmering blue in the rays of the sunset, to his beloved youngest son, Abrasha. This rare intimacy with father and the magic light emanating from the diamond, amid the shadows of the dark hut, made an indelible impression on Sutzkever and became the "glimmering essence" of his later poetry (see, for example, the poem "What Did You Expect to See, Praying"). His father died and was buried in the Jewish cemetery in Omsk. At the funeral, Abrasha felt a tremendous urge to leap into the grave, to join his father, but a dove appeared and pulled the child's eyes to the sky. The disbelief in the finality of his father's death and the miraculous snow-white dove saving his life are again magnified and mirrored in Sutzkever's Holocaust poetry.

IV. Youth in Vilna

In 1920, when the Russian Civil War had subsided, Reine Sutzkever returned with her three children and settled in Vilna, where they lived for twenty years in a small hut in the suburb of Snipishok. Her oldest brother (of ten siblings) had revolted against his father and left for America, where he did well. His quarterly checks supported Reine and her children.

All her life, Sutzkever's mother mourned her dead husband and never remarried. Through her, Abrasha adored his father's memory and his maternal grandfather. This grandfather was a rabbi in a small town, who devoted his life to writing a "sharp" book on a Talmudic topic in the Lithuanian tradition, and was nicknamed the "Gaon [genius] of Mikhalishok" (the book was published posthumously in Vilna in 1909). The poet's older brother went to study in France and migrated as a pioneer to Eretz Israel. His older sister, a beauty with long black braids, was admired as a genius, skipped three classes in school, and wrote poetry in Russian. When she died of "brain fever" (meningitis) at the age of thirteen, Abrasha fled home and wrote in the sand: "eternal." Again, the inexplicable death of a godlike, sick person was entwined with a sense of beauty and poetry and the child's imagination of eternal life.

Abrasha apparently internalized the images of the artists: his father, his poet sister, a girl dancer he met, and himself as a poetic child. By writing poetry he was fulfilling their dream and revitalizing their existence. In poetry he found something that will overcome death. He truly believed that only through poetry would he survive the Holocaust—hence it had to be a different kind of poetry, endowed with magical power to change reality, a poetry, as he often wrote, that both God and the dead would like to read. Of course, this is a romantic perception, reinforced by the romantic and symbolist poetry he read; but it also has deep roots in his own biography. Furthermore, a basic paradox underlies this perception: Yiddish poetry was secular in its very being but his mother conveyed an intense religiosity that transcended her own life (composed of widowhood, poverty, exile, and Holocaust). This may be the source of the poet's early attraction to a nonnormative, self-centered religiosity, as a base for his poetic mythology. First, he embraced a Spinozaist pantheism and, later, he resorted to a poetic pantheon for the dead, a denial of "realism" as a way to assert the subsistence of the annihilated world in some cosmic space.

Abrasha was a sickly child, suffered from headaches, and was unable to

Abrasha Sutzkever in high school uniform, 1927.

study in school. At first, he had a private rabbi (religious teacher), then he attended a religious school in his neighborhood and later a Polish-Hebrew high school. Sutzkever met Freydke, his life's companion and wife, when she was twelve and he was fifteen. Since the age of fourteen, Freydke worked in the bibliography section of YIVO, the Yiddish Scientific Institute, and knew a lot of Yiddish poetry by heart, especially the work of Moyshe-Leyb

Halpern. Sutzkever began writing poetry at the age of thirteen, first in Hebrew, then in Yiddish. But he never attended a Yiddish school or had any idea that Yiddish poetry had been written before. Now he elected a course of self-education, spending long days in the Strashun Library. At the age of sixteen, feeling enormous rage "against himself, his poems, and the world," he burned all his poems, against the protestations of his mother and Freydke. It was a traumatic and purifying event, marking a new stage of "religious" awe before the magic and power of poetry and a new commitment to serve it with no compromise. Sutzkever was influenced by the great Yiddish linguist and director of the YIVO, Dr. Max Weinreich, and by other scholars, including the literary historian Zelig Kalmanovich and the linguist Noah Prilutski. He studied Yiddish in depth, enriched and purified his language, wrote poetry in Old Yiddish, and began to translate the medieval Yiddish romance *Bove Bukh*, written in Venice in 1508, in precise *ottava rima* stanzas, by Eliyahu Bakhur (or Elye Bokher).

As a youth, Sutzkever joined the Vilna Jewish scouts' organization, "Di Bin" (the Bee), and was sworn in by Max Weinreich on the Buffalo Mountains outside Vilna, "faithfully to guard secular Yiddish culture." The Bee promoted love of nature ("all the birds spoke Yiddish," as nature teacher and cultural critic A. Golomb said, and Yiddish terminology for flowers and trees was avidly coined and learned). Both nature and literature were symbols of human dignity and an antidote to the confined life of the traditional Jewish "ghetto" (a mere symbolic designation, since there was no actual ghetto in Medieval Vilna). In that rarified Vilna atmosphere, it was just one or two interwar generations that promoted the ideal of a Jewish secular culture at peace with its past, embracing Jewish history on the one hand and lower-class folklore on the other, as parts of its integral heritage. There was an aristocratic conception of the purity of language and elitist literature, of Yiddish as part of world literature, measuring its achievements by the highest criteria.

As in other Jewish youth movements of that period, boys and girls of the Bee went on memorable excursions and summer camps in the beautiful Vilna area—an unusual pastime for Jews—sang around bonfires and discussed literature. The young poet developed a pantheistic admiration of Nature, as a mirror for the self-assertion of the individual, the free wanderer among forests and mountains, and for the rich life of his psyche. In the Bee, Abrasha struck up an intense friendship with Miki Chernikhov, the precocious son of a famous Vilna lawyer. At Chernikhov's home, the family read aloud all of Pushkin's epic poem, "Evgeny Onegin," written in a melodious and

Members of the "Young Vilna" group of poets and artists at a visit by the American Yiddish novelist Joseph Opatoshu. From right to left, first row: Shmerke Katcherginsky, painter Ben-Zion Michtom; second row: A. Sutzkever, Y. Opatoshu, Chaim Grade, Elchonon Vogler; third row: Moshe Levin, Peretz Miransky, Shimshon Kahan, Leyzer Volf.

flexible iambic tetrameter. Miki (later a survivor of the Soviet camps and subsequently American professor Michal Astur) introduced Abrasha to the best Russian Symbolist poets, and read and translated Edgar Allen Poe for him. Abrasha knew Yiddish better than any other language, but he imbibed the musical forms of poetry in the European tradition. He read Polish Romantic poets, steeped himself in the difficult poetry of Cyprian Norwid, and attended lectures by Professor Manfred Krydl, a famous Polish literary theoretician and critic, at the Vilna Polish university.

Through his neighbor and older friend Leyzer Wolf, a wildly original, grotesque Yiddish poet, he joined the group of writers and painters known as "Young Vilna." But Sutzkever was a loner and the leftist-oriented group looked askance at his poetry, lacking "social" (that is, political and leftist) commitment. At the same time, he was recognized and published by A. Leyeles in *Inzikh*, the journal of the New York Introspectivists, and his first book was published by the Yiddish Writers' Union in Warsaw. He befriended Jewish painters and was influenced by the ideals of art in Modernist painting.

World War II broke out. Sutzkever married Freydke. In September 1939, Poland was divided between Germany and the Soviet Union. The Russians entered Vilna, arrested many Jewish leaders of all political trends (including the attorney Chernikhov, who, once having defended Communists in fascist Poland, now disappeared in their jails), and turned the city over to independent Lithuania, which renamed it Vilnius. In May 1940, Lithuania too was swallowed up by the Soviets. Sutzkever's book, *Valdiks* ("From the Forest"), one of the masterworks of Yiddish poetry, was printed in tiny Lithuania, in a crevice of space and time: between the two totalitarian empires, Germany and Russia, and between the German-Polish war of 1939 and the world war of 1941. It is the most exquisite crystal of the Yiddish language and, perhaps, the last Yiddish book printed in Europe before the Holocaust.

V. Holocaust

On June 22, 1941, the Germans attacked the Soviet Union and two days later they occupied Vilna. Over 100,000 Jews of Vilna and the provinces were liquidated in the suburb of Ponar. *Ponar* became the terrifying symbol of the annihilation of Jerusalem of Lithuania and the Jewish nation in Europe. Only some 20,000 Jews remained, crammed into a ghetto of seven small streets, repeatedly persecuted and decimated by Germans and Lithuanians, and finally liquidated in September 1943.

From the first days of Nazi occupation, Jewish men were snatched up in the streets and dragged off to the horrifying Lukishki prison or to Ponar, from which they never returned. At best, they were taken to forced labor. Abrasha hid in his mother's apartment in Snipishok. For six weeks he lay in a crawl space under a little roof below their window, where he bored a hole in the tin roof and feverishly wrote his poems. When his disappearance roused suspicion, Freydke came at night to take him out, but he could not walk. Later, he joined Jewish worker brigades or hid in various places. On September 5, 1941, he was taken by the Lithuanians to be shot. He and the Vilna Rov, Rabbi Gustman, were forced to dig their own graves in the Sheshkiner Hills. It was a beautiful September day. The Lithuanians stood behind them and cocked their rifles. And then Sutzkever had a poetic experience: "When they ordered us to put our hands over our eyes, I understood that they were going to shoot us. And I remember, as if it were now: when I put my fingers on my eyes, I saw birds fluttering. . . . I never saw birds flying so slowly, I had a great aesthetic joy in seeing the slow-slow motion of their wings between my fingers." The Lithuanians shot over their heads and took them to the newly established ghetto.

In the ghetto he eventually found both his mother and Freydke. He succeeded in transferring his mother from the "second ghetto" (soon liqui-dated) to the first. During the "*Aktsia*" (round-up of Jews) of the "yellow permits," he fled the ghetto and found refuge in the cellar of a Polish peasant woman. His mother hid in a "*malina*" (a hiding place), but when Sutzkever returned to the ghetto she was gone. The *malina* had been discovered and all its inhabitants were taken away. In the beginning of 1942, Freydke bore a son in the ghetto hospital, but giving birth to Jewish children was forbidden and the Germans poisoned him (see the poem "To my Wife"). Writing poetry, or simply, as he puts it, "living poetically," saved his life in the ghetto: "It is a spirit that enters you and it is stronger than all the bullets." As Sutzkever explains: "There was a madman in Vilna, he walked into a synagogue and saw a painter standing on top of a ladder and painting the ceiling. So he said to him, 'hold onto the brush because I'm taking away the ladder.' That's how I was: I held onto the brush and held myself, did not fall down. That was the remarkable thing."

Soon, Sutzkever joined a group of intellectuals and young people who went to work every day in the building of the YIVO, outside the ghetto, in the so-called Rosenberg Stab (officially, *Einsatzstab, Reichsleiter Rosenberg*). This institution, organized by Dr. Pohl, Director of the Frankfurt museum for the study of eastern nations, prepared resources for the "Science of Jewry without Jews" (*Wissenschaft des Judentums ohne Juden*). Here, in the library and archives of the former Yiddish Scientific Institute, the Germans assembled books from the valuable Strashun Library and other plundered libraries and synagogues. Under the supervision of German "scholars" of Judaism (who knew neither Yiddish nor Hebrew), the ghetto brigade had to sort out the books and designate materials for shipment to Germany or to a paper factory. Risking their lives, Sutzkever and his friends smuggled

The young poet.

hundreds of rare books and manuscripts into the ghetto, often under the pretext of "heating paper," and put them in the library or buried them. Many of those materials were eventually brought by Sutzkever to Moscow or uncovered in Vilna after the liberation and from there were smuggled to New York and Jerusalem. Many valuable books and manuscripts were shipped by the Nazis to Germany, recovered after the war, and brought to the YIVO branch in New York.

The YIVO also served as a base for contacts with the city. Here, Sutzkever and his friend, the poet Katcherginsky, got the first machine gun for the FPO, the United Partisan Organization, which they smuggled into the ghetto. In the ghetto itself, during a lull between one *Aktsia* and another, an intense, illegal cultural life was conducted, as if continuing the prewar

With poet and fellow partisan, Shmerke Katcherginsky, in Vilna ghetto, July 20, 1943.

multidirectional activities of Vilna: a school was established, a hospital, a library, a theater, social and philanthrophic organizations, Hebrew and Yiddish literary events, music concerts, painting, and a youth club. Sutzkever taught Yiddish poetry and organized an exhibit devoted to the American Yiddish poet, Yehoash, whom he admired for the musicality of his verse and his love of nature. For his long poem, "The Grave Child," Sutzkever received in 1942 the literary prize of the Ghetto Writers' Union.

Sutzkever, Freydke, Shmerke Katcherginsky, Ruzhka Korchak, Michael Kovner, and other YIVO workers were members of the FPO. We shall not repeat here the well-known story of the failed Vilna ghetto uprising and the heroism of its fighters who went through sewers to the forests, where they joined the Soviet partisan army fighting the Nazis. Sutzkever, Freydke, and Shmerke Katcherginsky left the ghetto on September 12, 1943, with a group of partisans led by the legendary Zelda, who made dozens of forays from the forests to Vilna, to save surviving Jews. They walked for a hundred kilometers through hostile villages and German army units until they reached the same areas around Lake Narocz where he and Freydke had gone on excursions before the war.

VI. In the Forest

It was not a simple matter for city youth (especially the intellectual, idealistic youngsters who made up most of the underground movement) to live in the forests and swamps, through rain, snow, and starvation. The Gentile population of the countryside was hostile and denounced any hiding Jew or Jewish group to the Germans. The Polish rightist underground, *Armia Krajowa*, was busy slaughtering Jews in the forests. The only force they could join was the Soviet partisan movement, which became strong only at a later stage. But here, too, antisemitism was rampant.

Sutzkever's group was directed to the Byelorussian partisan Brigade headed by Markov, operating in the primeval forests and swamps around Lake Narocz. Only young Jews from the ghetto, capable of fighting and bringing weapons with them, were allowed into the forest—they had to leave their families behind, to be slaughtered in the ghetto. But in the forest, some five hundred Jews were mustered before Markov, including the fighting unit "Vengeance." The Jewish unit was dismantled, their weapons taken away, and most young people were taken out of fighting units and assigned to service units, while hundreds, including most of the women, were left in the forest to their own devices. Many were killed by the Germans. On Yom Kippur, over thirty thousand German soldiers surrounded the forest and began combing it. Markov and his fighting units fled, leaving the weak behind. Sutzkever's group was ordered to carry the wounded with them. Through deep, impenetrable swamps, they spread branches on the mire and crossed to a dry island. Even here, German spies arrived, but the Sutzkevers hid among bushes, deep in the freezing water, and survived. When the brigade returned, Sutzkever and Katcherginsky were summoned by Markov and assigned to write its history.

Suddenly, a cable came from Moscow announcing that a plane would be sent to rescue Sutzkever from the German occupied territory. Back in the ghetto, Sutzkever had sent a sheaf of poems, including the long poem "Kol Nidre," with some partisans to the forest. From there, the poem was sent on to Moscow, where it made an enormous impression. For the first time in the Soviet Union, this poem by an incognito ghetto writer showed the full horror of the Final Solution. Ilya Ehrenburg, then a highly influential writer whose columns in *Pravda* were read on the front, compared it to a Greek tragedy. Justas Paleckis, President of the Lithuanian government-in-exile in Moscow, had known Sutzkever before the war. Paleckis, a leftist poet, had spent years in Lithuanian jails with Jewish Communists, from whom he learned Yiddish and Hassidic songs. In 1940, when a Soviet Lithuanian capital was established in Vilnius, Paleckis had translated some of Sutzkever's poetry into Lithuanian. Now he remembered the poet and saved him.

Markov provided guards and a horse-drawn sleigh to take Sutzkever and Freydke to an airstrip in another partisan region, ninety kilometers away. The journey through German territory was filled with dangers; one of the partisan guards was an antisemite and tried to shoot them. Eventually the Sutzkevers were left alone to cross a railroad. Trees were cut down on both sides, to prevent partisans from blowing up trains, and the whole strip was mined and heavily guarded by the Germans. Dismembered wolf carcasses, human bodies, and limbs littered the field. As the poet recalls, he stepped among the mines to the rhythm of a poem, with Freydke in his footsteps, and was saved, in spite of German fire from the distance. Later he wrote that writing poetry is like walking on such a mine field—you never know where you will step next (see the poem, "A Winter Night"). When they finally reached the other partisan brigade, a small plane landed on the ice-covered lake. Sutzkever sat in its opening, with Freydke tied to his knees, and two more partisans were stuck in the rear. The plane veered through the heavy fire of the German front, diving suddenly, and eventually emerging on the Soviet side.

VII. Resurrection

In March 1944, the Sutzkevers reached Moscow. Ehrenburg wrote an article in *Pravda* about Sutzkever, "The Victory of a Human Being." For the first time, *Pravda* wrote openly about the Holocaust and about Jews participating in the war against Nazi Germany. Sutzkever received letters from all corners of the Soviet Union, including some from old friends, like Miki Chernikhov, who was still interned in a camp. Vilna was liberated in July and Sutzkever returned to his "slaughtered city." Surviving Jewish partisans from the forests took part in liberating the city, including the Hebrew poet Abba Kovner and Shmerke Katcherginsky. Together they dug up remaining cultural treasures saved from the Germans and built a Jewish Museum, which was closed and confiscated by the NKVD some three years later.

Abraham and Freydke Sutzkever in Lithuanian Partisan Headquarters, Moscow, March 1944.

As the poet tells it, "I felt that I must be the witness of all those events, that I was destined to be the witness. I entered a spectacle someone staged, I thought I played a role in it. Who staged the spectacle, I don't know. Who needed it? What for? In those years of destruction, I always felt I was a witness to an immense earthly and cosmic play. I felt a divine sense of messianic mission, those were the most elevated moments of my life." As we see, the mythical conception of his poetry permeated the poet's perception of his own life; poetic imagery and discourse entered his daily discourse, too. And now that this messianic perception was realized, Sutzkever was chosen to appear at the Nuremberg trial as a witness to the destruction of the Jewish people.

In 1947, via Vilna, Lodz, and Paris, Sutzkever and Freydke came as illegal immigrants to Eretz Israel, the land of his mother's dream. The pioneering, secular culture that built the young society of Israel was based on a miraculous revival of the Hebrew language. Like Yiddish, modern Hebrew conquered all areas of modern life and society and all genres of European culture. However, the scars of the "war of languages" between Hebrew and Yiddish for dominance in secular Jewish culture were still fresh in Palestine. Nevertheless, Sutzkever succeeded in raising the sentiments of Zionists from Eastern Europe (such as the scholar and President of Israel, Zalman Shazar). The Hebrew Trade Union Federation "Histad-

Vilna after the liberation, July 1944: sorting out concealed manuscripts. From right to left: Abba Kovner (commander of ghetto partisans, Hebrew poet), Elye Gordon (Soviet Yiddish writer), Abraham Sutzkever, Akiva Gershater, Arn Kushnirov (major Soviet Yiddish poet, captain in the Red Army, died during purges of Yiddish writers in Moscow, 1949), Shloyme Kovarsky.

rut" provided the means for the establishment of a high-level cultural and literary quarterly in Yiddish, *Di goldene keyt* (The Golden Chain), which Sutzkever has edited from 1948 to this day. One hundred thirty issues, of about 250 pages each, have appeared so far, bringing together the scattered Yiddish writers from Europe, North and South America, Israel, and the Soviet Union. A new haven for the last generation of Yiddish literature destroyed in Europe was found, gathered in the Holy Land.

Sutzkever has appeared at international poetry festivals, has been translated into many languages, and has received dozens of literary prizes, including the Israel Prize, bestowed by the state on persons of unusual achievement. Yet, the destruction of his people in Europe and the demise of his language permeate his words, along with the sense of the futility of words.

On Sutzkever's Selected Writings

The Selection

This book presents for the first time in English a comprehensive selection from Sutzkever's twenty-three volumes of Yiddish poetry and prose, as well as several uncollected poems. There are two exceptions: *The Fiddle-Rose*, a book translated by Ruth Whitman, and the book-length rhymed narrative poem, *Gaystike erd* (Spiritual Soil). Obviously, even a volume of this scope cannot do justice to Sutzkever's narrative poetry or, indeed, to many of his excellent lyrical poems.

Except for the first section, the poetry is arranged chronologically, in sections corresponding to the poet's published books. Within each section, the poet's order is usually preserved. In the poetry written during the Holocaust, that order is strictly chronological; however, most other books were constructed by the poet himself, using thematic or poetic principles. In several cases, independent sections are isolated from their original volumes, notably "Partisan Forest" and "Elephants at Night." The section "Blind Milton," however, includes poems from three books. The section "Faces in Swamps," written in the first days of the Nazi occupation, is reconstructed here, using poems from a collection of previously unpublished texts, *The First Night in the Ghetto* (1979), as well as poems from a manuscript in the poet's handwriting hidden in the ghetto and recently discovered in Vilnius, almost half a century later. With the exception of this section, the early texts are translated here from the 1963 edition of Sutzkever's collected *Poetic Works* (1,140 pages in two volumes). Several minor corrections or realignments were made with the author's collaboration (for example, restoring "Execution" as an independent poem, as it appears in the post-Holocaust volume *The Fortress* [1945], rather than as part of the cycle, "A Day in the Hands of the Stormtroopers").

The poetry in its chronological order, however, is preceded by 36 poems from Sutzkever's last published book, *Twin Brother*. Symbolically, 36 stands for twice 18, the *gematriya* (letter-count) of *ḤAY* (to live), for the poet's two lives. This section is titled here, as in the poet's earlier version, "Poems from My Diary." It contains the distilled reflections of the mature poet, looking retrospectively at his many lives and deaths, as well as the condensed recollection of some of his basic imagery. We felt that the reader too could only look back at the poet's long road from the vantage point of the present, rather than starting with a naive youth in the illusory calm of the nineteen thirties. The Diary section is arranged in an intuitive order by the translators.

The second part of this volume includes translations from Sutzkever's two collections of poetic prose, which, if space were available, should have been translated in full.

In the course of our work on this retrospective selection, between intimate and emotionally draining interviews and discussions of his life and poetry, Sutzkever responded with new poems, summarizing his life's road. Several of those poems were translated and placed chronologically as the last poetry section. Two recent poems, "The Bottom Line" and "On My Father's Yortsayt," close the book.

The Translations

Translating Sutzkever is an exceedingly difficult task. His poetry depends so much on precise and variegated meters, innovative rhyme, surprising sound orchestration, and complex strophic forms. Without these, the poetic texture threatens to become lax and flat. A word that seems to be the absolutely correct choice in the original, activating the full body of its sounds and connotations in an interplay with its counterparts, may not be justified in translation without those relationships. Free verse, prevalent in American poetry today, depends on a completely different selection and combination of words, which are more easily preserved in another language. Furthermore, Sutzkever's original rhyming foregrounds his neologisms, his play with the various linguistic components of Yiddish (Germanic, Hebrew, Slavic, or international roots), the ironies and tragicomedy of it all. Parallelism, so prominent in his poetry, serves as allusion to folk poetry as well as to symbolist poetry, and as background to variation and contrast.

It is hard to imitate these precise forms in another language. And even when it is done, the sacrifice on the semantic level may be considerable. We felt that in this almost lost, hardly accessible language of literary Yiddish (unlike the lower-class jargon that many Americans still remember), we should convey the original meaning as closely as possible. Moreover, a translator is not allowed the range of innovations, wordplay, and rhymes that an innovating poet can afford; thus, even when rhymed, an English translation cannot fully convey the freshness, surprise, celebration, and disruptions of the original rhyme and rhythm. But the main problem lies in the different relative functions of verse forms in Yiddish (and Russian) on the one hand and in contemporary English poetry on the other. Precise meters and symmetrical, rhymed strophes tend to be perceived as old-fashioned and "romantic" in American poetry, as some themes in this poetry are, even though the imagery is striking and modern.

Our response to this problem has been pluralistic. We chose a variety of solutions for different poems to promote at times the formal and at other times the semantic potentials of the original. "Siberia" was translated in its precise trochaic pentameter (unusual in English), full rhyme scheme, and "Byronic" strophic form. In the "Poems From My Diary," we kept the meter in most of the poems, though we relaxed the fixed line length, moving toward free verse wherever the semantic texture and imagery seemed self-sufficient. We approached rhyme in the same way. Several poems are rhymed, in full or in part, while others have their rhymes omitted altogether. In many poems (especially in the simple litanies and ballads written during the Holocaust), we felt that at least partial rhyming was absolutely necessary.

The narrative poem, "Clandestine City," is written originally in lines of four amphibrachs. We decided to transpose it into the traditional meter of English narrative poetry, iambic pentameter. Moreover, the full rhyme scheme seemed too rich in English for this kind of subject matter; instead, we rhymed alternative lines and closed the ten-line stanza with a rhyming couplet. Without rhyme altogether, the text would have fallen apart and the ten-line strophe, symbolic for "a nation of ten"—all that remained of an entire people—would have lost its conspicuous form.

"Ode to the Dove" is a precise masterpiece, composed in a solemn, dactylic hexameter, epic in tone, but fully rhymed, to indicate its sonnetlike, nonnarrative quality. It has exactly ten parts, of four times four lines each, fully encased in feminine-rhymed couplets. We tried to convey the tone by keeping a six-beat line (precise hexameters in English may sound too mechanical) and rhymed the last couplet of each part only, as a closure to the four strophes.

In some poems, for example, "Who Will Remain, What Will Remain?," "Soft Curving Air, a Rain of Rice," "Signs," or "Divine Comedy," sharp rhyming of short lines seemed so crucial that it had to be re-created. In other poems, such as "Sirius" or "Rain of Colors and Flowers," we were unable to do so; the irrational magic of the innovative sounds in these unusual poems is lost but we felt that enough is transferred to give an idea of the poem.

The Illustrations

Sutzkever's interest in art and his longtime friendships with Marc Chagall and other artists, resulted in a wealth of portraits and illustrations of his poetry made by survivors of the last generation of Jewish European painters (Marc Chagall, Jankl Adler, Mané-Katz, Artur Kolnik) and by some of the best Israeli artists (Yosl Bergner, Arie Navon, Reuven Rubin, M. Ardon, A. Steimatzky, Shmuel Bak). Bak, at the age of nine, was a prodigy artist in the Vilna ghetto, and is now the major Israeli Surrealist painter. Yonia Fain, a native of Vilna and son of the director of the Yiddish Teachers' College, became a painter in Mexico and lives and creates in New York; he is also a fine Yiddish poet and president of the Yiddish PEN Club in the United States.

This colorful dialogue between poet and painters deserves a book in its own right. Here, we have presented only a few examples, notably the intertextually fascinating Sutzkever-Chagall *Siberia* and some of Sutzkever's own drawings, published here for the first time. Most illustrations to the poems are excerpted from Sutzkever's published books. We are grateful to A. Sutzkever for permission to use these illustrations.

With lifelong friend, Marc Chagall, Israel 1961.

Acknowledgments

We are grateful to the poet for his intense and demanding involvement in our work and for the dozens of hours of talks and recorded memoirs that he shared with us. Benjamin Harshav had earlier experienced the tribulations of translating Sutzkever's formal poetry into Hebrew (in two books, *Chariot of Fire* and *Siberia*, as well as many poems included in the collective volume, *Wings of Granite*) and learned to dare to compromise in the process. His students in the Sutzkever seminar at the New York YIVO showed him how much excitement Sutzkever's Yiddish poetry can still generate.

We wish to express our warmest thanks to Stanley Holwitz, our friend, editor, and publisher. This often exasperating enterprise could not have come about without his understanding of its importance, his patience, and encouragement. Randall Goodall is responsible for the sensitive, restrained, and elegant shape of our books in this series. To all of them our thanks.

Poems From My Diary

(1974–1985)

אַברהם סוצקעווער

צווילינג־ברודער

Cover of Twin Brother *with portrait of the poet by M. Ardon.*

✳

Who will remain, what will remain? A wind will stay behind.
The blindness will remain, the blindness of the blind.
A film of foam, perhaps, a vestige of the sea,
A flimsy cloud, perhaps, entangled in a tree.

Who will remain, what will remain? One syllable will stay,
To sprout the grass of Genesis as on a new First Day.
A fiddle-rose, perhaps, for its own sake will stand
And seven blades of grass perhaps will understand.

Of all the stars from way out north to here,
That one star will remain that fell into a tear.
A drop of wine remaining in a jar, a drop of dew.
Who will remain, God will remain, is that enough for you?

A. SUTZKEVER   53

In the orchestra, we are the notes, just the notes,
Registered with human marks, more shadowy than motes.
We are read by others only, we philosophers, we hoboes,
We are read by the musicians, violins and oboes.

We are just the notes. We change, we mix, confound.
And we give for others only: tones and chords and sound.
And above the strings and keys, over every part,
Only the conductor knows us all by heart.

Lightning in a storm conducts. Revealed in disarray:
From within our silences, all abysses play.
White seagulls give themselves to clouds, a mating game —
With wailing joy, in a creation that has yet no name.

From within our silence, trees and nests emerge,
In the humming muscles of the orchestra converge.
But who, from inside us, can play the I, all it connotes.
We are just the notes, just the notes.

Explain? How to explain? When here
The sun — it did not freeze in rage,
But still it cannot melt a tear —
And only childhood does not age.

Like red grapes squeezed, a cellar's prey,
Youth has been trampled on a stage.
Your shadow's hair is silver-gray —
And only childhood does not age.

Its snows and violets are gone.
Old are its kingdoms, king and sage.
And all is said and all is done —
And only childhood does not age.

Soft curving air, a rain of rice.
Someone may like this food, this spice.
My hunger will swallow the sunset, or
The yesteryear up to today's warm core.

I feed my hunger, a panting hound,
On words, on every newborn sound,
A bit of aesthetic on the tip of a knife —
My horrible hunger is panting for life.

What more? To the druggist I run for a dram:
On a golden scale he weighs by the gram
The tears of serpents and bittersweet herbs.
My hunger keeps panting, torments and disturbs.

What more? Like a fiery red locust you thrive,
Your appetite growls to devour me alive.
And though I am older than time and my hunger — is younger,
The earth will not lie light on you, sated hunger.

Yosl Bergner, illustration.

My wandering fingers came together. They knead
From dream-clay, clay of other planets,
The shape of my redeemer. Painful and intriguing:
Like Eve emerging out of Adam's rib.

Pliant, flexible the clay, I sense an eye, an arm.
A miracle takes shape, assumes a wondrous form.
Its fragrance — honey in a buzzing field of clover,
The Milky Way, my nourishment, is flowing through its limbs.

The kneading, the enigma, puzzles on till dawn,
Till the morning star crows and the bees awaken.
Till the line between spirit and matter grows straight
And my fingers are only the hands of their redeemer.

But when the Morning Star crows twice and thrice,
The limbs of my redeemer fall apart like petals.
The fingers, the *Lamed-Vovniks*,[1] wander off,
Praise be to them: a lone gray hair grows younger.

Trees are made into wonderful paper. And I — the reverse:
I transform paper into a tree, the tree of life.
I'll graft myself onto its roots — till the dawn
Of its birdsong.

The birds will blossom. They'll flourish the first
Blessed sounds. Unique, inevitable, my mission:
Transform the transformations back to their source,
Transform myself into the protoplasm of my dream.

Transform the clumps of clay into their human face,
The precious jewels into a living jeweller.
Transform the isolated mysteries, miles away from words,
Into rays that reach the depths of tears.

I dip my seal ring in the sun and stand it in the dark
To watch the transformations. My future heir,
The cosmic poet, will seek and find them.
And my bones will smile.

✳

The mumble-hieroglyphics on your face are true
Legends of my age.

I read them with my eye and ear. Their contents
Weightier than libraries.

I read your mumble-hieroglyphics and admire
The heroes and the victims.

A conflagration that we lost,
Its last embers.

I read your mumble-hieroglyphics, strangely-true
I recognize in them my life.

I recognize the nail stuck in my soul,
The hand and hammer that pounded it in.

I recognize the ladder that pulled me up
Into an underground stream in an upsidedown abyss.

In your mumble-hieroglyphics I live
As in the first half of my memory.

I recognize in them my unstilled pleasure,
That I inherited in a world with no heirs.

In your mumble-hieroglyphics I live
Even now, reading them with eye and ear.

A white hair separates our ways.
If we could split it at the core —
No more wandering, no more space,
No angel, no demon anymore.

Praise to the flesh in drunk assault!
No dance of knives, no fear, no whims
Of life's hand sprinkling grains of salt
On gnawing wonders of our limbs.

Praise to the evil spirit that would
Reveal the glee and gleefully crack it
And liberate a hungry flood,
A rainbow later will bedeck it.

Scarlet in us the festive fear.
The coveted calm — a web so sheer.
A closeness that must separate:
To love till the last drop of hate.

✻

A funeral by day, a concert by night.
To be here and be there, that is your plight.

A yoke on your back, with its weight you are stuck:
Two pails overflowing with luck and bad-luck.

If one of the buckets were empty, may be
The other might also be empty, may be.

Salt would not know its own salty taste,
On seven grains of salt, a fortune it would waste.

Light would be wrinkled and terribly ill
If on shadows it couldn't drink to its fill.

A funeral by day, a concert by night.
To be here and be there, that is your plight.

To sense the coupling of music and muck:
Two pails overflowing with luck and bad luck.

Together-together, the flat and the steep.
A ray will bend to swim down to the deep.

Thus, the scythe and the stalk are bound,
Thus is the union of fiddler and sound.

Thus are entwined the *now* and the *then*,
Thus are entangled a wife and a man.

✷

Horizon — raging salt. Caravans of camels, brooding
Steps in covered camel-steps, a walking litany.
But over them, a silver string of storks
Reminds me of my city home in Lithuania.

My traces covered deep by dunes and dunes.
Oh, who has strung that silver string above?
The string will slice my memory world in two.
The camels touch the covered camel-tracks and move.

I seek my traces too, to end my wandering,
But it's too late to learn wisdom from the camels.
The silver string of storks has sliced above
A third domain of silence over sand assemblies.

A dune-spring floods my words, a sandy spring.
Above, the desert-devil plucks a string.
Fata-Morgana palaces crumble in the dust.
A splinter of a second — in my heart it bursts.

✷

Streaming muscles of death in the desert: dunes.
Underneath, rustling shards of faiths and ruins.
Night in the desert.
Desert is the night.
Burnt out breath of stars,
They guard thereafter.

A. SUTZKEVER   *41*

Somebody laughs.
Somebody laughs
A cosmic laughter.

The laughter rolls. Roll
After roll, in a craze.
Hollow, horrifying ball —
A desert cat in its gaze.

Does it laugh at the creation of the Maker,
Or does God laugh at what He has made?
Find out, you wise faker,
And tear up the last page thereafter.

Somebody laughs
At his own laughter.

How old are you, grasses?
To the one and only —
How many zeros are strung out
All over the earth?
More than you is their number
Or less, much less?
Now, when the sea breeze
Ruffles your hair,
More patiently can I count you
And remain more alone.

Different people and different plants,
Wherever the sea breeze sailed me away.
Only *you* stay the same
Under brimstone and fire.
Not a scythe has cut you down.
Not the thunder shoved you aside.
The hue of your soul stays outside.

How old are you, grasses?
I am trying to guess
When I stroll about later:
Older than me and my sharp-tongued question,
A tiny bit younger than your creator.

The red bricks of your body — you forgot their house,
Forgot the street, forgot the number in the lantern light.
A cloud remains, changing shapes and lines,
A yellow leaf remains, a memory of a summer.

You don't recall the face of the young first rain,
The address of your dove, the amulet in her beak.
The meadow, where you lay together in a onesome,
Now scorched by brimstone and by fire.

Forgot your papa-mama. Who brought you into the world?
The ash of fire is the same. Its victim, you don't know whose.
But in your heart you know, it still ferments,
The darkest, clearest word of all words: truth.

And in your heart you know: the glimmering essence,
More diamond than ever, you can cut with it again
The shadow world — till violins play from the shards
And calm in you another person's pain.

★

The clay of time grew soft. Sunset after sunset
Kneaded, and it rose. Soon, a grain of sand
Splits in your dream, unravels a riddle,
And only an owl will hoot from a silvery tangle.

The dead have risen long ago! Hastily,
They fled the other world, their heavy hump.
They practice Yoga, play chess, are free and easy,
Besiege the opera and snatch up all the tickets.

Does anyone recall who tore apart his limbs?
The teeth too shaky, too weak to chew it over.
The dead admire abstract art and petty quarrels,
No more a sign of Cain, Cain bears a sign of Abel.

Only a blind seer, flayed to the bone,
An ancient prophet, never died, that no one knows:
Is it he who rolls the dark or is he himself the sun? —
Runs from abyss to abyss to save the victims' smiles.

✳

Isn't — what a word! No rhyme or reason
And has a magic grip over my scene.
How palpable it is. Here I'll serve you, *isn't*,
You are my amulet unseen.

A fire-chariot tore from earth and hurled
Your contents, in a cosmic storm its wheels are seen.
Your biles of smoke have left me burnt pearls,
You are my amulet unseen.

Isn't, you're my is, my here, my real name,
Your names are youth, idea, feel and mean.
You cannot be uprooted inside me in hunter's game,
You are my amulet unseen.

I pray that in an alley dark as night,
In my last seconds, live, you come toward me and roam —
A choir of my wounds will sing to you with light:
Protect me further, amulet from home.

✳

A tree is born out of a seed, a fiddle is born out of a tree,
And you, you bear my star, so night will be for real.
You bear him far from here, his light belongs to us,
You bear him where no leaf, no smile will wither.

For a score of silences, we were not-here together,
A cosmic courage will not hinder our demise.
The earthy, the real, is earthy-real and valid,
And death has no more dominion over our breath.

A. SUTZKEVER   *45*

His kingdom cannot reach the green tree of life,
The past will not be past, for time is timeless.
Fled from the bustle, love is our silence,
The eye of our soul weeps new images.

The mating throb of two silences in one
Brings each closer to himself, to wholeness.
Wonder, nameless, is telling of its feats,
The language of atoms — as simple as a folksong.

You separated moment, like your sister
A million lightyears ahead. Easier to seal
In the air the sound of an orchestra
Than to bring you back for a moment to earth and know

You are mine again; to live again that delight,
The ruts of your plowing mouth; the springtime, raw
Torrent, the kiss-seeds in raked flowerbeds,
To drink your music for a second time, a second.

In my finger nest, your delicate flutter still lingers,
As if I touched a bird, the size of an eye,
A golden moment-bird, wounding with sweetness.
I want to draw it back into my empty finger nest.

But you are farther than my thought, as neverborn,
A myriad of lightyears ahead and barely glimmering.
I was not even able to follow you out there —
To live our joy a second time, a second.

✶

You say: There is no God. No world creator.
If so, my friend, it seems, the miracle is greater:
He isn't and created all that isn't, all that is,
Light and shade, rainbows of madness, all are his.

Created life, created death, in an eternal dance,
Where only once we come to taste his healing herbs.
Created pearls of sound in the seashell of remembrance
And little changing clouds the universe disturbs.

You say: You have to take fate in your own hand.
Oh, I do not disagree with you, my friend.
But where do you take it? Tell it to my pack
Of fingers. Easier to take the Eiffel Tower on your back.

Your shadow must have gulped a bucketful of cheer
But I'll confide a secret into his swinging ear:
Only an ant can carry on its back, alone, its fate.
It may take us ages to rise up to its state.

✶

Memory of a stroll with Marc Chagall. Flamboyant
Summer colors. Nature imitates Chagall.
Blue grapes the air. We descend the summer
Mountain. Could we but taste them all!

The same hand that created angels on our earth
Now rests on my shoulder. I accept the panorama.
He says: I hide from myself, from envy, from praise,
But I cannot hide from my own *tate-mame*.[2]

A. SUTZKEVER   *47*

Blue grapes the air. And lo: on a verandah
An old man in a straw chair. His fingers curl
Under a garland of light-and-shade, they cut
A dove of wavy paper, as delicate as pearl.

Chagall bows to Matisse. And frightened off,
The dove soars light into the sunset, it lingers.
In a diadem of ripe red grapes, the old man bows,
The scissors drop out of his frozen fingers.

Remembrance of three flamingos at Lake Victoria,
Revealed to me in their full splendor and glory:
Three fiddle-strings taut on a wave, a bow
Moves over them, a rainbow bow.

Such a music will not be born of a fiddle or a lyre.
Such a threesome instrument, it seems, does not exist.
Its maestro had a dream: to try out his creation,
To play on living strings with his own hand.

Skeleton days have turned into a desert.
Three stringed flamingoes I cannot forget:
Luminescent in the same revealing pose,
On the same wave, pink as the sun at dawn.

And what gnaws at me is the curious question:
Three stringed flamingoes, do they remember
To whom they belong?
Once in a lifetime are you granted such an encounter:
To see, to hear, to long.

✳

The chopped-off hand belongs to me, my catch
Of years ago in a tomato patch.
A human hand, no owner anywhere, I made it mine.
My third hand. Without it, I can write no line.

To a dozen curious readers, confess I must:
Not I who feeds them magic words, not I entrust
The ear of paper with memories that match:
It is my third hand that I found in a tomato patch.

No Jewish knowledge will decipher what it writes.
I teach myself its tongue. I stray at nights
In its dark paths, stumble on thorns, till a stretch
Of dawn unravels it in a tomato patch.

To me belongs the chopped-off hand that used to stroke
Perhaps a woman's hair, before its owner broke.
I found it where he lost it. It was without a scratch —
September nineteen forty-one, in a tomato patch.

Ever since my pious mother ate earth on Yom Kippur,
Ate on Yom Kippur black earth mixed up with fire,
I, alive, must eat black earth on Yom Kippur,
I am myself a *yortsayt*[3] candle kindled from her fire.

The masts of sunset mercilessly sink, mast after mast.
Like little birds, one star hops over to another.
But ever since my mother eats earth and doesn't fast,
I eat black earth on every Yom Kippur, like my mother.

A locust has left nothing on my lips
But two thin stalks of syllables: *Ma — ma.*
Separate from life-and-body, they swim, my lips,
To the kingdom where she used to fast, my pious Mama.

The silence between us grows deeper. To the dregs.
And she, who eats Yom Kippur earth, she sees her son's thoughts sprout:
Oh, that her prayer should guard his steps, she begs,
When her one *yortsayt* candle flickers out.

No more, the green eyes from long long ago. Green
As a pine forest. But if I see the eyes, it means:
They see me. My envy is pine-branch-green, my envy
Of hungry spirits, of sounds and voices.

Had God only created their dark-green green
He would have been the same God. How could they not-be?
I stray in a deep forest: the sun gleams in spiderwebs,
From green caves green tears rustle among roots.

If that green pair of eyes had disappeared for eternity,
Instead of eternity, we would have worm-eaten moments.
I stray in a forest: it's night. A root still throbs, believing,
The sun in spiderwebs still here, it has not vanished.

Dark-green eyes that see me, waiting for a sign,
With their face, they flutter, facing me.
Rustling tears from green caves swim into
My vision, leave their gleam for me.

The biting tartness of the last cranberry
Plucked from under snow, a wolf ripped by a mine
A moment before your foot trod on it in vain —
Pieces of reality in glowing vise, remain.

Your wounds, glued to the leather of a boottop
As you sink in a swamp, and to your eyes revealed:
Stars sing with frogs and snakes, a choir so insane —
Pieces of reality in glowing vise, remain.

The bread shared with a dead friend, his portion
Larger than yours, for friends stay undivided,
Even if a rustling field of stalks won't fill his need again —
Pieces of reality in glowing vise, remain.

But oh, how strange: your face in whirlpool of a mirror,
The warm butterfly that keeps you imprisoned in a ring,
Your smiling postman, bland people in your entourage —
All these are distant from the earth, a mere mirage.

✻

For my friend Rachel Krynski-Melezin,
who reminded me that I asked a surgeon to allow me
to be present at a brain operation in the hospital of the Vilna Ghetto.

Tell me, what did you expect to see, prying
Inside a cut-open skull, in Jew-City cut up with no reason or sense?
— Maybe The Eternal that stays outside of dying,
I named it: Glimmering Essence.

The skull — agape. Its armor, a thin presence.
It was my lot to see its Glimmering Essence.
Creation looked like this on the first morn.
Thus light bore light. Bore and was born.

The skull — agape. I stare into its abyss
When Jew-City is cut up, piece after piece:
Thin veins of writing. Name-with-no-name. Intense.
I close my eyes: Glimmering Essence.

The hospital went dark. Its pillars kneel.
The city's skull agape. Nowhere to rush, I reel,
Drunk on the vision, drunk beyond sense:
Guarded from now on by the Glimmering Essence.

✻

The same saw that sliced my body seven times, part after part —
And yet I stayed to live and tell it all by heart —
The same saw still survives, my body underneath,
And high above my mind, the stars are its teeth.

Above the graves of millions, on both sides of the world,
I see the same saw still, by two demons unfurled.
Superfluous my body. Its pain, perhaps, a hole.
The saw comes close and closer to my runaway soul.

To and fro, they pull the saw, deliberate, they never age:
They want to slice the calm in me and slice the rage.
To slice the world unseen, the essence that remains,
My body — grass over my bones. Still living, my remains.

A saw on both sides of the world. Two creatures in contest.
"His soul," I hear, "is sawed to pieces, let him rest."
"Still quivering, it knows our face," a voice growls brash.
The vision of two demons and a saw has crumbled into ash.

In laughing solitude, in a flea market in Paris,
My boyhood friend bought a laughing skull.
Good evening, I say to both. And to my friend: Who is he?
— Call him: The Happy One. A man who will not die.

I lost everyone. My rescued jewelry —
A bundle of manuscripts. Now I have an heir.
And in the mirror, in the same outside-of-existence,
Laughs a second skull, a man who will not die.

Two goblets rejoice with miniature sunsets.
L'Chaim,[4] sounds and colors rhyme with each other.
L'Chaim, two echoes approach with other worldly courage.
The happy ones who will not die drink too.

The skull's head is spinning. *A bientôt*, my friend,
I deciphered the manuscript planted in your wrinkles.
A tongue of sun licks out the gray dampness of a moment.
Arm on shoulder, we both laugh: We won't die either.

✳

Is it from a moving train: I see the trees in snow
For the first time, last time, or, floating, out of breath,
White-crowned nurses, eerie smiles, come and go —
On the scales of their looks: life and death, life and death?

The long corridor is shorter than a moment, perhaps.
I still have time to calm my friend, perhaps.
A nurse points down the hall: a door where I'll remain.
The white nurse winks a dark spark, now in vain.

But before I get down that way, to the door of fate,
An ash-blond woman, bony and disheveled,
Cuts me off, a visitor appeared so late,
An aging Gioconda, her smile bedeviled:

I am that young dancer with fluttering glance
You once desired. Now, I end my dance.
But if you split your sounds and syllables apart,
I will dance out of them and snare again your heart.

✳

The far-away comes close. After all journeys, all adventures,
Australian crawl on paper in the shadow of a hawk,
Leave two lines, rhymed like day and night, two verses in a century
And let your young heirs share them on a rock.

If that won't do, pull out a third verse from your veins:
Why leave behind your cat with outstretched arms,
An orphan? Weren't you enthralled in her domains?
Or did you leave her in your will a pack of charms?

At her green *yortsayt* candles in a midnight hut,
You've seen what no one saw, a vivid vision:
Endowed with tiny wings, a dozen stones have risen
And over them, the gate of mercy no more shut.

And when you give away all your possessions
And pay for all your wounds and poetry confessions,
Flee to the desert where the stars grow dry and dryer.
Their light dies out. Go water them with fire.

Drawing by the poet.

Twin Brother

I

My twin brother in the red dunes of a mirror,
Don't say: I have no time. Say:
There's so much time and I
Had no time
To build a temple of its breath. No
Crack in the whole universe
Where your time can
Slip through, sneak across
The border.

Life-and-death in love, your time:
Twintime,
And both dwell
In the crevices of your face.

II

You are my second I: my first friend,
My first enemy.
Loyally, you'll accompany me to the Kingdom of Dust
And then return home
To become I,
Truly I.
Not like anybody else in the world.

It was good to live. Just to live,
To string wounds into a dream-figure,
Even that
Was a grace.
Now, from the Kingdom of Dust,
From above, I shall accompany your steps,
Twin brother.

III

Too late?
Then turn yourself into Ezekiel's prophecy.
Tune your bones with veins
No one has ever stretched before.
Breathe into yourself
A savage force
To conjure up a rock
With your words.

IV

Twin brother in the red dunes of a mirror,
A jealous sword cut off your wings. Come nearer.

Do you hear, in distant cloud, how lightnings rustle?
Your wings long for their shoulders, for their muscle.

Sometimes: a sudden shudder shakes your empty shoulder
(Thus grass, sensing rain, grows taller, bolder),

Then you are time-wise more than time, that on your face is crying —
Too young for being born, much older than the dying.

V

You are not older by a year, you are a lifetime older.
Numbers are a trap for joy in sun's reflection.
Inhale the smell of silence, take a deep breath:
You are not older by a year, you are a life-time older.

Soon, you are the age of your Creator.

VI

There is a forest where fireflies wing,
Lead you astray in a narrow ring
Where colors bathe in a black spring.

Colors bathe by themselves. Their whirling wail
Draws you in deep, if you walk on the trail
To the black spring wrapped in a silver veil.

In that magic spring, a sign will still hide
Your earliest sounds, mute voices abide.
Swan begets swan, on the water they glide.

Where to? To you. Through you. A miracle white,
Only for you, for your delight.
Bow to the miracle, wondrous sight.

Syllable begets syllable in your ear —
Silent as in an ear, you hear:
To change one moment into ever-here.

You hear a seed suckling in its bliss.
Echo of silences, deep in abyss.
The unknown calls you: name it if you can.

Blessed be the unknown. Amen.

VII

Twin-brother,
Twin-time,
We unique,
We double,
Should a thorn prick my skin,
You'd feel a drop of trouble.

Should a beak peck at my brow,
With a sound or mute,
Your brow too will feel with me
Pecking so acute.

On the whetstone of a sound
A tear is being honed,
It will light the cloud's abyss,
The darknesses we owned.

Twin-brother,
What will be
When we part anew?
Twin-time,
Is there no
Kingdom for us two?

Let's say, with my head
I will crack the mirror,
What will be?
— The red dunes
Will shudder ever nearer.

1984

Blond Dawn

(1934–1937)

Yankl Adler, portrait of Sutzkever for his first volume of poetry, Warsaw 1937.

Away From the Four Walls

Away from the four walls,
Where the traces of my footstep sear,
Vast panoramas of granite
Appear.

Fiery rocks. Abysses deep.
Music flows of melted gold:
— Beloved, your unknown name
Will be told!

I climb upward, climb
Over steps of stone, over gorges in sight,
To the blue gods of genesis
In the height.

My touch, in ecstasy, will melt
The colors — blue and violet —
On the face of a rock I etch
My portrait.

Strides and valor overwhelm me:
My gaze from granite's face.
I descend from rock to the earth,
Enveloped in grace.

White flame — a veil on the mountains,
My step — silver echoes on the planet.
Today I breathed my will
Into granite.

Here I Am

Here I am, blooming as big as I am,
Stung by songs as by fiery bees.
I heard you call me in the shining dawn
And rushed to you through night and dust and sweat.
Cities and villages tore off from me.
Lightning set thin fire to my old, gray home.
A rain washed away the red traces.
And I stood before your name
As before the blue mirror of conscience.
Like flayed branches, my hands
Rap hastily on your bright door.
My trembling and baffled eyes,
Like two sails, are drawn to you.
Suddenly: the door is open.
You're not there.
Everything's gone.
A poem left behind.
Silly weeping.
Incomprehension.

1935

In the Knapsack of the Wind

In evening-gold,
A barefoot wanderer on a stone
Casts off his body the dust of the world.
Out of the forest
Darts a bird,
Catches the last morsel of sun.

A willow on the riverbank is also there.

A road.
A field.
A quivering meadow.
Sly steps
Of hungry clouds.
Where are the hands that create wonders?

A living fiddle is also there.

So what remains for me to do at such an hour,
Oh, world mine in thousand colors?
Just
To gather in the knapsack of the wind
The red beauty
And bring it home for supper.

Solitude like a mountain is also there.

1935

from **Autumn Dances**

I

Give me your hand, sister, I'll lead you
To autumn. From its jug shall arise
Flaming punch, we shall drink it until
We grow ripe like the autumn, and wise.

Over there on the hill lies a shepherd.
A windwolf has devoured all his sheep.
Sunglow freezes on his pale hands,
At his feet, a tree bows deep.

In the field — a bright sheaf, embracing
A lady sheaf, strolling by in the light —
A bridegroom leads his bride where a cloud
Faithfully makes them a bed for the night.

But a windmill is already grinding their sunset,
Grinding legends, grinding the wind on the run,
And paints with dream-color your brow
Till you yourself go down in the late sun.

Rolling stones shiver like lyres,
Rolling words grow drunk and rancid.
Let us scatter our cares in the field,
Let us dance the autumn dances!

IV

Noisily, zestfully, in haste,
Cavalcades of trees on the road —
Entwine me in their branching fantastics,
In a treetop vision of halfdream.

I become a part of their tangle,
Gallop along with the trees —
To the stars! I, their friend, slice
With my head through the horizons.

Over fields, beam-children are dozing.
(Whose hand has planted them here?)
Through shadows of bowing assemblies
I ride with the riders in the night.

Rivers. Villages. I hover over them.
What I hover over becomes *mine*.
Just a boy, I grow up to be a hero
With a new goal, a new being.

Suddenly — an amazing moment:
Wild swaying. Shoving. Terrors range.
Over me — the diamond Vega,
Close to me — my life, large and strange.

Gypsy Autumn

On spungolden horseshoes the autumn is galloping through.
A wind with red blood on its fingers gropes every hue
And sings over fields a sad drunken ballad of old.

A gypsy band huddles together like sheep in a fold
Around sunset's bonfire, spraying its sparks all about.
A heart weeps away in the broad sorrow-dome and goes out . . .

An old gypsy sits, with an earring of fine silver leaf,
With a knife from his belt he unravels his hoary gray grief,
The dark cores of his eyes fill with blood, but no fear:

—Hey brothers, dear brothers, I see how the end's coming near
To our gypsy race. We shall sink in abyss and expire,
We shall be extinguished, die out, like the sparks of our fire.

Strum all mandolins! Let us scatter our dance to the wind!
Let us plait burning thorns into wreathes on our head, let them spin
Till the wintery snow covers up every spark, every trace.

For then there will be in this world no more gypsy race,
And only the howling wide steppe and the trees in the vale
Will see us in dreams and will tell of our colorful tale.

On spungolden horseshoes the autumn is galloping through.
A wind with red blood on its fingers gropes every hue
And sings over fields a sad drunken ballad of old.

A gypsy band huddles together like sheep in a fold.

1936

A Stack of Hay

A silvery stack of hay under my head,
In a meadow, I dream. No, I'm awake.
So many stars above — as drops
Of dew on earth. A white road
Rises in my stiffening eyes.
The stack of hay
Reminds me of my fate, she's close to me,
Rocking me slowly in her cradle.

Smell of blood like blooming honey.
Hot lust gushes from the raw plain.
The stack of hay washed in dew and moon,
And I — it seems I'm lying beside myself,
Breathing in fresh hay the smell
Of green time. I feel, walking through me
Flower and scythe. I lie on an altar
Of colors and smells. Every rustle and sound
Comes strangely close, streams through my limbs.
The tiniest blade of grass, I ache its pain . . .
I lie in hay — a weary wanderer,
Till I myself become a stack of hay.

1936

The Gates of the Ghetto[5]

I

A long arm of fire
Burst the gates of the ghetto.

A blind beggar, the day
Stands at the corner
Of an old wall,
Weeping pennies in his fists.

He would shake the old gates,
Bring down the walls,
Like imprisoned Samson
The marble columns,
And fall with the ghetto!

(Oh gates — wailing moons,
Caressed
By the fingers of my thoughts!)

This is the truth of the knife.
From green roofs
Stars take off —
Homeless children,
And hear
The fever of a mute generation.
A generation of fighters, singers, and hoodlums.

This is the truth of the knife.
In shards of windowpanes
The sun is a red toadstool.
Every face an autumn leaf,
Chains — every sound,
Unrest
Slithers up like a serpent —
Over roofs,
Over gates,
Higher!

II
An organ-grinder like a Purim clown
Clamors on his sick instrument.
A cross-eyed yellow parrot
Wobbles on his bony hands.
The man is a singer too
And he intones
A ballad flashing in your ear:
    "Seven brothers slaughtered in the pogrom,
    The eighth one fell at the gate."

Children touch
The dusty organ-grinder.
And he who cranks the song
And the children — blue and naked,
Along with the parrot
And the little water carrier
Carrying his prayer in a cracked bucket —
All tangled up
In a magic ring,
Each a mirror for the other.

III

But sometimes, the ghetto rocks in a trance,
Violet windows sway in a dance.

Through thin golden dust, like a brook in a valley,
Blue-eyed youngsters flooding the alley.

Sleeves rolled up, strong arms like a steeple:
"From their own ghetto, we shall free the people!"

The echo falls on the houses like thunder,
The ancient walls are amazed at the wonder.

A blinding flash. Eyes rising and bright.
And sounds reach out like bridges of light . . .

The alleys huddle, fearful and gray
Watching the blood of freedom's day.

A blinding flash. Extinguished the light.
The golden vision has vanished from sight . . .

IV

Evening. The ghetto turns blue.
Hot colors take their course.
The Gaon appears in the *shul-yard*[6]
From behind copper doors.

A girl sits on a stoop,
Inhales the letters of a book.
Dreams of a rare pleasure:
Bread and shoes in her nook.

The shadows grow thick and wide.
Like a peacock, the sun will depart.
A youth pulls a knife like a beam
Out of his boottop's heart.

The moon would have fit in this scene.
Aha! she's lurking in wait.
But it seems, a bullet-torn flag
Rises behind a gate . . .

June 1936

Siberia

(1936)

Marc Chagall, illustrations to Siberia, *1953.*

In the Hut

I

Setting sun on roads in icy blue.
Sweet, the slumber-colors in your heart.
From the valley, shimmering toward you,
In the snow of sunset shines a hut.
Wonder-woods sway wide on window-panes,
Magic sleighs ring in a ring. A niche
In the attic: doves. Their humming rains,
Humming out my face. And the Irtysh,[7]
Flashing crystals on its icy deck
Trembles, half-unreal half-beguiled.
Silence-soaring cupolas protect
Blooming world: a seven-year-old child.

II

In the shining-dark, the snowed-in home
Of my childhood in Siberia's waste,
Eyes of shadows blossom in a dome —
Quicksilvery flowers, light-encased.
In extinguished corners, one after another,
Blows the moon her breath, her dazzling bands.
White as face of moon, my looming father,

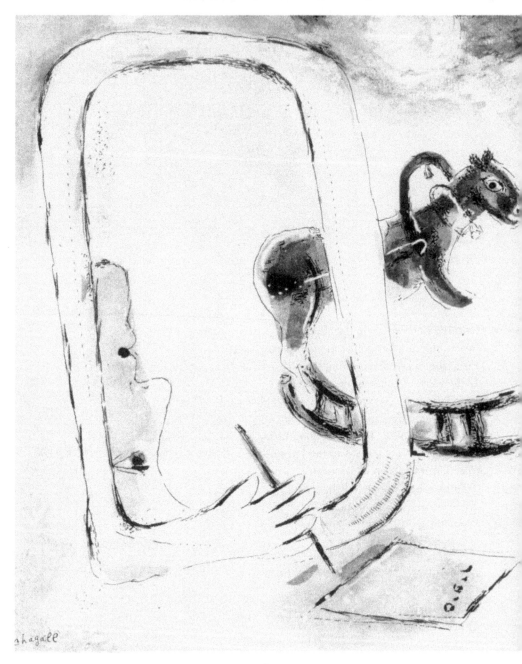

Silence of the snow is on his hands.
Father cuts black bread with shining knife.
Merciful. And blue, his bearded head.
And with freshly sliced ideas rife,
I immerse in salt my father's bread.

III

Knife of mercy. Father. Smoking brand.
Childhood. Shadow pulls a violin
From the wall. And sound-flurries descend,
Snow-sounds falling on my head, thin-thin.
Silence. Father plays. Each sound, each hue —
Etchings in the air. Like in a frost
Silver slivers of your breath hang blue
Over moon-glazed space, on snowy crust.
Through a pane engulfed in icy furs
Peeps a wolf to sniff the music's flesh.
Silence. In our dovecote now occurs:
Baby-dove pecks out of eggshell, fresh.

Dawn

Signs of paws — an animal has sown
Like blue roses in the white snow's gleam,
When the sun, new risen and unknown,
Like a baby, casts its piercing scream —
Barely gilded on their rims. Below,
Darkness still. The roots of forest's trees
Gnash their teeth in deep ravines of snow.
Harnessed to a sled, a dog will wheeze
Living steam. The steam climbs straight and high,
Meets a chimney smoke, just slightly bent,
And a human breath that's drawing nigh —
Hovering in air at dawn, a tent.

Recognition

I

"Papa, tell me where the whole world ends!" —
Philosophically, solution I request.
Answers he: "See, where the sun descends,
Just behind that hut, beyond hill's crest."
Really? If it's so — I would not think:
Catch up with the setting sun! I run,
In a silver net of tears, up, to the brink,
Where the whole world ends and hides the sun!
Eyes are begging the Siberian God
Not to make my longing all in vain.
All the zillion years before me nod,
Trembling in the snow: Be blessed again.

II

Back of me, my father — tiny dot.
Toward the sun is galloping my heart.
Now, I run uphill and reach the hut!
Eagerness still beckons, won't depart.
To the bonfire, over howling pit,
Stretch my lips, my body would descend.
Papa, see, the world goes on a bit,
And there is no, is no, is no end.
Papa cannot hear. A star will blanch.
Papa cannot see, out of the blue,
How a boy becomes an avalanche
Made of light and wonderment anew.

Like a Sled Bedecked with Longing Bells

On the blue, the diamond snow, I write
With the wind as with a magic pen,
Straying in the shimmering depth and light
Of his childhood. Never seen, as then,
Such lucidity, which grips, compels
All the lonely shadows of your mind.
Like a sled bedecked with longing bells,
Thin and long, my life will toll behind,
Through the evening steppe. And in its mirror,
Moon will press her nose against the glass,
With two wings, reflecting brighter, clearer,
Sparkling brass.

A Fur of Fire

Fields around — of shiny dazzling metals.
Trees — in icy rock, all climbing higher.
Snows have no more room to drop their petals,
Sun walks in the sky in fur of fire.
With his diamond brush upon my pate
Artist Frost paints as on window pane
Snowy legends of his color palette,
Signed in flight of dove, in sky a strain.
Sun sets inside me. Ended her route.
Just her flaming fur alone arose
On a stretching branch. And I — a mute —
Would put on the fur before it goes.

In a Siberian Forest

I

Infant sun, forever born anew,
Rolls in snow with me, with light enriched.
Papa says: "Come on, the sky is blue,
Let's go fetch some wood." And so we hitched
To a sled our silver colt. And went!
Shining axe. In flames of snow, the day
Sliced by whetted sun-knives. Sound is spent.
Sparkling dust — our breath! We run — away,
Over silent steppe of sleeping bears,
Through the sunweb. Ringing fields aglow.
Yesternight has scattered all its stars,
Frozen now they lie, calm in the snow.

II

Forest. Fresh the glimmer on the trees
Breathes the howling of the wolves. Around,
Glowing echoes of the silence breeze,
Shoot hot arrows in my heart, resound.
Every snowflake is a bell of winter,
Touch it — and it rings, a paradox!
Till the ring splits in a thousand splinters,
From a snow tent comes a little fox,
He sticks out his tongue and disappears.
— "Foxie, do not fear!" A spark that cracks
Warms my cheek and takes away the fear,
Till the sun sets in my father's axe.

III

To our quiet hut we travel back,
But my soul still straying in the forest.
Good old forest, calm and deep and black,
Warms it and includes it in his chorus.
Stars blown by the wind, sailing on high,
Crown me with their song, with sparks at play!
For the stars above I want to cry . . .
Till the forest's last tree fades away,
Just the ruts in snow, as in a bed.
Father's voice awakens me, we roam,
And I see: the moon is in our sled,
Traveling to the valley, to our home.

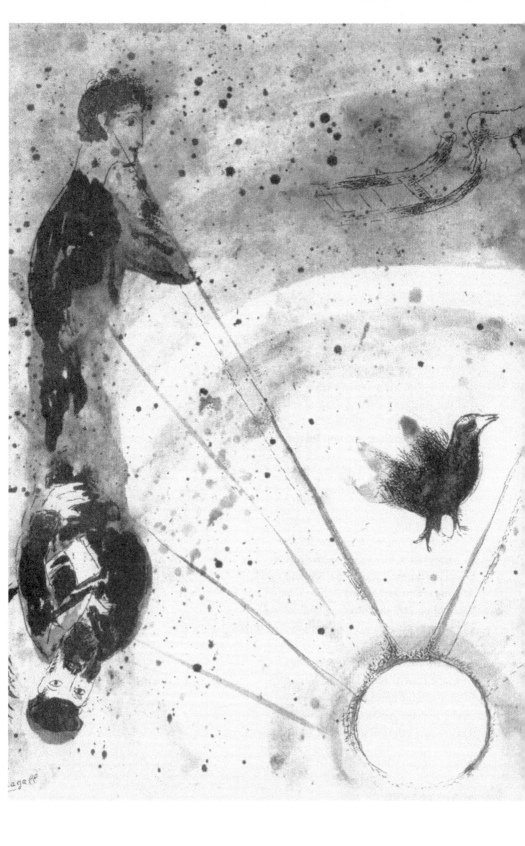

To Father

Pa, behind your coffin on a sled
I ran after you, I wanted to
Catch up with your memory that fled.
At my breast a dove as white as snow.
When a pole, with pulsing heartbeats, hollowed
In the ice a hut, for you to stay,
And the white abyss has quickly swallowed
You — in ice, you sparkle to this day —
I too wanted to jump in with you!
But my dove burst out of my embrace:
Evening sun crowned with white gold that flew —
And to life she drew me in her trace. . .

Irtysh

Hush! From what new source springs such a ringing?
The Irtysh is fleeing from its shore!
Seeks in cold waves, whirlpooling and swinging,
Faces of the days that are no more.
From a circle cut in ice, it opens
To the stars its eyes: "Oh, spring, how long
Will you overlook my praying, hoping?
Will the ice be broken by my song?"
Then the night has muttered to his beard:
— "A new sun is being forged!" A shiver —
And a star fell from a thread and sheered
Down, to kiss the stirring winter river.

Snowman

I

Snowman, monument to childhood, guard
Of a frozen treasure! Not in vain
Do I still believe you are my lord.
Hail to you, my snowman, hail again!
You're the god of children and of wind,
At your feet, my rainbow dream arrives.
Wolves come up in packs to you to spin
Prayers: Snowman, watch over our lives!
Snowman, you're eternal, never melts
Your white, sparkling crystal coat of mail.
Beautiful your dancing on your stilts
For the human stars down in the vale!

II

Snowman, clumsy, with a pot so triste —
On your head a crown! Come and surprise:
One more time your smile out of the mist.
All my loneliness warm with your ice.
If my longing reached you left behind —
In the traces of my footsteps go:
In a hut of sounds, there you will find
Me in holy prayer to the snow.
If you don't find — you alone will last,
We have missed each other like a rhyme.
You inherit then my small-hut past
And you finish breathing out my time.

Siberian Spring

I

Multicolored wings begin to flutter
Over *taiga*[8] wilderness in wind.
And a melted mirror springs and shudders
Over miles, where green seams just begin.
Snows sing a farewell, a wet, gray chain,
Wings and mirrors full of hues and sound.
With the lion's roaring of the rain
Flares the childish wish to run unbound,
Catching up with all wild streams he misses,
Flying like a bird, he'd soar away:
Over people, forests, rocks, abysses —
To the new, the shining festive day!

II

Shimmering in bright green, the Irtysh
Polishes its metal on the stone.
Wants to find again its waves, its fish,
For again the floes of ice are flown. . .
And instead of looking dark and grave
Through its only eye, a sawn-out wheel —
It observes through every tiny wave
How the world is spinning in a reel
Round the sun that, daring, from its perch,
Hurls its swords, and now it licks the sweet,
Sparkling ice-shine of a budding birch
As a child licks eagerly a treat.

Kirghizes[9]

From afar, hello to you, Kirghizes
At Irtysh's bonfires, gilded hues,
Where, among the dancing spears still breezes
Your old melody, in dance you lose
Melancholy hearts, and fall asleep.
Everyone his weeping sips like brandy.
And the camel's hump, he smiles so deep
With his creases, wisely understanding
All the music of your yellow fever.
When my life, a lantern that flickers —
Far, to you, I bend my song forever,
Open seven ears — hear deeper, quicker.

My Childhood Friend Changury

I

Are you still alive, my friend Changury,
Or a snowman amid frozen seas?
From the clouds your flickering face is luring
With two pupils borrowed from the trees.
Let us play again and find anew
All we never had in childhood past.
At the early breath of dawn, still blue,
Let us kiss each leaf and blade of grass.
Let us gulp mare's milk from goatskin bag,
Start a hunt of owls in light of day.
Let us, after long carousing, sag,
Fall asleep as then, slumped by the way.

II

Come, my brother, riding on your deaf
Humpy camel, quickly hoist me up
By my shirt and hold me like a staff—
Let us soar into the wind and gallop
To the quiet corners, there to meet
Birth of shadows ere the fall of night.
Grasses sparkle, charming at our feet.
Splendor doesn't know its own rich sight.
Spots of life dark in the tundra wide,
The Irtysh is clouded, on his own.
Camel steeped in blue. And we both ride
To the lustrous rocks of granite stone.

III

When the haughty mountains disappear
And a violet forest floats aloft,
A long evening-hand brings close and near
All that's separate, is merging soft.
The last flicker dances on a fir.
A last word is dancing on our lips.
In grass dream, our camel doesn't stir.
Only silence sails off on its ships.
In the sky a rake combs a wet cloud.
Opens up its secrets. Night comes mellow.
And we eat the moon (it is allowed!)
Like a sliced-up piece of watermelon.

At the Bonfire

I

In the forest, night stokes up a fire.
Youthful trees grow ashen gray in fear.
Among crackling branches, climbing higher,
Shadows fall where axes sharp appear.
The Kirghizes, sitting in the glow,
Mirrored in their flashing blades, awake.
Branches crackle with a rooster's crow.
And like pearls when a necklace breaks
Falls the dew on praying hands, clasped tight,
Falls the dew on sparks, all rising higher.
And a soaring bird, sunk in the night,
Flutters in, its violin on fire.

II

A bronze figure leaps, a daring star
At the bonfire, comes in with a bound,
In a dance with silvery guitar,
Whirling with the forest all around.
Whirling. Drums. An ardent tune, a spell.
Till in sparkling rhythm of the rite —
All the forest swinging like a bell.
Last stars fall into the beards of night.
Drunkenly dance with him the Kirghizes
In a chain around the flaming dish.
And with waves like running spears, he freezes,
Tickles the horizons, the Irtysh.

The North Star

North Star, you who walk along with me,
I'm your snowman in a cloak of skin.
From my coldness, all the neighbors flee,
Just the birches at the fence stay in.
North Star, faithful to the death, I see
How much mildness you recall and stir!
Every summer, fire snows on me,
Winter brings your ringing in my ear.
Let the memory that never passed
To your bluish smile above be sent.
Let these sounds, let this demanding quest,
Over me remain a monument.

From the Forest

(1937–1939)

Drawing by the poet.

✭

All is worthy of the roaming of my eye,
All is noble, precious for my verse:
Grasses, trees, a spring, a vessel, earth,
And the distant rainbow hues of sleep.
    In everything, I come upon a splinter
Of infinity.

I see my body in the white of a birch,
I feel my blood in the blooming of a rose,
And out of nature's metamorphosis
I spin of consciousness a house.
    In everything, my master is revealed
Deep and great.

Simple dusts speak of forgiveness,
Silent dew — of shining grace.
Apples announce wise love
Of the white, isolated orchard.
    Every moment without a hymn —
Is a loss.

A. SUTZKEVER   *95*

All I can feel is mine.
Wherever my word can reach, there I am.
Like a spring in the desert, pleasure gushes
And draws my life's caravan.
    In everything, everything, there is a trace
Of my footstep.

From the Forest

Of grass and flowers, the substance dissolves
Into drops of dew.
And he who wants can see
The subtle play
Of black and fire, silver and blue.
All around,
Trees sleep, sprawling on the ground,
Their shadows grow high.
The air is cool and soft
As dry
Water.
Silent, calm,
Mute paths kiss.
Here-and-there,
Green glows wink at you.
A nest trembles,
A spring shines.
You see:
Worlds spin on their axes
And dews are mirrors for the cosmos.

If someone screamed right now,
All the skies would dissolve
In cosmic panic.
But all is hush. Just shadows
Cast by a spirited nightingale:
Following the star notes, he reveals
His lonely night

> And his travail.

Lost Nest

See
A lost nest on the road?

Its tenant, its tenant ran off.
> The wind blew it up — right
> Here. And you, whose home is the night
Found a nest warm and soft.

Landscape

Sky — the dream of a lunatic.
No sun. The sun blooms and gushes,
Metamorphosed into a hot, full,
Wild rosebush in the field.
The wind is a magician. He buttons
   Day with night.
A root chatters with a root.
     A cloud laughs
     In sleep. A flashing eye
     Winks from the forest.
     Like falling stars, birds fly.

Rain of Colors and Flowers

I

Rains fall,
Serpentine, stalk-like —
Hordes of wet winds gallop over the earth,
Lightning,
Etching
Dreams unheard-of
Into the air,
   Thoughts freshly branching
Green-flowering,
   Downpouring,
     Torrents

Scared of the noisy valor
In the sky.
Behind them — a flower-bordered evening.
Behind it — a village
Looming up out of the earth,
A road,
   A cherry orchard
And
   A man.

All this illuminated by the rain.

II

I am the birth of the forest
That wants to sky up from the earth.
You are the sunny herald
Announcing that my thought is heard.
Whence your going and coming
I know, from my lucid words,
Oh, fiery-flodding joy,
Oh, rain of colors and flowers.

I lie in the grassy damp,
Entwined in the thought of your light.
I feel on my body a river
Blending dream and wine.
Your beauty words my palate.
Your fire kindles me like silk.
I beg you: enliven me, cut me
With streams, with colors and flowers.

You, like a starbody pure,
Perceive the speech of my spirit
That whispers trusting to you,
All my blood you release
From its embalmed muteness.
I do not feel how I soar
Upward to you from my rest,
Oh, rain of colors and flowers.

You cloak me in your cape,
You purify my body with your grace.
Forests glimmer gold-green,
Festooned with light and mystery.
I feel: You perceived my prayer,
Gave it flesh of vision, in such hours:
Now I forest up in the air,
Rained in with colors and flowers.

Electrical Content

Stars storm and startle —
Flood of electrical flows
Into granite cisterns —
Through the dark a castle glows.

Black caves breathing gold —
No one will gather it fresh.
Someone anoints with blue oil
A thought seeking flesh.

Do not touch the grass, the leaves.
Lightning in each speck of dirt.
Swim away in silent ether
To a second heart, a third.

Birds hover. Strangely falling
Into an abyss of mood.
And the white goddess Luna
Dances naked in the wood.

In a Summer Morning

I

A tapestry of sapphire ether,
My daybreak paths. Through
The latenight dark they led me
To mountains, where a rain
Of planet calm hovers
Over frightened windflowers, weeds,
And the freshly-cut raw earth.
But the young sun pours its clarity
Behind mountain forests, spraying
A geyser of colors, its radiant
Thoughts flicker lightnings
Over water. A silver lyre,
The air, and a chirping melody
Breathed into strings
Swayed by the wind. Far away,
The wheat-stalk dunes, waves
Of humid ochre — until

All the images of morning
Rise in wise awareness
   In the tapestry of my words.

II

Oh, whence the green crystals, seams
Of shimmer on the mountains all around?
And the rosy, grassy valleys,
Where stars lie feverish. My blood
Blooming. Like the mind of a genius,
Zephyrs flow with warm puffs.
In the desert of the air, blues flourish
Like pellucid oases. The grasses
Forgive the footsteps that tread
On their green thought. A rivulet
Sings out on a violet plane,
Its rhyming voice of a lamb.
Through squirrelly, nutty woods,
Now losing all measures,
The sun strides with its fiery train —
And the cloverleaf covered with red.
The creator of plenty girded up
My feeling, he throbs in my pulse.
And my daybreak spirit warbles
   Out of sleep, and awakes.

III

You, pitchblack, slender firtree,
Apart from the sun's stream!
You, transparent, turquoise spring well,
Whose mirrorsoul sings and amazes
My thought! You, diamond poppies
With hairy, sticky stems!
And you, dear chirpers, enthroned
In the air! All that is transient
And eternal — to you all now

My blessings! For all my senses
Are primeval, my body — armored
With time's garb of all times,
In your eternal bloodstreams
My blood streams too, and under
Your lovely, peaceful glances,
I am earthy — a trunk in the ground.
My life's mysterious destinies
Spring out of your depths.
We are bound by the same joys
    And the same fire.

IV

Man, encountered on the road
Near ripe and scarlet orchards —
Our happy early meeting
Is a miracle, your every barefoot
Stepping trace — a tale
Of your fate's bloody struggle —
Though the sun has endowed its part
To you too, as to the dewy stalk —
You are close to my heart. I greet you:
Goodmorning, and offer my hand, we are
United by the colorful morning.
The sun, our primeval mother, cleanses
All the shadows, and smells of a garden
And of bluish perfumes of hay,
The breeze's trembling caress
Is a balm for our grief.
Silent brother, let us together
Plumb the foundations of the world,
The concealed stem of all stems,
    The above and below.

Stars Become Sheaves

Sheaves gazing cold — pink swans
Want to swim away,
    Take in the words
    And the meaning
    Of seven stars
    Hanging on the sky-tree,
    Listening.

Now: The seven stars as fire arrows —
Down to the field.
Down,
Down —
They rush, they want to become sheaves.

    Miracle. The sheaves swim off,
    Sing a farewell, and forgive
    The wonder-stars from afar,
    Who become sheaves, crocheted into time.
    And kneeling to the miracle of change —
    The seven.

Sirius

Blue flickering flames
Near-far splendor
Over the dreaminess
Of gold turquoise
Lucidity
Of latenight!
You, bonfiring
Heavenly composer —
See the heat of my rage,
My word embrace,
In your memory-glow
Seal my face.

On a Mountaintop

There is a tone that blares
After all the music died away . . .
  — Yehoash[10]

Where the blue has swallowed every green,
Runs a waterfall. Into its stream
The sun weaves her last glances, flows
Down together with the stream.

The stream, through folds and crevices, dazzles in the valley.
Sunshine trembles lightly in his depths.
But he cannot conceal his treasure
From the inexorable blue.

Airy nature forces in collision.
Fire-echoes. The blue gives birth to springs
Of calm. Its kisses stir the vitality
    Of the earth.

    Now is my hour,
    Rejoicer, ruler, you!
    I am a sound, a tremor
    In your deep blue.
    On a soft haystack
    You created me,
    And a red bird
    Pecks, pecks, pecks
    Genesis syllables
    In my skull, and flutters
    To celestial Sirius.

Like camels, caravans of shadows
Kneel in awe at the water,
Remain deep in sweet doze,
On soft knees. Dew rustles

Among white leaves. Blue children
Blend with the grass. A wind
Descends from the sky as a link
Between song and time. Silence ignites

Violet drawbridges over the valley.
From the forest — mood calls.
A blend of honeysap and wormwood,
    The air.

Destiny mine, let
My footsteps not falter —
Be my oracle now,
When the evening blooms
Under my thoughts
And in the crown of a fir
And at sky's fence
Flashes, flashes, flashes
The soul of the
       Black forests.

Eternity? Who knows: is it eternal,
Will this same evening
Not return sweeter, loftier
Through the forest parting of roots?

But the mountain believes. His memory
Recalls the generations when he was
Still a valley, and how, much later,
He became a mountain, a giant.
All is metamorphosis, renewal.
A moment — and the mountains
Seem different. Old becomes young.
       Small grows big.

       Evening, come, inspire,
       I want to be a shadow
       Of your cosmic fire,
       Against the stars, a tree
       Under your coattails,
       Here, where I lie,
       Rock me, sing me a lullaby,
       Be my faithful dome.
       Give, give, give
          For my body a home.

A. SUTZKEVER   *107*

Beyond the Sun

Beyond the sun who can reach?

. . . Once, in an evening purple soft,
When the air was kindled wool,
I met a boy rolling a wooden hoop
From a backyard,
Through alley and street,
Uphill, where the ball of the sun
Was suspended —
A roll and a rush and a run —
And he set
In the sun,
In the red transparence,
Tore apart
The heart of the sun with his hoop
And, drunken,
Rolled it on,
On and on.

My Temples Are Throbbing

My temples are throbbing —
Galloping, galloping:
Two riders, two riders,
Each dashes,
Each whirs,
Through skull and through head,
With horns and spurs.

One rider is white and the other is black,
Both armored like heroes, no slip and no slack.

The white one is joyous, the black — is in wrath.
The white is up front and the black — is like death.

Blackwhite and whiteblack — over trees, over gullies;
Whiteblack and blackwhite — like the hues of a *tallis*.[11]

The white — with a sunny flag of a ranger,
The black one — danger, danger, danger.

The white one rides off in direction of light,
The black will extinguish each spark, he is night.

Clipclop and clipclop,
By destiny's will,
Two riders are riding
To a single sill.

To the only sill only one will arrive.
(The white one, the white?
The black one, the black?
The eyes are blinded, the bones crack.)

Rolled by the storm,
Two hoops in the rain —
Two riders that run
Through throbbing brain —
On and on.

And the one who arrives,
And the one who accedes —
Will be written
With blood
Over grasses and weeds.

from Ecstasies

Imprisoned, imprisoned
Am I
In the polished sounds
Of the sky —
No escape from its fences
That flame —
As before the eyes of a fly
In a glass
Overturned.
And beyond the glass — words bloom,
Blossoms grass
(Let me smash the glass walls, oh please!
Release!)
And above —
A flock of opal doves,
They cannot break out
Of the tangle of tunes,
Of the melody swing,
And remain
Imprisoned
Inside a ring.

Pity.

＊

Like a rain on a field all of a sudden —
And there is no hiding, no home outside it —
In the middle of the roads,
In wild encounter, love fell upon me
And illuminated
The other side of my yearning.

— Why like a rain?

You don't know whence it comes, whence it rolls,
You see only the spot where it falls.

＊

When with eyes shut
I wrote a poem, suddenly
My hand got burned,
And when I started
From the black fire,
The paper breathed
A name like a lily: God.
But my pen, in awe and wonder,
Crossed out the word
And wrote instead
A more familiar word: Man.

Since then, a voice unheard
Haunts me like an unseen bird
That pecks, pecks at my soul's door:
— Is that what you traded me for?

A. SUTZKEVER   *111*

Epilogue to the Forest

(1939–1940)

War[12]

The same ashes will cover all of us:
The tulip — a wax candle flickering in the wind,
The swallow in its flight, sick of too many clouds,
The child who throws his ball into eternity —

And only one will remain, a poet —
A mad Shakespeare, who will sing a song, where might and wit is:
— My spirit Ariel, bring here the new fate,
And spit back the dead cities!

1939

Anthill

Anthill, subconscious of the forest,
Poked up by a curious stick —
Your labyrinths, storey on storey,
Collapse into dust. Be aware:

I am like you. My skull
Crumbles into shards
Carried off by ants — by words.

And every word — up, down, over — roams
From nerve to nerve, through smoke and powder keg.
And all are running from their homes,
Bearing in their mouth a snow-white egg.

1940

Gray Time

Oh, love your dog, your bed, your platter,
But do not love the gray time.
A faithful dog will not so flatter
As gray time will flatter you.

Your eye is not a nest for it.
Your mirror, not a test for it.
Your palate feels: won't go away.

It burns your pearls in despair.
And you wake up: your wisest hair
Is fooled and gray.

1940

Madness

Through alleys of sunset, a woman does hover,
She weeps: Give me back the straw, my lover.

Behind her a crowd, with water and rope,
That would not give back her straw and her hope.

Her yellow shawl slips off of her shoulder,
From afar — a firetruck comes, ringing bolder.

And no one in the crowd, shouting and raw,
Will grasp: can you fall in love with a straw?

1940

In a Garden

I dream: I am a sun that sinks
Into a swamp among lilies. Nearby, rife
With leaves of time, hangs a garden, sings
A weeping bird: Where is your life?

But like an amoeba, I split in two:
Just my earth half will descend in a cave.
As I see my image in the red of an apple,
From the swamp screams my second I: Save.

Is the dream over? — I do not know.
When I awoke in a garden so fair,
In sun's dew laurels — my world
Screamed: *Save me*, as there.

April 1940

Faces in Swamps

(June–July 1941)

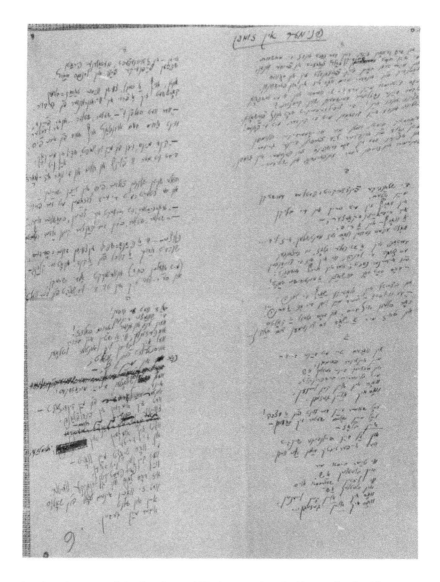

Sutzkever's poems of the first days of Nazi occupation, in his own handwriting,
Vilna 1941, discovered after 49 years in Vilnius, Lithuania. (See introduction to the
cycle "Faces in Swamps.")

Faces in Swamps

The cycle, "Faces in Swamps," was written in hiding during the first days of the Nazi occupation of Vilna. Subsequently, it was hidden in a ghetto cellar and discovered forty-nine years later in Vilnius. The manuscript contains nine poems with the following note in the poet's hand:

> Note. I wrote the nine poems of "Faces in Swamps" in the first 10 days, when the Plague marched into Vilna. Approximately between June 25 and July 5. I wrote them lying stuck in a broken chimney in my old apartment on Wilkomirska Street 14. This way I hid from the Snatchers who dragged off every Jewish male they could find.
>
> My wife carried the poems through all the horrors and tragedies. They were with her through the first provocation, were covered with blood, in prison under Schweinenberg's whip. Miraculously, my wife fled back to the ghetto with the poems, where I no longer was — I had fled in the middle of the night, during the Roundup of the Yellow Permits. When I returned, I found my wife in the hospital where she gave birth to a baby. In her labor pains, she was clutching the poems in her hands.
>
> A.S.
> Ghetto Vilna, May 16, 1942.

The text translated here is from the manuscript. The titles of two poems were added later.

I. *Faces in Swamps*

. . . And overnight our thoughts grew gray. The sun
Sowed poison salt on open wounds. We choke.
White doves turned into owls. They're poking fun,
Mocking our dream that disappeared in smoke.

Why tremor, earth? Did you crack too, in trance?
Your nostrils smelled the stench of victim's flesh?
Devour us! We were cursed by overconfidence,
Devour us with our children, with our flags so fresh!

You're thirsty, earth. We, wailing pumps, will fill
With gold of our young bodies your newly opened pits.
A spiderweb of faces in a swamp will spin to kill:
Faces in a swamp — over the sunset, over huts . . .

II

Serpents of darkness: nooses choke
My breath.
Horseradish in my eyes, I toss
In a grater dungeon —
Each toss grates my skin.
Were there anything human, familiar . . .

My hand gropes: a piece of glass, the moon
Trembles imprisoned like me in the vise
Of the iron night. I grow tense:
"This was created by a human hand!"

In the glass edge I stroke the moon:
"You want? — I give you my life as a gift!"
But life is hot and the glass is cold
And it's a shame to put it to my throat. . .

III. Leaves of Ash

I warm tea with your letters —
My only treasure,
Thin leaves of ash remain,
Sprinkled with glowworms
That I alone can read, can ask:
I warm tea with *your* letters,
My only treasure?

Let the wind be mute as a tombstone!
Let my shadow stand still!
One puff —
And all your healing beauty
Will stir jealousy
On all the roads.

How dear are you to me in leaves of ash,
How shining do you die in leaves of ash,
That I alone can read, can ask:
I warm tea with *your* letters,
My only treasure?

July 6, 1941

A. SUTZKEVER   *123*

IV

Above — in a death swordplay, metal pirates
Spit whistling arrows into the heart of the moon.

Below, on a hill, among white tobacco flowers
A woman twisting on pain-and-wonder of birth.

"Who will help?" — "Hush, hush. . . " And her beloved
Weeps the glimmer of his eyes in the dust at her feet.

"My child, melody of my love, play on inside me, don't rush,
You are merely flesh and dream, and reality — is murder."

Slices of light swallow the fields. Fish in rivers scream.
The earth trembles along with the woman.

"Ghosts of death, don't dare touch, I beseech you. . . "
"Hush, hush, I am the armor against all evil."

Suddenly . . . like a piano playing among hordes of thunder,
A voice of a child slices through. And this sound —

(Whence the strength?) subjugates all fears,
And the love of the world turns the dew red.

V

Soon it will happen!
The black hoops
Grow tighter and tighter around my neck!
Impersonally, like a stone in a brook,
I shall remain lying under hooves,
Redeemed from the world.
But deep inside me —
Three ants still stray:
One,

Under the laurel of my childhood —
Will return to magicland.
The second,
Under the armor of my dream —
Will return to dreamland.
The third,
The one who carries my word —
Will have no path,
For the land of believing words
Is covered with plague.
In the valley of shadows, it will watch,
Alone and solitary,
Over my bones.

The Circus

Tell me, brother, our dog's struggle
What does it mean?
Our heart's gone mad.
All words fled —
Bees from a hive embraced by smoke.
But in a backstreet of the mind,
Still throbs
A flickering nerve saved from destruction,
A last groan
Defying that blind silence
Sealed by a handful of earth.

Who are we? What is
The sense of our suffering?
If only
To be victims of a bloodthirsty lord —
Let frogs be born instead of us!
The tongue is swollen with the rusty promise
That wolf and lamb will dwell together.
As a child resembles father-mother, we
Inherit the resemblances of generations' plague,
Of being waiters at the world's set table,
Grateful for a coin tossed to us.
Is this the golden chain that binds two thousand years,
The tear chain burdening our souls?

It seems, just yesterday,[13] forms lost their measure,
Abysses straightened out their hunchback necks
And covered the unburied skulls of generations
With hope —
    And we were ready
To accept the blooming wounds as medals,
Boast of them in a pagan parade:
— Ho, ho, we too take part in the dream-plundering,
With our blood, pay dues to revolutions!
We, we.
But a lion overlooks the branch-covered pit
Lurking at his paws.

Today — at dusk, in a circle,
Around bonfire's coppery wings,
Under whips of steel guards,
At the laughter of yesterday's comrade —
Naked, with striped backs,
We dance: I in the middle.
With our own hands, we are forced
To tear the silver parchment
And toss into the bonfire
Like our own limbs, singing
Happy Russian songs.
Look! Between sword and sheath
The voice of paradise looms,
Letters from Babylon flutter,
Inscribed on the blackboard of night.
And farther, on high coils —
Rising, the "I am"
From a consumed parchment,
And nothing —
He too went up in smoke.

✶

Circle, circle, dancing round,
    If you have a feeling — burn it,
    If there is a bath in hell,
This is where it will be found.

And without a stick the lame
    And the rabbi — blind and old,
    They're all hopping in a ring
For the joy and for the game.

Peasant woman hops to see:
    What a circus, God is One!
    Says a neighbor: Pay them stones,
For a circus costs a fee.

One whore points out in the clatter
    To another: See them naked!
    Stones are falling. Fire devours.
Climbs a *sheygets*[14] on a ladder.

Rabbi falls with stones that fall,
    Kissing sparks in ashes flying.
    And his *Sh'ma*[15] is drowning too
In the coldness of the All.

✶

And I, who was the clown in that disgraceful spectacle,
Had no courage to stammer a curse,
No strength to throw myself into the death,
As did my brothers in the time of Hadrian the Roman
When faith stifled in their body all the pain
(Though my heart is poisoned with coal glow
And the eyes of my spirit are speared with smoke).
Worse: I knelt naked before him,
Who defiled my father in his grave,
And with tears like black pox,
I begged for mercy.

    Cursed one! Where is your old shield
    That bent the spears of nations?
    The colors of that image, don't they reach you?
    The blood of your forefathers, was it never revealed?

    This is your punishment: to gasp half dead,
    Gulping death rattles of your brothers, insane.
    For you have not deserved the last bread
    Of joy: being naught — which means: becoming again.

Written in a hiding place, early July 1941

Written in Vilna Ghetto

(1941–1943)

They Search

A search all around. Any peep is a knife.
The bloodhounds — steps of a wrathful God.
But who protected us both with a fog?
Do you see? It envelops us . . . You nod . . .

Do you see the palace of gray, where all colors
Like suffocated babies sink in the gray.
We lie there in tandem like naked sheaves:
The fog and us two — all the rest swam away.

But in the no-one-ness, my mouth clinging tight
To red glints. Only now can I see how they part:
Out of the gray, your lips are abloom!
But who has created this purple art?

The fog has created them! See their red tips
Sever themselves from bodies and mind.
They float. For this is the nature of lips:
To love only others, drunken and blind.

Vilna Ghetto, 1941

A Pack of Music

I

Over a pile of steaming horse dung,
I warm my icy hands.
I warm my hands and regret:
Not enough have I known, have I listened
To the greatness of smallness.
Sometimes,
The warm breath of a pile of dung
May become a poem, a thing of beauty.

II

With such moments
In a forest of snow
You have to wrestle
Worse than a dying man
Fighting his microbes.
If you win —
They will become your own,
Revealing
The meaning of struggle,
The birth of fates
Locked up in snow.
But if you lose the furious fencing —
Your own breath
Will freeze you to death.

III

Alone. Pure, frozen calm.
Under the stillness —
My naked body.
Just two yards of ground are mine —
Here I lie, covered by the moon.

I sharpen my ears
For a voice of a friend,
A voice of a friend!
But like my own echo coming back from afar —
Music of wolves
In a shimmering semicircle.

Is this the only faithful thing
I have left:
Music of wolves —
The last faithful thing
Frozen howls over forest snow?
Let it be!
Relentless as steel,
It closes in on me,
A pack of music!

Come close, my wolves,
My dearest wolves!
Let us be friends, let us prowl together
On hostile man, on the devilish whirl.
Pack of music —
Conquer the world!

Vilna, Zakret Forest, December 1941

Execution

Digging a pit as one must, as they say.
I seek in the earth a solace today.

A thrust and a cut — and a worm gives a start:
It trembles below me, breaking my heart.

My spade cuts him through — and a miracle, see:
The worm divided — becomes two, becomes three.

I'm cutting again: they are four, they are five —
Was it I who created all of those lives?

Then the sun breaks through my darkest mood
And new hope makes me proud and firm:

If a worm will never succumb to the cut,
Can you say you are less than a worm?

May 22, 1942

Am I Guilty

— Am I guilty, must I pay for guilt?
And to whom: the present or the past?
— No difference, you fool, there is a *guilt*,
You may be a mistake — but pay you must!

— Was I created of my own free will?
Think about it, please, and spare your scorn!
— Nothing to think about, don't ask what, when,
And do not hang your faith on any thorn.

— Am I and Fate a one or strangers two?
If two, reveal — I'll beat him to the ground!
— Decide yourself. In the flash of your pain
You see him in the stormtroopers around.

May 1942

A Day in the Hands of the Stormtroopers[16]

I

Don't hit. My limbs do not hurt anymore.
These limbs are not mine, like an hour that's passed.
An unseen hand pulls me out to a world
Where there is no death,
None.

I take off my body like a cover of dust.
Like a road wound up on a wheel, I spin in time.
But the pit is not covered with shuddering panes —
It's really a shame,
A shame.

II

Cranberries torn by the storm.
Bunches of beads on snapped twigs —
My body in lime.
Is this I? Where is my I?
Every limb will try
To touch, to feel itself:
     Here.
     Here.
     Here.

Pieces of quicksilver
That won't come together.
Reality has no grip on by body.
No pain — like knifecuts on nails.
Dream is truer —
Drumming in my head:
    Madness.
    Madness.
And stains before my eyes, just stains
Like radiating hearts of carrots.
How did I get here?
Fled.
When? From whom?
How do you flee? Who gives the order?
The arrow sees sharper than the eagle,
Though he is ruler, she — a slave.
Hush. Live it backward, recall.
No, forget.
No, no, recall again:
Escaped.
You from death or death from you?
No matter.
The mocking man just played:
Instead of you, he shot the dog.
Now the dog howls in your head:
Madness.
Madness.

III

Dawn,
As if I were born anew:
The stains — gone.
One white stain of lime,
Dissolved in water,
Seethes and sees:

I lie steeped in it,
Half-drowned,
And melted rubies emanate from me,
Drip, run away
In lines like poems, plant
A smiling rosy sunset in the lime.

I grow fond of the limepit.
I lie and contemplate:
    "I shall not cease to be amazed —
    Till night, till late —
    At the loveliest sunset
    That I myself create!"

Vilna Ghetto, May 1942

Three Roses [17]

From the Poem "Three Roses"

I

Slivered sunset — shards of hot hail.
Time on my tongue lost its mind.
I run and fall like a stone
Into an abyss.

Falling, I pray to oblivion:
Splatter my memory with acid.
Later, I lie in the depth of an abyss,
On delicate,
Rosy-soft serpents
Of a dream.

The serpents suck out my memory,
Extinguish the smells,
Deepen the colors.
The knife of darkness cuts open a vein.
Time seeps out of my skull.
But my mind cannot
Free itself of itself:
Under the ash of what once was life
Splinters of God's image
Still glowing —
A vision of my mother
In her flowery shawl
And eyes: two candles in the storm.

II

You were hiding, hiding, hiding your tracks.
A wall split and swallowed you up in its cracks,
When Satan's mignons, like worms,
Sought your breath.

Sought — not found, and drunk, moved away,
Suddenly: who's breathing the wall, looks for prey?
A Jew . . . *Mogen Dovid*[18] . . . Is it you, my child,
Or perhaps the savior?

S. Bak, illustration to Sutzkever's ghetto poems.

Wrong, wrong, the Jew has betrayed.
He drags by the hair, you are stunned and afraid.
Your hair turns white,
Covered with snow.

III

An untouchable scale
Swings back and forth:
On one pan the world topsy-turvy
And I, crucified on a gate,
On the other — a teardrop.
The world swarming with me,
Has no idea what man is.
But the teardrop that would not be split
Can tell you of death.
It weighs deeper.

IV

Who runs through the dead city with flapping wings
Like a chicken with its throat slit,
That tore out
Of the slaughterer's stained hands?
Night enfolds him
In black smoke,
Unrecognizable.
But my heart,
Sensing what cannot be sensed,
Beats in time to that running.
It runs faster, faster,
Beyond all measure.
Five times,
A hundred times
As fast as him.
It hovers to the gates of the ghetto
Marked by a plague with screaming letters:
Achtung!
Plague.
Off Limits to Non-Jews.
And there, it grabs the figure by the collar
Like a thief

And in the light of broken eye-white panes,
It sees:
A man as big as a thimble
And bigger than everybody else,
Windy naked.
His skin of blue, wavy glass,
Transparent,
Reveals (it's scary to believe):
All the inside, the hidden:
A horde of senses fettered in chains
Like criminals
And over them a purple whip.
And every single sense
Bites the other's throat:
— It's your fault, yours.
And screams in Yiddish . . .

The right eye is gold-blue,
A monument to a childhood
In the grave of a diamond.
The left eye, seen everything,
A cloud empty of lightning,
And on the cloud, a cataract —
A yellow *Mogen Dovid*.

V

Either because my Golem-head wants to break through the earth,
Or because the soles of my feet long to see the stars —
I am drawn to fly off the roof with the sharpness of a sword
And, out of vengeance, to destroy myself.

VI

No, your words are too gracious, too maternal.
Consolation won't heal when sin is defiled.
If I'm too weak to stab your murderer —
On myself I must bring a vengeance wild.

Payment must come. I, your offspring,
Of my own fate I must be the judge. I wail:
As a broken bone wants to flee from its pain,
My soul wants to break out of its jail.

And maybe this reckoning is abysmally false
And *this* is the punishment: myself to torment?
And maybe your love has remained, keeping me
From leaping into freedom, forever pent?

VII

I open a window to let in the frost,
Let the moon hang me in the noose of her shine.
My budding gets warmer as I freeze,
Farther from home and closer to you.

VIII

You had swum across the river —
You are free
And your life-color
Went off with the waves.

On the other shore
There is no memory.
You don't even recall
How you got there,
For you left death
On *this* side.

And on this side am I
With our dying in my brain,
Suckling me, feeding,
Like your milk in the beginning.
But I cannot touch you, Mama.

For *you* are a mist
Spun out of tears,
And I — a tangle
Of sliced-up words
(Just one word: vengeance
Still gasping).
I wait for the river
To pull off, stream away
Under my footsteps,
And my life-color —
To catch up with yours.

IX

I shall take a spade and walk off to seek you,
I shall plow up fields, dig up graves.
I shall ask the grass, I shall taste the thorns
And feel your shadow on my arms.

And if I cannot reach out to you,
I shall dig into words and spade into sound.
Until I shall free the beautiful roses
Of the dark land where they went down.

Vilna Ghetto, October 1942

My Mother

I

Friday evening in an attic, cooing.
You flicker at the moonshine in a *Siddur*.[19]
The points of your yellow patch are praying,
Like human limbs, they flicker and endure.

The pupils of your eyes drip with moon.
Mama-drops illuminate my faith with love.
Your prayer brings to me the smell of warm *challah*,[20]
With fervent prayer you feed the doves.

In each of your wrinkles my life is concealed.
I hear you cough. You tremble, trying
To hide it, lest anyone hear — for there in a corner,
Covered with earth, my bones are lying.

Your hand on my forehead is dozing: be calm,
Just a day or two, salvation — is near.
Your other hand on my ear is resting:
The voice of the murder I must not hear.

II

You won't fool me: I know you are dead.
Though you live in my dream. Why do they char
Your heart, three roses in scarlet red?
Don't cover up.
I know who they are!

Don't cover up, Mama, you can't fool your child!
How can they bloom here, three roses unheard?
I see three bullets, purple and wild:
The first, the second, the third.

III

Bring on the cymbals,
Bring joy to a laughter, mute the scream of a crow.
Through fields
They chased my naked Mama,
Her body a ray in the mirrors of snow.

And she, as to redemption,
Runs somewhere, faster, fast.
And through her frozen tear, where the sun glows
Imprisoned forever, she sees me at last.

And amid her confession
She sends a blessing to her son.
The rifles pound.
She falls like a dove on the throne of the sun.

IV
Where was I,
When cymbals crashed
And they dragged you to the scaffold?
— in a dog's kennel; I buried my bones,
With a dog's joy that curses itself,
On lips — a leech,
In ear — a spider,
I peeped through a crack to see:
Under the moon — mirror to the night,
The wind plays with pearls of snow.
Snow-orchestra,
Mysterious swirl
Against the moon —
Whence such splendor?
Each tiny pearl
Of snow played
With its own shadow and the image
Gave me such pleasure
That I burst into barking — — —

V
For me, in the night, three bullets shine.
I run, from shadows dark to set them loose.
I reach a yellow gate with watching sign:
"Achtung! Plague. Off limits to non-Jews!"

With my teeth, I bite through the stone
In light of slivered eyewhite panes, I falter:
The houses — with no souls. I am alone.
The streets — a burnt-out altar.

And I fear to watch your window pane.
Breathing with your dying, every stair.
With my mouth, I seek your smallest grain
Of dust. I feel you in each tremor of the air.

I drop to a threshold of stone, gray-white:
— Mama, here I am, I'm returning!
And the bullets, painful and bright,
In the turmoil of my conscience, burning.

VI

I seek the dear four walls
Where you once breathed.

The stairs dizzying under me
Like a whirlpool moiling.

I touch the doorknob and tug
The door to your life,

It seems: A little bird cries
In the cage of my fingers.

I walk into the hollow room
Where your dream darkens —

Barely flickering, the oil lamp
You have lit.

On the table, a glass of tea
You didn't sip to the end,

Fingers still throbbing
On its silver rim.

Begging for mercy, the tongue of light
In the flickering lamp—

I pour into the lamp my blood
So it won't stop shining.

VII
Instead of you, I find a coat of many colors.
I press it to my heart, bashful and raw.
The holes of your shirt become my days
And the seam of your shirt in my heart like a saw.

I rip the clothes off my body and creep
Into your naked shirt as into myself.
No longer a shirt—your shining skin,
Your cold, your everlasting death.

VIII
You are talking to me
So palpably bright:
— Don't, my child,
It's a sin, it's a sin!
This is our parting—
Accept it as right.

If you are still here,
Then I exist too,
As the pit in a plum
Bears in it the tree
And the nest and the bird
And the chirp and the coo.

Vilna Ghetto, October 1942

From a Lost Poem

Mama,
I'm sick.
My soul is a leper.
And maybe more:
Yellow madness.
The balm of your kiss —
Too holy
To breath
Into my wounded abyss.

But if it is true
that you love me as ever,
Next to God —
My last plea and commandment:
— Strangle me!
Strangle me with your Mama fingers
That played
On my willow cradle.

It will mean:
Your love is stronger than death.
It will mean:
You trusted me with your love.
And I will go back
To before-my-becoming
And be and not be
Like a star
In water.

A Wagon of Shoes

The wheels they drag and drag on,
What do they bring, and whose?
They bring along a wagon
Filled with throbbing shoes.

The wagon like a *khupa*[21]
In evening glow, enchants:
The shoes piled up and heaped up,
Like people in a dance.

A holiday, a wedding?
As dazzling as a ball!
The shoes — familiar, spreading,
I recognize them all.

The heels tap with no malice:
Where do they pull us in?
From ancient Vilna alleys,
They drive us to Berlin.

I must not ask you *whose*,
My heart, it skips a beat:
Tell me the truth, oh, shoes,
Where disappeared the feet?

The feet of pumps so shoddy,
With buttondrops like dew —
Where is the little body?
Where is the woman too?

All children's shoes — but where
Are all the children's feet?
Why does the bride not wear
Her shoes so bright and neat?

A. SUTZKEVER   *151*

'Mid clogs and children's sandals,
My Mama's shoes I see!
On Sabbath, like the candles,
She'd put them on in glee.

The heels tap with no malice:
Where do they pull us in?
From ancient Vilna alleys,
They drive us to Berlin.

Vilna Ghetto, January 1, 1943

.

My every breath is a curse.
Every moment I am more an orphan.
I myself create my orphanhood
With fingers, I shudder to see them
Even in dark of night.

Once, through a cobblestone ghetto street
Clattered a wagon of shoes, still warm from recent feet,
A terrifying
Gift from the exterminators . . .
And among them, I recognized
My Mama's twisted shoe
With blood-stained lips on its gaping mouth.

— Mama, I run after them, Mama,
Let me be a hostage to your love,
Let me fall on my knees and kiss
The dust on your holy throbbing shoe
And put it on, a *tfillin* on my head,
When I call out your name!

But then all shoes, woven in my tears,
Looked the same as Mama's.
My stretched-out arm dropped back
As when you want to catch a dream.

Ever since that hour, my mind is a twisted shoe.
And as once upon a time to God, I wail to it
My sick prayer and wait
For new torments.
This poem too is but a howl,
A fever ripped out of its alien body.
No one to listen.
I am alone.
Alone with my thirty years.
In their pit they rot —
Those who once were called
Papa.
Mama.
Child.

Vilna Ghetto, July 30, 1943

On the Anniversary of the Ghetto Theater

I

. . . We walled ourselves in
And live apart.
From your freedom outside, do not smile at us,
Do not pity —
For us, even death can blossom into wonder.

How can we sit together
With you in one place?
Your hatred for us will poison you like mice,
Our wounds — love will heal.

As long as the outside is yours —
Ours is the ghetto, here we will lie
And from God's heart, we will knead a redeemer
And polish a melody . . .

II

Perform, Jewish actors, in tatters and in walls,
Where life shrivels like hair that caught fire,
When red drops of your loved ones are seething on stones,
And the alleys convulse like half-slaughtered hens
And cannot arise, fly away, flee. . .
Perform, friends! Let us think: it's a shtetl of yore,
They celebrate a wedding at an autumn graveyard
With Jewish singing and dancing light,
In a joyous circle around the bride and groom!
Perform! From your mouth, let Yiddish sound,
Pure and clean as the ghost of a slaughtered child,
Harsh and hoarse as the voice of our rifle and gunpowder,
Performing tomorrow
Over the rooftops. . .

And you, melancholy fiddlers,
Who stole out at night
Into the lurking outside,
Shuffling past houses,
Evading patrols,
Creeping to your ruined old home
And digging up your fiddles
Planted before your march into the ghetto —
You play too!
Pluck out the deepest tones!
Let them carry above your bones
And stray far, where a Jew still shimmers. . .
Where a heart still trembles, waiting for good tidings.
Let them carry over fields, over front lines,
Pure and clean as the ghost of a slaughtered child,
Harsh and hoarse as the voice of our rifle and gunpowder,
Performing tomorrow
Over the rooftops. . .

Vilna Ghetto, December 31, 1942

How?

How and with what will you fill
Your goblet on the day of Liberation?
In your joy, are you ready to feel
The dark scream of your past
Where skulls of days congeal
In a bottomless pit?

You will look for a key to fit
Your jammed locks.
Like bread you will bite the streets
And think: better the past.
And time will drill you quietly
Like a cricket caught in a fist.

And your memory will be like
An old buried city.
Your eternal gaze will crawl
Like a mole, like a mole —

Vilna Ghetto, February 14, 1943

Grains of Wheat

Caves, gape open,
Split open under my ax!
Before the bullet hits me —
I bring you gifts in sacks.

Old, blue pages,
Purple traces on silver hair,
Words on parchment, created
Through thousands of years in despair.

As if protecting a baby
I run, bearing Jewish words,
I grope in every courtyard:
The spirit won't be murdered by the hordes.

I reach my arm into the bonfire
And am happy: I got it, bravo!
Mine are Amsterdam, Worms,
Livorno, Madrid, and YIVO.[22]

How tormented am I by a page
Carried off by the smoke and winds!
Hidden poems come and choke me:
— Hide us in your labyrinth!

And I dig and plant manuscripts,
And if by despair I am beat,
My mind recalls: Egypt,
A tale about grains of wheat.

And I tell the tale to the stars:
Once, a king at the Nile
Built a pyramid — to rule
After his death, in style.

Let them pour into my golden coffin,
Thus an order he hurled,
Grains of wheat — a memory
For this, the earthly world.

For nine thousand years have suns
Changed in the desert their gait,
Until the grains in the pyramid
Were found after endless wait.

Nine thousand years have passed!
But when the grains were sown —
They blossomed in sunny stalks
Row after row, full grown.

— — — — — — — — —

Perhaps these words will endure,
And live to see the light loom —
And in the destined hour
Will unexpectedly bloom?

And like the primeval grain
That turned into a stalk —
The words will nourish,
The words will belong
To the people, in its eternal walk.

Vilna Ghetto, March 1943

A Moment

A moment fell down like a star,
I caught it in my teeth, for keeping.
And when they chopped open its pit,
It sprayed on me a kingdom of weeping.

Each drop mirrored back to me
Another dream, another sense:
Here — a road winged with thousand arms.
Here — a bridge to a dream ascends.

Here — my grandfather, a snake at his head.
Here — my child smashed on a stone.
I also found there one free drop
In which I closed myself alone.

Vilna Ghetto, April 7, 1943

Yonia Fain, illustration.

Moses

Who is the woman fluttering toward me,
At her breast a baby with no name?
She hovers through to the Viliya shore
And at her breast the child — a flickering flame.

She dashes to the shore, into the river,
Digs deep into the rushing torrent's hiss.
She sets the baby on a floe of ice
And she — starts sinking, sinking in abyss.

How far is the Viliya from the Nile?
Same water flows, days other days beget.
The horror of eternity makes it a habit:
Return again — so man should not forget.

For one last time she reaches out her fingers
And pulls the sunset down. The waves, they race
Over her head, now stormier and lighter,
And on the shore — just I remain, a trace.

The ice floe bears a present to the spring:
A dreamy baby swimming to the sea.
And I accompany it to the moon
And bless it: A new Moses will you be!

Vilna Ghetto, April 15, 1943

Teacher Mira[23]

With patches on our bodies, striped and parching,
They chase us in the ghetto, streets are marching,
Our buildings say farewell eternally,
Stone faces walk with us at each decree.

Old people wearing tfillin like black crowns,
A calf walks with a village Jew in tow,
A woman drags a person by the nails,
Another pulls a bunch of wood on rails.

Among them walks a woman, Teacher Mira.
A child is in her arms — a golden lyre.
She clasps another child by his frail hand,
The students walk around her — trusting band.

And as they get to Jew Street, there's a gate,
The wood still warm and raw, they huddle, wait.
And like a sluice for torrents of a flood,
It opens up and swallows in its blood.

They chase us over ruins, no bread, no light,
Bread is a book, a pencil shines so bright.
She gathers all her children on the floor,
Teacher Mira goes on teaching as before.

She reads Sholem Aleichem's[24] tale aloud,
A sparkle in their eyes, they laugh so proud.
She ties blue ribbons in the girls' braids
And counts her treasures: hundred thirty heads.

And Teacher Mira, like the sun, at dawn
Awakes, waits for her children to go on.
They come. She counts. Oh, better not to count!
For overnight, some twenty were cut down.

Her skin, a windowpane in stains of dusk,
Mira must not reveal the darkness thus.
She bites her lip, of courage she will tell:
About Hirsh Lekert,[25] how he fought and fell.

And overnight, gray covered all the town,
And Teacher Mira's hair, her silver crown.
She seeks in cellars for her mother blind,
And seventeen more children she can't find.

When sun dried up the blood, with branches green
She trimmed the orphaned room, so neat and clean:
— Gershteyn[26] the teacher came and we shall sing,
Over the walls, our children's choir will ring.

They sing: "Not far is spring." But in the street,
Axes and bayonets smash, crush, and beat.
They drag from cellars, hidings, but the choir
Sings on "Not far is spring," sings higher, higher.

They are but sixty, with no sister, mother,
Now Teacher Mira is one and the other.
A holiday approaches, little doves,
We shall prepare a play, a play she loves.

The fête — and only forty children left.
But each in a white shirt, each child bereft.
The stage is fresh, a garden in the sun,
A river you can swim in, you can run.

When Peretz's[27] third gift took all the bows,
The peril has cut down the rickety house.
People were caught by snatchers![28] Save us, Heaven!
Of a hundred thirty, Mira remains with seven.

Till axes split her mind, she on her knees,
A flower, and her children — buzzing bees.
Gray is the flower, and the time is awesome.
Tomorrow in the dew, again she'll blossom.

Vilna Ghetto, May 10, 1943

The Fortress

I

The fortress is old,
So gloomily old,
Its dust — crumbled stars.
The grandfathers molded its hidden mold
Of clay soaked in tears.

Half a milennium, they built and built —
Oh, distant grandfathers,
Patient and great!

Bones kneaded into the walls
Stand guard —
Witnesses of fate.

Hear their voice:

> Recover
> Your trace,
> Ignite
> The steel,
> Unite
> The race.

> A wall against fear and a wall to endure,
> In the fortress, your own body immure!

II

At night the fortress is dark,
Only the glow of hate.
The street lost its tongue —
Galloping steps of fate.

S. Bak, illustration to Sutzkever's ghetto poems.

But deep under iron and clay
Layers are moved in the night:
In secret, they drill and they build,
Through channels, traces of light.

A second fortress they dig,
In stormy rage — a mine.
And wicks feverish, ready
To ignite for the battle a sign.

Vilna Ghetto, July 14, 1943

On My Thirtieth Birthday

At thirty, my father's heart burst
While playing
Rebbe Levi Yitzhok's melody[29] on a violin at night.
The fiddle trembled on his shoulder like a child
And its tongue —
A shining magnet —
Attracted
The wide world to the shadowy hut
Where I, a seven-year-old dreamer,
Wound around
My father's knees.

It was in luminous Siberia.[30]
Was.
A sunstain
Or the hot tongue
Of a freezing wolf —
Licked the snow on the windowpane
And could not melt it all. —
Its light
Illuminated the staccato sounds
Of the violin
And striped my wet eye with sparks.
Suddenly, my pale father
Clutched his heart,
Twitched,
Shook
With outstretched arm,
And on my small hands
His body fell
Along with the violin,
Like a heavy branch
Falling on a light wave
And the wave bears it away.
Above us, hovered a melody.
Below, on the floor,
My father gasping, breathless.
And either I made it up
Or my words are true:
Lying thus,
Bound to a cold silence forever,
His lips entrusted me:
— That's how, my child,
Try out on your hands the weight of life,
So you get used to
Bearing it later.
That moment
The poet in me was born.
I sensed:

Somewhere in my body a seed lies waiting,
Carrying in its entrails
A special mission.
It seemed: I became the lord
Of forests,
Men,
Things,
And all I see
Is my embodied wish.
Since then it follows me,
Father's lucid will:
— That's how, my child,
Try out on your hands the weight of life,
So you get used to
Bearing it later.

Now
I have myself run up to my father's age.
Run up —
And no road back
And none ahead.
And when I see my face
In a mirror,
From its waves flows up
My distant father.
And maybe I am *he*, and my years
Are just a link
From his departed life?
The same face as his,
Evoking snow on windowpanes;
The same heart,
Prepared to burst,
And like my father,
I have a red violin:
See, I tear my veins
And play on them my melody!

But no one is there
To wind around my knees
And weigh my life,
To carry on
Like a wind
My yearning cloud
To a clear goal —
There
Where all words come to rest,
Where days meet
Which never met before.

Like a stone, I clutch in my fist
My thirty years
And hurl them in the abyss
Of a cold mirror.

Vilna Ghetto, August 1943

The Lead Plates of the Rom Printers[31]

Like fingers stretched out through the bars in the night
To catch the free light of the air that is shed —
We sneak in the dark to grab up, as in spite,
The Rom printing plates, with old wisdom inbred.
We dreamers now have to be soldiers and fight
And melt into bullets the soul of the lead.

S. Bak, illustration to Sutzkever's ghetto poems.

And now, once again we broke open the seal
Of a strangely familiar, a timeless dark cave.
And armored in shadows, with candles concealed,
We poured out the letters — in lead lines engraved.
Thus did, in the Temple, our forefathers wield
The golden menorahs, poured in oil that was saved.

A. SUTZKEVER   *169*

Liquid lead brightly shining in bullets so fine,
Ancient thoughts — in the letters that melted hot.
A line from Babylonia, from Poland a line,
Boiled, flooded together, in the foundry pot.
Jewish valor, hidden in word and in sign,
Must now explode the whole world with a shot!

And he who saw Jewish youth in their prime
Clutching the weapons in ghetto halls —
He saw the last struggle of Yerushalayim,[32]
The heroic fall of those granite walls;
Took in the words, poured in lead, out of time,
And heard in his heart: their ancient voice calls.

Vilna Ghetto, September 12, 1943

Partisan Forest

(1943–1944)

Portrait of Sutzkever by A. Bogen, drawn in the partisan forest, 1943.

Stalks

Two years I longed for stalks,
Silent stalks in a familiar field.
When I struggled in the vise
That caught me
And blocked
The road,
The green road to those stalks —
But not the stalks in the familiar field.

And when my breath melted the vise —
A wind in my veins
Whistled and called:
— "Get up, son of man, the stalks are ripe.
Now your own body is like a stalk."
And as fate walks, so walked I
Through burned cities
To that call.

But when I came, weary, through the sunset,
I reached my longed-for field —
They lay there, my brothers,
Killed over the field.
And the stalks with glowing spears,
Layer upon layer, grew through
The skulls, the ribs,

And climbed higher, higher, higher,
o the sun that gathers back its light,
As if each stalk rushed to overtake
The others.
One stalk
Went wandering
Through a mouth with clenched teeth!
Two stalks crept through shoulders.
And there, a stalk searching for a way —
A hand reaching out of the earth.
And a cornflower through an eye, weeping —

What do I see now in the evening light?
I see a field with stalks, blood red.
And rushing to me closer, comes a mower
And mows the afterwar fresh bread.

Narocz Forest, September 1943

To My Wife

I

Don't count the toll of wounds,
The suffering, the scar.
You have ignited once
A newborn baby star.

And at your feet, a spring
In our dark cave has curled,
And suddenly a baby's
Cooing has touched the world.

And like the purest spring
The word was then revealed,
But up above us no one
Must hear what must be sealed.

I knelt for you in thanks,
My spirit too did lift,
I brought you from above
Two blades of grass, a gift.

II

A child is not an other —
It's you alone and me.
It leads up on a ladder
Close to ourselves, you see.

But still before we thought
A name for him that's right,
The axes and the crowbars
Have plundered in the night.

The babe knew not a thing,
It dozed off in its rest,
A German came and ripped him
Away from mother's breast.

And what can take its place,
Dear, desolate and wild,
When from afar they glow,
The small bones of our child.

III

— And breathlessly we rush,
Through swamp and growth so wild,
You hold in hand a rifle —
A shadow of your child.

And every time the rifle
Spits out the chunk of lead,
In its dull glow we see
The child that we have bred.

As air fills up the world,
It fills our minds, a shield.
In pink of dawn, it rises,
Appears here in the field.

And over all our wounds,
Our suffering, our scar,
It did not disappear,
The newborn baby star.

Narocz Forest, September 30, 1943

March Through Swamps

Swamps.
Swamps.
Swamps.

We splash
Through flooding copper.
We carry
Forest-partisans on naked shoulders.
Behind us —
In wheeling circles, the enemy.
Ahead —
Breathing in moon-scales —

Winks, draws us in, the melting soil.
The legs, sunk somewhere deep . . .
On frog-keys
They play
A hymn to the swamps.

Deeper.
Nightier.
Abyss.

Glimmer —
A star in the mud —
Is rest there?
Knees — ensnarled in phosphor-nets.
Bellies — bound with glowworm belts.
Hail
Pounding on naked bodies
Frosty flaming sweat.
Soon — soon —
The naked bodies will sink,
Arms — no longer strain to stretch
High up, clutching the guns.

Only a lost sigh over shoulders
Floods consciousness
Over our maddened senses.
They grasp how real is
The serpentine intoxication,
And tear apart net after net — —

We harden the swamps with our will.
We draw to the island, the hidden hill.
We shall get there. Bold, bolder!
We carry wounded partisans on our shoulders.

Zazherye Forest, October 13, 1943

Farewell

I

Oh, not to mourn for you I come, city of my song.
For wet is still your soil, though your face is scorched.
I want to enter you like a night with glowing stars,
To shine into all windowpanes,
Wells,
Malinas.[33]
To shine into the Gaon's shul, where, from the HGRA,[34]
God's H was torn off and what remained is GRAY —
(Where is the letter H,
Does it wander now within my soul?)
And into the Great Synagogue, left alone in the Synagogue Yard[35]
With fortress walls that guard the past, the muteness.
And on Straszun Street 6 —
The very last barricade,[36]
And in the canals beneath the earth
Where Jews
Hoped for liberation and celebrated May Day.

I want to enter you like a night with glowing stars,
To shine into every house — standing or destroyed.
Into faces, living or not — for me they live!
For, as a person feels his arm just now cut off
And sees the golden ring on his severed finger —
So I feel the link
With houses,
Friends.

II

You are my first love and my first love you will remain.
I bear your name through the world
As my distant grandfather bore
Through the desert flame the Mishkan[37] on his shoulders.
(Oh, grandfather, you too hoped to see a shore!)
And anywhere I wander —

All the cities will
Transform into your image.
I will not strike roots
In any other soil,
As the water lily torn from its umbilical cord
Cannot strike roots again
In a scrap of soil under water's pressure —
And swings, lost over abyss of waves,
And no one, no one sees that the cord is torn —

III

. . . And dear to me as never before is your Yiddish —
The flickering wick
Of an orphaned Eternal Candle,
For only in *mama-loshn*[38] did a tiny baby cry:
Father,
Of all the words in the world, I lack one: *Mama*!

IV

I am the child that carries a blade of grass
When they lead him to slaughter.
I am the woman hiding in the sewers
Along with her newborn babe, not severed from her belly,
Where the gloom is so infinite you think
Of mice splashing in the mud:
Angels are singing!
I am the old man, gray and wrinkled as a walnut,
Who needs, to cheat about his age, to look like twenty.
I am the boy "younger than need be"
Who must scratch his face and stand on tiptoe.
I am the last word of one fallen into the pit,
I am the helplessness of one paralyzed
Who cannot bring his arm to his throat —
To free himself.
I am the man returning from the city with gunpowder in his boots,

Creating from it a savior
As the Maharal[39] created a Golem.
I am the one madly in love on a creaking gallows.
(His eyes suck in from afar a smiling woman.)
I am already burned.
Frozen.
Beheaded.
But with the stream of the Viliya — swims to you my song.

V

Not to those who defiled you —
Not to them will you belong.
They will crawl blindly on their knees to your gates
And thorns will prick a second time their blindness.
No mercy in the cloud above Ponar —
It will answer prayers with rusty lightning.
Graveyard stones will tear themselves off the earth
And every single letter will hurl into their face.
And the Saint Anna Church, red like our blood,
With no mercy, will lock its narrow doors,
And like a curse forged from copper — will toll
For them the old bells in my dusk city.

And if no more Jews remain in my city —
Their souls live on in its alleys.
And he who thinks a house is *empty*
And walks in
And puts up an idol, a table, makes a bed,
Puts on an abandoned shirt,
A dress,
A shawl —
At night, he will hear the crying of children,
And the shirt will become a grater, shredding his skin.
Until he runs madly out of the house

As if his conscience,
Turned into a crow,
Went back into his brain.
And he will run — his own shadow will not catch up with him.

VI

From the whole world, barefoot scouts will come
With green willow-branches to your gold-stripped temple.
And everyone will dip into your heart
For a handful of ash
And take it home
To light his long slumber.

But I, who grew in the shadow of your splendor,
I carry you whole — a bloody scroll.

Vilna Ghetto and Narocz Forests, 1943–1944

Frozen Jews

Did you ever see in fields of snow
Frozen Jews, in row upon row?

Breathless they lie, marbled and blue.
Of death in their bodies, no hint and no clue.

Somewhere their spirit is frozen and saved
Like a golden fish in a frozen wave.

Not speaking. Not silent. Just *thinking* bright.
The sun too lies frozen in snow at night.

On a rosy lip, in the freeze, still glows
A smile — will not move, not budge since it froze.

Near his mother, a baby starving, at rest.
How strange: she cannot give him her breast.

The fist of a naked old man in surprise:
He cannot release his force from the ice.

So far, I have tasted all kinds of death,
None will surprise me, will catch my breath.

But now, overcome in the mid-July heat
By a frost, like madness, right in the street:

They come toward me, blue bones in a row —
Frozen Jews over plains of snow.

My skin is covered with a marble veil.
My words slow down, my light that is frail.

My motions freeze, like the old man's surprise,
Who cannot release his force from the ice.

Moscow, July 10, 1944

Clandestine City

(1945–1947)

(Episodes from the epic poem)

A Nation of Ten

Remember how the autumn sun sent spiders
To spin our houses in a net of fire?
Remember people on that day, disheveled
Half-slaughtered chickens, straying in the mire?
In crucible of Jew-set melted down
A silver candlestick, a chimney dark with age,
A gutter, splintered panes, smouldering wood,
The slaughter-house, the *shul-yard*, hatred, rage,
A child in cradle, rifle raised in terror,
And all the figures drowned inside a mirror.

A welding of that crucible, my body
Was buried deep, till night stood at my head.
Was it the rain, tin-tapping over me,
Locking the lightning into drops of lead?
Or did a dream command my sight to cut
Through layers, seek some meaning in the sight?
My every limb opened an eyelid wide
To see through agonies a blinding light.
Glass in my hair, like glowworms turned cold.
I slithered through the alleys ghetto-old.

Yosl Bergner, illustration to Clandestine City.

Two-legged curse, who has invited you
To pose so slyly as a godly splinter?
My question broken off — I heard steps shuffle
Like dry leaves crackling on the eve of winter.
A woman stops, espies me in the ruins,
Life cuddles in her arm, as fresh as dew.
She stretches out her other arm: No stranger,

I am as rich as you, as poor as you.
If now you have no better way, or task,
Come to Clandestine City and don't ask.

What can I lose? I, soaked in searing fires,
Leaping in clay of silence on mute stages,
The last remaining man, the very last
In narrow streets set up like scorching cages.
The air still flashes lightning, stung with sparks,
Riddled by bullets, and with torments filled.
The woman, old and gray now, limped ahead
And lifted from the ground a rusty grill.
The sunshine was unable to pursue us
When we descended in abyss of sewers.

Now, would it ever have occurred to you
That there, where filthy sewer water splashes,
Our sole, our only sanctuary be?
You would have said, that prophet mocks and rash is.
But now, with silly skin on waist and thighs,
I swim in the thick stench, through sticky dark
Of mouse-hole cupolas. To whom to turn?
Where is a place for rest, a ray, a star?
We stopped, the waves rolled over us and moved
And giggled in mouse language: "my beloved."

My memory will not recall how long
I swam through pipes, some narrow and some broad —
An hour? A year? Eventually we came
Upon a clearing outside of the road.
Abandoned sewer, like a cellar clear,
Where murky waters hadn't coursed for years.
But human voices muted the dank calm
And figures faintly in the dark appear
Like shadows cloaked in fog, emerge cloud-gray.
And she who brought me here greets them: Good day!

Yosl Bergner, illustration to **Clandestine City.**

Black eyeballs in the dark, they sniff my flesh
Like animals around a newborn babe,
Their fingers — graying motions, stretching out
To touch in me a kin lost with no grave.

— A Jew still living? — and a murmur thin:
Are we the last remaining ten? (Above,
An iron grate, we saw a speck of sky
And hovering in air a sunny dove.)
— Of ten — a breath curled bluish in the hollow —
A nation will arise, to spite the Moloch.

The stripe of sunshine falling through the grate
Flees like a thief where murky pipes their war had.
I see: one shadow has a yellow patch,
Another — *tfillin* blooming on his forehead.
And in the dark, springs up a shimmering sound:
Swaddled in kerchief, singing baby-cries.
Behind the melody, the tear-filled echo —
A child! — How could we then believe our eyes?
But she who brought me here began to tell:
I found the trembling nestling in a well.

The child was sobbing loud. Its echo went
To seek redemption far, in other worlds.
— How goodly are your tents, *Ma tovu*, Jacob,
Somebody rumbles on, when tears are pearls.
That moment, what would be the baby's fate
None in Clandestine City dared imagine.
A hand swam in out of the cosmic shores,
Transforming our last *minyan* into legend.
Reality thus met me underground
When I departed from my slaughtered town.

The Sewers

We were just ten of us in underground,
Each of the shadows' dreams cut us asunder.
The darkness slashed me with an ancient sword,
With copper vaults, with dark medieval wonder.
Little by little, in each moving shadow
I smelled myself — the part of me I lack.
I tasted of his mind, kneaded myself in him,
My world did not so gloomily wail back.
And as I yearned for Vega and for Sirius —
They flashed before my eyes, bright and mysterious.

And like the pupil of my eye, growing familiar
With all the dark, has nimbly turned it into
White light that window-covered our black lair,
Where the reflections of a thousand splinter
Rivulets waved — so an outlandish force
Has wrestled with the dreadful stench, abhorring,
And finally exchanged it, as forever,
For scent of fresh mown hay on a cool morning,
For scent of Friday nights, of rolls with cream,
That each of us still savored in his dream.

The sewers, channels, pipes are different,
Like highways, roads, and lanes in forests deep.
(We shall discuss it clearly in its place.)
Most times the water is subdued, you creep
Out for a "stroll." In raintime, it will rise
With shrieks and whistles like a witch's song,
Flow over through oblique cracks, slits, and holes
Into the "storm canal," neck-slim and long,
Roaring under the broadest street, it goes.
Galloping like a horde of buffalos

Yosl Bergner, illustration to **Clandestine City.**

And thundering down into another stream,
Runs into the Viliya. Brotherly
Accompanied by various side pipes, branching
From under narrow streets that suddenly
Contribute to the flood in time of rain.
The flow brings from all backstreet yards
Eternal filth like an infernal fire,

Strikes on your swooning brow — hard, stinking shards.
At night a smaller stream, mute, barely born,
The pipes — they gurgle soft like organs torn.

And in a pipe where "Springs of Vingree Street"
Flow all together, sweeping their discards,
And branch out underground as stammering strings,
There in a pipe not wide, three-quarter yards,
Above the junction — hollowed out a moon,
A hole in metal ceiling. Through the hole
You can creep in, without the slightest danger,
Into a cavern, walk erect and bold.
This is our own, dug out and safe *Malina*.
We dwell here under wings of the *Shekhina*.[40]

Who are the "we" that secretly inhabit
The water palaces that may astound?
I'll modestly describe here all the figures.
I'll tell the truth as witnessed underground:
Elul,[41] five thousand seven hundred three.
No Jews in Vilna. The last transports left
Not to return, to sounds of autumn wailing.
The Teacher Gdalye jumped out through a cleft,
Searched for a hiding, slid down to this trench.
Slid down — and fraternized with all the stench.

Next morning — he encountered someone, Folye,
With him his mother, the leaseholder Esther,
And plaited close his further lot with theirs.
The mama, used to dark holes that would nest her,
Crept out of swampy night into the air
And gathered among ruins, empty houses,
Trampled potatoes scattered in the mud
And peas. Her generosity arouses
Our praise for all the presents that she shares.
There is a lot to tell of all her cares.

S. Bak, illustration to Sutzkever's ghetto poems.

Meanwhile, there came Arona, refugee
From Hamburg, does not like our Yiddish speech,
He sees the language as the greatest danger,
Caresses his own fate in cotton. Each
A character. The water roared and thundered
(A sign that in the city rain is falling),
And brought, as on a swaying motorcycle
Of waves, a guy out of the blue came calling.
He leaps down from the saddle, like hot news:
"I'm Doctor Lippman! You don't know me, Jews?"

And then they found in a calm, far-off corner,
Where only moon-mice splash and moon-bats hover,
A man enshrouded in his tfillin bands,
His countenance — the face of a cadaver.
His locks slathered with lime. Instead of clothes —
His body wrapped in parchment. The hermit Nathan.
Perhaps an angel pointed out the secret
Where Jews hide in the earth, to show his faith in
His fate. The parchment letters worn outside,
Their meaning is unknown here, far and wide.

Meanwhile did Esther, "hunting" for some food,
Bring from outside a shining ray of fate,
A girl, chased in a free-for-all domain.
Her name is Debby. Then, under a grate,
Did Deborah discover a blind man.
And later came to our retreat, in fear,
A pregnant woman, escaped from a mass grave
With snow-white hair. We call her Kreyne here,
Her story will be told, but where and when?
And I was number ten. A group of ten.

The city sank. The world is topsy-turvy.
A dozen buried characters remained
Where just a moldy demon lurks in wait.
But right before our lips, hope moved unchained,
An unseen rose . . . incessantly it called,
Winking and beckoning with mystery of hues,
Opened a morn in morning. But before you could
Touch with your fingers her delicate dews —
The rose has vanished. It glimmers from afar,
On the far side of death, a shining star.

Yosl Bergner, illustration to Clandestine City.

The House on Vingree

Nation of ten! With due consideration,
Folye distributed our functions here:

To carry out precisely, till the hour
Of our release from sewers will appear.
"You, Gdalye, Teacher, write a chronicle
For future generations, day by day.
You, Lippman, Doctor, guard us if you can from
All illness, you are good at that, they say.
Make sure that we all wash, keep up our will.
Make sure the drinking water does not kill."

"And you who are about to be a mother,"
So Folye mumbled into Kreyne's ear,
"You feed the baby that my mother brought
The other day. Get used, it will endear
Itself to you. I'm sure the doctor will
Help you. A cradle we will shortly get,
A primus, and a sheet, a lamp of oil,
I'll bring a jar of milk, rely on that.
It's said and done. The worries of a child
Need mother's hand, caressing, firm, and mild."

"And you," he went on, "Mister So-and-So,"
To the blind man who didn't give his name —
"You'll guard the entrance, and you must assure
That sudden torrents do not come and maim
Our hiding place. And you may sleep at night,
When we are all awake, you'll be alert
In daytime, guard our house, hold in your hand
The pulse of sewers, hear their noise and dirt.
If a suspicious sound you hear, beware
And pull the hanging cord I shall prepare."

The refugee Arona, trained in finance,
Folye appointed to become the master
Of gathering money from us all and hiding
Our state treasury somewhere in plaster.
Aside from that, he's crowned to be the guard
Of the larder. We'll try to get some bread
And nimbly he'll distribute it to all
So that the hunger will not strike us dead.
At first the refugee was skeptical a bit ,
But then, no questions asked, accepted it.

"And you," Foyle appealed to Rabbi Nathan,
"Decide your task." But the old hermit, gray,
Still wrapped around in his tin parchment,
Invisibly crept closer up, to say:
"My friends, allow me to become your cobbler,
I want to help with something, good and sound."
We heard his words as a refined example
Of human loyalty not to be found.
We looked with joy and fear, with awe and rage,
With admiration for the hoary sage.

"And you will wash our clothes, our dirty shirts,"
Folye has whispered in young Debby's ear;
"If difficult, I'll gladly help, we must.
You comrade poet, come light up our drear
With poetry. A nation of just ten
Is still a nation. Food is Mama's task.
And I will bring the warm hard bread of vengeance,
The victim never must forget his ax."
This is how Folye, with his reasoned gait,
Divided for each one his share of fate.

Written in Moscow-Lodz-Paris, 1945–1947

Resurrection

(1945–1947)

Resurrection[42]

I searched for the Shofar of Messiah
In specks of grass, in scorched cities,
To awaken my friends. And thus spake
My soul of bones:
See, I glow
Inside you,
Why look for me outside?

And in my great
Forged rage,
I ripped my spirit from my body
Like a sharp horn
Of a living animal
And began to blow:
Tekiya,
Shevorim.[43]
Come to life, the world is now free.
Leave your not-being in the graves
And leap out with blessing.
See how pure
The stars are rocking for your sake!
But the earth — like a river —
Flowed away with grass and stone,
And human words I heard:
— We don't want, go away, your earth is foul!

— From the punishment of living we were once freed!
— We don't need your time,
Your blind limping time,
And not the stars —
Our non-light glimmers brighter!
— Reality, that's *us*,
Vanish, cursed dream!
Gambled away, played out is your war.

Only one, with a voice unheard
Like the blooming of a forest, called to me,
Yearning: Redeem me, destined one — —

— Who are you, that your command should be heard?

And grass language answered me: God.
I once lived in your word.

Moscow, 1945

Black Thorns

On my mother's house
Thorns grow —
Yesterday's mad, piercing gazes!
And I —
In their thorniness I dwell.[44]
I seek my meaning
In black thorns.

I feel my mother's spirit
Hanging on the thorns —
The black thorns are now my Psalms.
At dusk,
When only dews know no tears,
I climb up to them,
Aching with devotion,
And my lips — clouds over words,
Prattle up a homey moon.

To him
Who planted the black thorns
I pray:
Plant me too like them,
I want to live here,
This is good, is good.

I undress.
Start dancing,
Dancing,
Dancing,
Till the thorns flower with my blood.

I want to live here,
This is good, is good.

Vilna, May 1945

The Woman of Marble in Père Lachaise

The woman of marble
In Père Lachaise
Ensnared me.
I walked in Père Lachaise
With a fresh bunch
Of jasmine
For Chopin's remains
Transformed into sounds.

Just the fact
That letters on the stone
Spelled out where
The master was born —
Touched me to the quick.
According to the place
He is almost my brother.
And according to time? —
But what is a century
Compared to our own minutes?
I swear I'm hardly jealous about the present!
I pressed my ear to the stone
And heard: a piano raining.

But then my puzzled ear
Sensed a warm throbbing,
A gesture.
I raise my head —
A woman-gravestone bends down to me.
The woman-gravestone came to life,
Opened lips of moldy green.
She runs her fingers through my pompadour
And speaks her stone tongue to my face:

"The heart of the one I guard
Left long ago for his homeland.
And only his dust blooms
In this red, dead tombland.

But you, if you wish, Monsieur,
Like my lord Chopin, long ago,
To enjoy — could you say where your heart
Should be brought — do you know?"

The sun shriveled
In my branch of jasmine.
I was left in Père Lachaise
Numb, no words:
Was it worth collecting
Thirty years,
Losing all my loved ones,
Hanging by a thread,
Emerging from the oven
With unburned tears,
That I should now,
At Père Lachaise,
Hear
That my almighty heart
Is worth a farthing.
And if I write a will that says
My heart should be brought home —
The entire, sad, eternal world-people
Will laugh.

Paris, 1947

In the Chariot of Fire[45]

(1947–1951)

Drawing by the poet.

Mirrors of Stone

If you wish, just once, to see eternity
Face to face
And, maybe, not die —
Hide your eyes,
Dim them
Like wicks in your skull,
And, ignited inside yourself,
Go where till now the time
Of your wanderings
Could not encounter it —

Then, gape open,
Facing the stone mirrors of Yerushalayim.

1947

On the Road to the Wailing Wall

On the road to the Wailing Wall,
In a leaning well of clay,
A Jew, hairy as an owl,
Sits and etches a chalice.
The melodies
Of his mute lips question
The cloud
Watching over the roofs:
When will *He* come walking toward us?
And he etches the answer on the chalice.

Thus he may have sat
On the road to the Wailing Wall
In biblical days and nights,
When the Prophet
Jeremiah with the yoke around his neck
Hammered of himself a monument.
Thus he may have sat
When no mother's son was left after the battle.

Today, in nineteen hundred and forty eight,
At the downfall of states,
He still sits there, the goldsmith, in the same garments,
In the same leaning well,
Against the same cloud over the roofs
And etches the answer on the chalice.

Like juicy rubies of a pomegranate,
Shot through with summer lightning,
Shines his face.
— Will you, grandpa, ever find the secret?
— I have patience, I etch.

Extinguished. No more face.
Cold, blue soot.
Just the hands —
Bony omens of redemption,
Not burned out, etch the chalice.

Extinguished too the fingers, the nails.
Bleeding in the air, the chalice's band.
With a prayer he makes a pilgrimage
To the moon rising in the land.

Jerusalem, January 1948

A Vision

For David Pinsky

Whence the storm on Mount Carmel?
From a rock.
I saw
A cloud-hammer cleave the rock
And from inside its stone burst a storm —
A chariot of fire,
Its wheels — four stars
On blue, diamond axles —
Plowed my body
Under the clouds.
And in the chariot
Looms a figure, into its face are kneaded
The faces of all people, animals, plants . . .

And it was, as I thirsted out my yearning for the vision,
A wheel of rays engulfed me in its eddy.
And I flew in the wheel
Between sea and clouds —
A star in the talons of an eagle . . .
And ere my thought filled up my eyes,
And ere my lips bled with a word —
Swam up a city of black pearl-fogs,
A primeval legend, encrusted with volcanic lava.

And I recognized:
The city of all my loved ones,
The city with no one, no one but my tears.
And the city was split asunder
As a moment ago
The rock on Mount Carmel . . .
And from the earth,
In a chariot of fire,
Rise all my loved ones.

. . . Soon
We fly
Together with the city
Back to Mount Carmel,
And the figure filled with faces of people, animals, trees,
Blesses all who dwell in the city
As Jacob blessed his sons.

1951

Shabazi[46]

Three hundred donkeys loaded with poems
— As it is told —
The poet Shabazi
Drove them from Yemen
To Eretz Israel.

Three hundred donkeys loaded with poems.
On a white donkey
Among his poems
The poet rode
Into the distance
Chirping like a bird
From his own Siddur.

Poet Shabazi,
I envy you —
Your donkeys did not tread in vain.
At your grandson's wedding, your sounds hover
Like doves adorned with golden bells.

And my donkeys,
Not so stubborn,
Did not get here with their songs.

1950

Yiddish

Shall I start from the beginning?
Shall I, a brother,
Like Abraham
Smash all the idols?
Shall I let myself be translated alive?
Shall I plant my tongue
And wait
Till it transforms
Into our forefathers'
Raisins and almonds?
What kind of joke
Preaches
My poetry brother with whiskers,
That soon, my mother tongue will set forever?
A hundred years from now, we still may sit here
On the Jordan, and carry on this argument.
For a question
Gnaws and paws at me:
If he knows exactly in what regions
Levi Yitzhok's[47] prayer,
Yehoash's poem,[48]
Kulbak's song,[49]
Are straying
To their sunset —
Could he please show me
Where the language will go down?
Maybe at the Wailing Wall?
If so, I shall come there, come,
Open my mouth,
And like a lion
Garbed in fiery scarlet,
I shall swallow the language as it sets.
And wake all the generations with my roar!

1948

The Longing of Yehudah Ha-Levi [50]

In the sea,
Between the death and birth of waves,
You can sense his longing. Music
Of self-begotten silence. Music
Ultrasound,
Somber.
And around the music,
Small as a star
In the distance
And big as a star
Nearby,
Imprisoned storms lie,
With desiring, pearl-bedecked faces,
And hear, and feel —
Can barely yearn up to his yearning —
With its silence
Their silence
To silence.

With Archaeologists

Sunstones fall into seagold. No apologies!
I came here with a group of archaeologists.

Under the white sliced up hill
A city is dreaming, an infant still.

The sleep of a hidden epoch shatters,
The hiding itself endlessly chatters.

A. SUTZKEVER   *215*

Silences smile, eyes shut as in pleasure.
Silence — form, and silence — measure.

Silences dazzle with color dynamics —
The archaeologists find here — ceramics.

Not the souls of humans, of suns —
Somebody finds a shard all at once.

A flash of joy struck the old professor —
Here is a knife of Tiglath Pilasser.

And I want to say, with no apologies,
To the archaeologists:

Nonsense, brothers, vanity of vanities,
Until you find the dream of those humanities.

1950

Silences

I saw an assembly of silences, all in blue.
I eavesdropped
On the purity of their muteness,
As the blood in sealed violins.
Describe them I cannot. Unless my heart stops.

From times and lands they came to hover here —
Souls that cannot die. Here in Eilat[51]
They long for the bodies they once inhabited.

The silences glanced at each other. And I —
Covered my face, lest they hear
My breathing. And between my fingers, I saw:

Unmoving, a snake
With a silvery head.
A deer stands awake
In a dry desert bed —

An enchanted island
By the cool of the sea,
Like a syllable of silence —
Lost, and gentle, and free.

And a breeze from a land
Of invisible sills —
Has lost in the sand
Its red pearls, its frills.

Like a paper burnt to ash
Hangs an eagle in the sky,
And his shadow — a flash —
Lights my dreams and goes by.

But in tigery gorges
Someone moves in this frame.
And the silence that forges
Will remember his name.

1950

Poems from the Negev

The Ascent of Scorpions[52]

Here you are at the workshop of all creation.
Hire yourself out, an apprentice —
Eternity will pay you
With its currency, if your work is good.

To the Ascent of Scorpions, you didn't come late —
Here, Genesis exhibits its art:
The Pillar of Smoke kisses his love —
The Pillar of Fire.

How simple. Not a shred of miracle.
You see the Creator through glass of sand.
Cities in the air: here dwells prophecy,
Not older, not younger — just as you left it.

Red-Headed Cities

I saw them: cities of muscled fire,
As yet undiscovered by makers of maps.
Cities unfurled from mighty music,
No one created their form, filled their gaps.

It seems they molded their own foundations,
Poured lava over their shapes like a dome.
Alone with their own will, they affirmed
For naked Adam and Eve a home.

Red-headed cities in the breath of dawn,
Dreams with no people, full-blooded, reach higher — —
In you they will dwell, the red-headed tribes,
Shaped of the same unsated fire.

Joseph's Bones

"Here is where Moses carried the bones
Of Joseph — to home's blue ridge."
My heart weeps: my generation did not
Fulfill a will, restore a bridge.

The bones of Joseph, still warm embers,
Left behind in dead cities, abandoned layers.
And with them — the eternal light of the language.
Came here naked, without grandma's prayers . . .

The bones of Joseph here, under sand,
The bones of Joseph there, under Poland —
They don't know each other, act like strangers,
And cut like knives, and glow like coals.

And You Don't See the Rain

For thus saith the Lord, Ye shall not see the wind,
neither shall ye see rain; yet that valley shall be filled with water.
   (II Kings 3:17)

And you don't see the rain, and you don't feel a drop,
Flaming madness straying in sand;
And streams like warhorses wildly gallop —
From the rocks, into bony *wadi*'s[53] band!

Where to? From secret regions they rush,
Busting dams, granite locks brought to life,
One stream meets another in a crush
And flows into him a sparkling knife.

Not for long. The juicy streams
Disappear. At the bottom, all that remains —
Grass in the *wadi*, full-blooded it teems,
Like green, long-trailing comet trains.

Deer at the Red Sea

Stubborn, the sunset insisted on staying
In the Red Sea at night, when they first
Come to the palace of water — the innocent-pink,
Noble deer, to still their thirst.

They leave their silk shadows on the shore.
With violin faces, they lick the rings of gold
In the Red Sea. And there it happens,
Their betrothal with silence — lo and behold!

Finished — they flee. Pink spots
Enliven the sand. But the sunset deer,
Moaning, remain in the water, and lick
The silence of those who will no more appear.

The Last Line

Dark. The last, the primeval last line,
Crystal-unique, quivers on high.
It glitters three times in the air
And teaches me, flickering deep in my eye:

Last is first. My rest is running.
And had not the void been shaped by my rhythm —
You could never have touched the palpable line
That trembles in man and draws him, is with him.

— Line, you are right, be blessed, for in me
Your colorful treasures you sparkle and flutter.
But if I crumble into glowing dust —
Where will you carry my human shudder?

1949

Small Hymns to Sodom

I

You hewed out of me a smile: In my heart
A blue pyramid of vowels fell apart.
Black suns with twisted mouths — a blaring art.

Soul of salt masked in diamond, oriental stunning,
You fooled the poets, blinded their cunning,
To me alone your mystery not shunning:

Just barely created — the created is lame,
To attain perfection, it must burn in a flame.
You burned. My ancient thought — the same.

Sodom! Since then, your shadow, red of blood,
Passed over times and lands, to the venging God.
You alone are pure, an image of the flood.

II

The sun — black from too much light,
Polishes my brow till it bleeds. . .
My first minute is still alive,
Here, under seven layers of heat.

The nonexistent and what exists —
Pupils of eyes on mountains all around.
A sculptor with volcano hands
Left his work unfinished, unbound.

Separate parts lie:
Souls, thoughts, hands, hide — — —
They want to be whole, to heal.
But it's not for them to decide.

A firetree — a personality
Stands on guard at the bottom.
I find a rare similarity
Between my dream and Sodom.

III

He who in his art has molded angels
Didn't know they would betray him and fall
In love with the beautiful little woman
Whittled of dreamsilver, a toy for his pleasure.
Like lions chasing a hare,
God's children
With kindled muscles
Ran after the little woman,
And she beckoned to them,
Though she liked only one.

Then a drop of salt fell from God's eye,
Poured over His creation at the Salt Sea,
Dressed her in a garment of eternal coral.

And so she stands, frozen in mid-running,
Under the coral, still quivering
Young breasts,
Her head — turned to her shoulder,
Her eyes — no-and-yes —
Flicker to the pursuing men,
And put temptation in my way. . .
— — — — — — —
Silence. The men
No longer pursue.
They crouch on their knees.
Roots — tresses of their heads
Baked into the ground.
Wild goats lick the tears off their necks.

IV

I could have made
The following experiment:
See, an ant
Runs at the same Salt Sea,
A little naked Lot's wife —
What if I
Poured over her a burning salt drop —
Will she remain eternal — like the other,
A white cloud under her head?
And there will appear a prophet,
A pen to tell the story in a lightning tongue,
Visionary and viable.

If ants have a Bible.

V

There is a cave on the road to Masada —
In the depth of a volcano, shunned
Even by a flock pursued by lions.
They call it "the cave of patient suffering."

I entered it against all prohibition:
Honey for me is solitude and terror.
A graveyard of shadows, the cave,
Its bony air — *the skeleton of the Creator!*

Pure darkness. Timeless silence. Not the slightest
Memory of light. Not a tremor of faith.
I wandered an hour or a year in the dark —
And suddenly the sun appeared from above.

A dewy sun over lips of the crater
Refreshes the skeleton in the bowels of the cave.
Tormented shadows abruptly flutter —
Their blackness polished off by the sun!

Oh Sodom, be blessed! In your cave I shall lie
Until you pour sun on my days and nights.
From the crater, my Sodom melody will flood,
And crows will bring me my daily ration of food.

1950

The Cherry of Remembrance

Self-Portrait

The city —
As if a lake
Stood on its hind legs
And froze in fear,
Covered with ice scales —
Its hoary violet creases
Trembled
When my fingers
Ruffled its glass face.

Echo of shadows.
Crucified sounds.

And I walked.

Pillars of light
Like broken stalks.

And I walked.

Where?
To find a human breath.
A living word over lips of clay,
A face I could greet with "Good morning!
With you, the world still has a meaning,
And snakes crawl no more from the sleeves. . ."

And I walked.

Once, hunger dazzled me like Lilith
And I gulped a swallow in the attic.
Now, recalling, the swallow chirped
Out of my eyes her swallow vengeance.
No more tears in them —
The bird
Pecked them all out
In mad chirping.

Once, as I lay in a cellar,
With a corpse like a sheet of paper,
Lit from the ceiling by phosphorescent snow —
I wrote with a piece of coal
A poem on the paper corpse of my neighbor.
Now, there is not even a corpse —
Disgraced whiteness
Draped with soot.

And I walked.

The snows of yesteryear fell.
Tiny flickers appeared —
My home,
A temple
Nibbled away by lightning. . .
I recognized it by the childhood dream.

Like a lock, bolted behind my back —
A breath.
And nails,
Pounded into my body
By iron silence.

Straying over the snows in the temple
A hairy man appeared to me,
Bent like me,
Disheveled and bony,
Lit by an over-rotten moon.

— Hey, wanderer, who are you?
And, dully, the hairy man howled:
— Who are you?

— You recognize me?
And he, returning the question:
— You recognize me?

— Soul?
And the hairy man danced closer:
— Soul?

But when I saw the wrinkles on his face,
When I lunged at him in triumph — alas!
Someone seared my skull,
And I fell
On the border of glass.

1951

Commentary on a Face in a Mirror

And if you paint over the image of the Jewish street
With a brush dipped in your new, sunny palette —
Know: the fresh colors will peel
Someday, the old image will attack you with an ax
And wound you so the new will never heal.

1949

I Had a Neighbor

I had a neighbor. In a deaf attic,
Among red sunweb and dreamy doves,
All his life he gathered bread, and bedecked
With bread his attic — gripped by a passion.

No one felt the taste of his stinginess,
Perhaps just the doves, the winged madonnas.
No one felt, no one older or younger,
And protected by bread, he died of hunger.

Tonight, the miser stammered in my dream
And stirred my thoughts: all my life, like him,
I gathered words and bedecked with them
The empty walls of my hut — gripped by a passion.

No one felt with a poet a recluse,
Not even dove madonnas told their gentle secrets.
No one felt, neither older nor younger,
And protected by my words — I am dying of hunger.

1949

The Silver Key

The footsteps on the stars, above our attic,
You think they're human?
An unearthly creature from the stars
Seeks us, human berries in an attic forest.
Strike a match and you'll see:
Over there, it devoured a whole shingle. . .

My neighbor in the attic strikes a match —
Tshhh, tshhh —
A yellow spot reveals the fog.
Goes out, the wood untouched by fire —
No more oxygen,
No life.

Armored in spiderweb, the child who had
Brought life to yellow darkness
With his crying —
Succumbed
To long fingers on his throat,
Fingers of all of us, all of us,
And more than all of us, of God Himself.
With a piece of glass, the young mother caresses her veins.
A moon-dwarf forged in glass —
Slaughtered.

The man who struck a match
Coos like a dove:
— No death *outside*.
Death has snuck in inside, among us,
Let us leave him behind in the attic
And flee!

And he runs first to a corner,
Opens a rooftile and, raving, falls back:
— Jews, we're on fire!
Hide your hair in your pockets!
Hide your hearts, the attic is on fire!!!

A column of purple soot breathes through the crack,
Stains the attic-faces, feathery as owls,
Won't let them flee.
The end.

Only the sly spider, like a centipede diamond,
Swings on a column of soot
Undisturbed,
Shakes his head in farewell —
Disappears.

A little Jew unfolds seven rags,
Pulls out a herring
And draws it like a knife across his throat.
Someone sings:
    — *Let us all, all together*
    Greet our fiery guest![54]
A boy, Tsalke, cries:
I've never kissed a girl in my life.

Suddenly, from out of the bodies, a girl unfolds
Blooming like a cherry tree in spring,
Her voice — Goldsound
Of a bird meeting its mother:
— Jews, I have a key
To save us all — — —

Madness like a shadow
Separates from brains.
Eyes — oozing poison —
Blue amazement reigns.
The dead child too,
By curiosity inspired,
Senses the wonderful tidings
Of the girl messiah.

And the shining figure says:
— Yes, yes, I have a key
Of silver. A white clad old man
Gave it to me and said:
Gather the Jews in the attic and flee —
Fast, faster, to Castle Mountain,
To the palace built ages ago
By Prince Gediminas.[55]
The key is to the palace,
And no one, no one
Will find you in its bowels.

The crowd is excited:
— Holy girl!
They kiss each other.
Like a fox, Tsalke
Cuddles up to her knees:
— My dear, who are you?
And the little Jew who just now slaughtered himself
With a herring,
Savors his herring —
If it's a holiday, let's have a holiday!
But the man who lit the match
Breaks the spell:
— Could you be so kind as to show us the key?

The girl trembles:
—Yes, of course,
Right away, just a moment — — —
Seeks it in her garment,
Near her heart,
In her stockings.

— Mamele,
Just now the old man gave it to me!

— What old man?
What was his name? How did he seem?

— Oh dear, the key remained
In his hand,
In my dream — — —

1949

Eternal Garments[56]

I

In our hovel, as far back as I can recall, loomed dark
A hunchbacked old ruin, an otherworldly room.
As if someone has spun a canopy of clouds
Over shadow figures, born of shimmering glow.
The mute walls howled with dog mushrooms
In grandmotherly-blind darkness, knotted up in an elflock.
And suddenly, silvery flickers would flood
Like drops, leaking from cracked wooden buckets —
It was the moon, dropping by through the chimney,
Sneaking out of the stove, and straight — into green
Cat eyes hanging alone like untimely plums.
Then, it would leap, caught in a net of spiderweb —
A young mermaid in the hands of an old fisherman —
With silvery spasms, it would torment the room,
The clay ribs of the ceiling, the hook in the middle,
And all the figures born of the shimmering glow . . .
The hook — a question mark, hanging upside down,
A twisted leather strip always swinging on it,
Here, a man once hanged himself like a chicken,
For a girl poured poison on his words.
I loved to hide here alone, against my will.
To lie on a meadow of garments — and dream,
Facing the cat in the crumbling, cold stove,
And see the mermaid gushing in through the chimney.

II

A pleasure overcomes you feeling the mystery of solitude,
Inhaling the fragrance of homey, flowery garments.
Here my poem splashed, floating in seas of beauty,
I would not have traded that room for a splendid palace.
The sooty stove reigned hollow with fears.
Like lusterless black pearls, the darkness under the bricks.
Here my mother hid the eternal garments —

A bundle of linen like dazzle of angel wings.
A young widow at thirty — she bought them in advance,
In holy longing for father. His face, lucid
In the Siberian *taiga*, yearned from afar.
With eternal garments, it's nicer to live here without him.
And once, oh God, when I was still a boy,
In secret, she donned them on her living body.
The room, illuminated by the sun shining from her golden ring,
Beaming from the cracked mirror's tear-filled eyes:
Four brides with the same faces flushed with happiness. . .
Four brides with golden rings in silken flames . . .
The dark little door was unhooked at that moment —
And, like a stone, my *oy* struck my mother.
Ever since, the eternal garments are hidden away
In the dark stove along with bottles for Pesakh.
Only in her hair, a thread from the linen remained,
Fanning out threads, thin whitenesses, all around her head.

III

Oh, destiny, shadow with bloodshot eyes, you swam,
Invisible, after me and my thoughts, you swimmer!
And lo, you yourself were transformed in a flood,
A flood of two-legged men, sweeping her room.
Mama quickly dipped her hand in the stove,
Roamed among the sounds in the darkness-violin,
And soon the bundle of linen bewitched with sparks
Hung on her little shoulders, in the coffin of her room.
Instead of a mermaid, a crow flew in from the chimney,
Hitting its beak on the old, wounded mirror.
And the widow shone in her sunny snow —
A cherry tree under a saw in a circle of buds.
But a five-cornered abyss was impaled on her heart,
The image was left of her own soot-dipped fingers.

Blackness gushed like a spring in the sunshine of her heart,
And her eyes alone sparkled younger.
This is how mama walked to the light of sacrifice,
To father the snowman with his red violin — she walked,
A snowstorm's yearning ignited them both together.
And then, the room too went down in the storm.
And I, all alone, an Adam thrown out of Hell,
Am still a slave to the Voice that makes me a singer.
My flesh is cloaked in her white, eternal garments
And my heart is sealed with five soot-dipped fingers.

1950

Encounter

In the middle of a street,
Hands of fog
Blindfolded my eyes, my world:
— Guess who?

Familiar names popped up:
— Miriam, Golda, Reyzel . . .
— No, no.
— Whose hands are those, whose?
— You were the rainbow-grass in my tears!

And all of a sudden
The voice changed
Into a living soul.
Had I met my own self?
It would not have happened:

— You? How did you come back, resurrec — — —

And she smiled with her violet eyebrows:
— The fire didn't like me.
Well, no is no.

Then I mutely whispered to my dearest:
— I could not believe that fire
Would have a heart to swallow you. Now
A life long I won't be able to believe,
And disbelief torments my rest like dew:
That you are living, intimate, you, you.

1949

Ashamed

Among us they wander, the ashamed,
Their number
Seared in their arm
With red coal of hell.
No one wants to see it,
Seared in terror,
As a hump will not see its own shadow.

See, among us they wander, the ashamed,
Small, thin,
Hiding their shame in a cave, in a ruin.
Thank God, from their gums
No one has yet
Sucked their drop of hatred.

But once, in shameless night,
When the ashamed lie
With eyes green like cabbage in Maidanek —
The number alone,
Cutting patience,
Tears away from their skin
Like a melody —
Hovers into the palace
Where a butcher dance is performed
By a freshly lunatic Belshazar.

1951

Chords from the Proud Forest

Dr. Atlas

To Sh. Kacherginski

— Commander,
The Lipichany forests are ablaze
And the Shchara[57]
Will melt by night.
Give an order! As long as the ice holds,
We have a retreat from the battle.

But Doctor Atlas,
Used to mishap and sensation,
In a hut of branches, shimmering
With tar drops,
Answers coldly:
— Not now,
First, I'll finish the operation.

Huddled in a fur,
As if a calf had grown
Out of his bones —
Lies a peasant, moaning,
His pipe, stuffed with snow,
Stuck in his teeth —
As a suffering rod.
For nothing in the world would he give up
His pipe — not even to God.

Doctor Atlas will not dim
His pleasure.
Nearby, crouching on one knee,
A king lies on the other —
The peasant's rotting leg.

The half lens of the doctor's glasses
Glimmers like an icicle in sunset.
The leg,
Forged in a boot with a lucky horseshoe
Will not part from its boot.

— Commander,
Soon it will be over,
We are *ten*
And they . . .

He cuts them off:
— Mulya, wash the saw with snow
And have the boys saddle the horses,

The Lipichany Forests are ablaze,
Woe, woe.
The peasant grimly bites his pipe,
Woe, woe.
And Doctor Atlas takes a deep breath
And saws off
His leg.

Ten horses gallop.
Doctor Atlas — in the lead
With the peasant on his saddle —
Make way!

And the horseshoe suns ring
And sing
Over the shifting ice
Of the Shchara.

Blackberries

"Hungry warriors! Let us gather
Black berries in the night."
An idea to remember:
Black berries in the night?

Darkness. Just a yellow owl
Playing cards in dark of night.
In the forests green with firs —
Black berries in the night.

Crouching over, creeping out
To the berries in the night,
Goes an army with its weapons,
Gathers berries in the night.

People, gotten used to killing —
Kneeling for a grass at night.
For like flutes they pipe their magic,
Black berries in the night.
And the glowworms play along
And the yellow owl laughs bright.

Elephants at Night

A Trip Through Africa, 1950

(1950–1954)

✴

All the noises, all the sounds, asleep.
Under seven streams sleeps fear.
And the elephant, so deep in sleep,
That you can sneak up, cut off his ear.
All the noises, all the sounds, asleep.
No rough axe will wake them, make them hear.
All the noises, all the sounds, asleep
In two eyes, two eyes still open deep —
The two eyes of God, still open deep.

On the Nile

Even on the Nile I have no mother —
I shall weave me a wicker basket,
Seal it with the red clay of my wounds,
Take along the reflection of a dream —
And abandoned to the sighing Nile,
Rock on the golden shards of golden idols,
Until a king's daughter. . .
                    Oh, consuming malaria!

Rain Dance

A lion's heart bleeding red,
Hoisted on a spear —
To the Rain God.
Rain God Shango
Will not see,
Will not appear.
The sun — his armor —
Blowing heat.
The water of the roots is molten iron.

The prophet
Blares on his horn,
All his veins dance along with him:
Shango! Shango!
A lion hides his heart
As you hide the rain.
And you, you love a heart offering,
Fresh from a roaring lion.
Let the heart alone roar, roar, roar. . .

God of Rain!
The heart is roaring, bleeding on the spear,
Take pity, send your tongue — the cloud —
And pay with silver coins of water.
Water.
Water.
Grant us water.
Ostriches lay eggs baked in the sand,
Not a drop in them, not a drop of water.

Look at the pointed,
Pregnant women's bellies —
Instead of bushmen, they bear skeletons.

Take away the shimmering armor.
I shall dance around the spear nonstop,
Day and night,
Until you appear.
Even dead I shall go on dancing.
And if you kill me, the dead one,
My tears will dance
Around the spear alone —
And roar:
Water.
Water.
Until you and the tears
And the drops of lion's heart that fall,
Into my arms, fall, fall, fall.

Dance of the Pygmies

Pygmies of Sahara in the circus of the moon —
Living chess pieces moved by madness,
Glimmering with bloody knives,
Black-silver bodies —
Dance their *vengeance against tallness*:

Tallness must be sliced with bloody knives.
Tallness is stupidity striving to the lord.
We, short-grown, devouring locusts,
We shall destroy all tallness to the core.

Oasis

A land where trees are leaf-covered dreams . . .

Under them — a man of black marble.

Red lips burning on his leg.
A serpent has tattooed
Her jealousy on the beautiful Bantu Negro.

Next to him — the milk-white bones of his horse.
But he himself — as if asleep.
The strong poison
Marbled his limbs.
The night hyena
Will not dare approach —
Dreads the poison.

It seems: death has no more power over his victim,
With his brush, he cannot paint him gray.
Who will care for the dead Bantu Negro?
The black crow dreads the poison.

Suddenly, festive birds arrive at the oasis.
Golden birds!
On their way to a wedding.
Rest a while on the leaf-covered dreams,
Tinkle with their hearts in shimmering fatigue,
Glitter with colors a man cannot merit,
Tune their fiddles . . .
And when they fly off,
They take with them
The dead rider.
To the wedding, they take
The beautiful dead rider.

Zunga

Thus said King Zunga
To the children:
— He who would be king,
Let him answer fast:
What is the color of God?

They call out colors. . .

And King Zunga laughs like a skull:
— No one deserves to be king.
He is not white,
Not black,
He has no color,
And He created all colors.

Elephants at Night

Hunting Song

Elephants at night, heavy ghosts
Coming one after another
Bathing in the river,
Are not elephants,
They just wear the mask.
I, the hunter of the night,
Who saw how stars
Turn into antelopes —
Once upon a time, was lurking
At the river, among grass, for seven
Moon elephants
Walking to the shore.

A. SUTZKEVER   *257*

Each of them pondered the river for a while
To see if all was clear,
And took off his elephant mask.
Took off his ears, his tusks, his long trunk —
And before my eyes, appeared
Seven girls.
Seven girls slice the water with their breasts,
Bend like tempting rays,
Swim, swim.

I knew: soon they'll swim back and don
Their ears, trunks — will be elephants again.
Quieter than a serpent, I crept up to the masks,
Took one and hid myself.
And when the seven girls, in a veil of pearls,
Began to don their elephant costumes —
One missed her mask, remained naked,
Naked on a stone, her skin trembling,
No friend, no caress, no warmth.

And I, the hunter,
Married her — a girl with no mask.

Elephant Graveyard

Skeletons of ships on the floor of the sea —
Lie elephants with ripped-open bellies,
Where the moon comes to bear her children. . .

Black rocks all around — tombstones
With silver epitaphs in a wise elephant tongue.

No one brings them here. They walk
One by one through weeping forests,
Months, years, when their time comes to die.

An elephant walks.
His feet — four thumps of thunder —
Drum the dust of his wrinkled years.

But the striped jackal already rides his back.
And, when the elephant calmly chooses his bed —
The jackal will devour his childish eyes,
And the ivory is sawed off
By hunters.

The Immortal

Yonder, where the fireox, the sun,
Drags a red cloud like an enormous plow,
At his animal lair crouches a naked man.
His face —
As if all old men, ever since old men have been on earth,
Before their death, pawned their wrinkles to him
And their last fears redeemed from mourning.

The people here, chirping like birds,
Call him: The Immortal.
They're all afraid
To pass his cave.
Only the blind —
For the blind gain their sight in the smoke of his gaze.

The people here, chirping like birds,
Know that The Immortal is older than the rain,
Older than the locust,
Older than hell.
He was not created in a belly
Like you, like all of us —
Bellies are graves,
Where, in man's image,
Death is created
With a curly head.
The people here, chirping like birds,
Swear:
The Immortal wants to die but cannot.
Fire would help him —
Does not reach his skin.
The cobra would help him —
Its venom has vanished.
It bites and bites and cannot poison him.

Witness the tigress
That lives with him.

The Monkey Merchant

Father, see:
The day lies stretched at the tent
Like a dying elephant with his feet to the sky.
And the flamingos are burning in the river, where toward us
Oxen swim.
Thirteen oxen, like my years.
Thirteen oxen, with the monkey merchant at their head,
To buy your faithful daughter.

Father, hear:
The oxen toll with their heavy bells.
And the monkey merchant at their head
Wants to plow with them
The flowerbeds of my body.

The dead monkeys will not forgive him.
The living ones
Will curse him from the trees.

Song of a Sick Girl

After my death, from my belly
A forest will swim out,
And I myself will live in that forest.

My kisses will turn into birds,
And I myself will sing
Out of the birds.

A. SUTZKEVER   *261*

I shall don the dress of a gazelle,
A young hunter will see
And think: A gazelle.

But before he pulls his arrow,
Quickly I shall undress in the bed of grass,
And the arrow, taut in the thin bow of my brow,
I shall hurl at the hunter.

Lovesong

Fire is the wife of storm.
She, whom I love,
Is the wife of my tears.
Tears that bind
My soul to god Moari
Like steps of love-oxen
That bind two people.

Beautiful, chop off my hands,
If they are fit to be your earrings.

Give me, woman, your future grayness,
I shall rejoice to be gray.

Lament of a Young Widow

Since you are not in my arms, I do not need the stars.
I live on the sad earth with two souls.

Our child did not have time to sing: mama,
Remained half in you, half in me. Forever!

My dear, like the sun in the sea
The world shrank. And only my love
Grows in the smallness.

They say: I am beautiful. Had you said: ugly,
I would have liked it better than beautiful.

While eating corn, I think:
Your lips.

The stormy red ox reminds me
Of your virility.

In lion's roar I feel
Your mighty passions.

Since you are not in my arms, I do not need the stars.

Bride of the Thunder

On the shores of the Tugula River
A girl went to fetch some wood.
All the trees were cold and wet as fish.
Suddenly, a thunder, a silver axe in his hand,
Saw the girl. He liked her.
The little silver axe laughed in the forest,
And the girl saw a heap of branches.

Says the girl:
— Good man, how will I thank you?

Says the thunder:
— Be my bride, this will be your thanks.
If God could see your eyes
And your beautiful belly,
He would weep with joy that He created you.

And he takes a lightning, makes a nosering
And puts it on the girl.

Says the girl:
— If I am to be your bride,
I must know, dear man, your name.

Says the thunder:
— My name is Thunder.
There is none like you among the cloudgirls.
If God could see your eyes
And your beautiful belly,
He would weep with joy that He created you.
And he takes a rainstring
And dresses her in pearls.

Says the girl:
— I am flesh and bone,
And like your heap of branches, in a fire
My eyes will go out.
See, in the Tugula River swims one like me,
Wearing the same nosering,
Dressed in pearls,
She is of the same flesh as you
And will love you . . .

On the shore of the Tugula River
You can still see a heap of branches.
Under them a grave. Passers-by, take in the sight:
Above it cries a thunder day and night.

Song to the Lord of the Clouds

Little children fall with the rain from the clouds.
Not the clouds bore them.
What will be?
They were born of cloud women —
Young mothers you swallowed up.

The young mothers are yours. Ours — the children.
They fall with the rain, with the storm.
What will be?
They mix with children of the earth,
Become young men, beautiful women.

The dead mothers yearn for their children.
And all human lips are yours.
What will be?
You give one puff—
And gray like salt are all black colors.

The end is close. We are all dying.

Song of the Lepers

Warrior, dip your arrows in our blood,
And the enemy will lose his feet.

Our blood is not from father-mother,
But God's spit in crippled limbs.

When we die, the earth boils like pitch,
Our blood can enflame a stream of water.

Warrior, dip your arrows in our blood,
One struck by such an arrow—will not live.

Just touched by its shadow—will not live.
No one struck, a fire still remains.

Lightning birds in high nest of thunder
Fall singing dead into the abyss.

We alone, we have no fingers,
We cannot rush upon the enemy—

Warrior, dip your arrows in our blood.

The Suicide of the Herreros

The rainbow doesn't care. Its many-colored sword
Stops the rain. Tells him: Stay in the sky.
And we commit suicide in the folds of the earth,
The hyena darts along, green as mold.

The rainbow doesn't care.

The rifle carriers with the white slave dogs
Lure us into gold mines with all kinds of tricks.
The rainbow doesn't care that our blood runs out,
That the girls slaughter themselves.

The rainbow doesn't care.

Oh, bird Insinguizi, smaller than a tooth,
Of our suicide in your realm, tell the gods.
The rainbow doesn't care. Horribly doesn't care.
It will let the rain go — later.

The rainbow doesn't care.

The Locust

The locust
Has bitten into our flesh.
He thought:
Stalks, we are stalks.

A. SUTZKEVER   *267*

Soft eyes of donkeys
Swim in his blood.
He has devoured
All shadows of trees.

He has devoured the moon.
Now she reflects diamonds from his wings.
The stars kneel: We shall be your slaves!
And now the locust darts to God . . .
To God who created the locust.

Gray Fire

Who creates the gray in your hair?
Don't you know, brother:
Between earth and sky, a spinning wheel —
On the spinning wheel hangs the gray fire,
Nearby, on a cloud,
Sits your own skeleton,
He cherishes your dying,
And spins for your hair
The gray fire.

Farewell to an Arrow

You, with lion blood anointed at a red bonfire,
Sated with flesh and love like a pregnant woman —
Come closer, closer to your lord the hunter!
Now, when the hyena prepares salt for my muscles —
Oh, closer, closer to your lord the hunter.

A man dies —
At his funeral, his wife seeks another.
Children think: they bore themselves.
A man loves a man in a mirror.
You — will not betray.
With lion blood anointed at a red bonfire,
You will descend with me into the kingdom of death,
Where the hunting will go on and on — —

Eulogy for an Ox

Oh, come admire my ox.
He is beyond compare.
His father was the sun,
His mother — moon.

Whiter than a woman's
First milkspray
When she gives to suck —
The whiteness of his forehead.

In his eyes you see the future.
But do not dare
To open them
When they doze.

The horns are masts of a ship
Carrying treasures in her belly.

Girls change in the shimmer of his splendor.
In their blood —
The warmth of strangers' mouths.

Oh, come admire my ox.
He is beyond compare.

Where he bathes — the rivers turn sweet.

To a Tiger

Suddenly we saw each other. Time vanished.
You guarded the gates of paradise.
Above you, two cascades —
Streaming wings.

Brother! My gaze of weighty lead
You melted in your fiery mildness.
Cowardice played a trick on me —
Did not let your lips taste me.

Instead of lying dumb in the ground —
My blood would have gushed in a tiger!

Too late. Separated from you
By ten thousand miles.
Back to the eerie word, unsated scars.

And though we both are free — we walk behind bars.

Blind Milton[58]

(1954–1962)

Portrait of the poet by Marc Chagall.

Ode to the Dove

I

Seldom, once in a childhood, dazzling in rainbow of colors,
An angel descends from the stars, his tune will be with you forever.
An angel appeared — and vanished on the other side of the world,
Over my chimney he left me a sign — a beautiful feather.

Not just an ordinary angel, how would one have thought of a boy?
A wonder! A dove is the feather in snowing magnet of dawn.
Newborn, hovers the dove, learning — it takes just a moment,
Till she glides down at the steps of his porch in silvery rings.

Soft finger nests of the boy keep her warm, stroke the down.
Her snowy plush comes alive, cooing with a sunny breath.
The boy will teach her to fly, to peck the mist like peas.
"You saved my life, dear boy," she nods her snow-white head,

"What gift shall I grant you, think fast: perhaps you would like
The mystery of my whiteness, an eternal snow, an amulet?"
Groggily, answers the boy: "My dearest, if you I inspire,
Come whenever I call you, in rain and in snow and in fire."

II

Sounds imprisoned in lips, like pearls in ocean castles,
Mute for thousands of years, and over the muteness — a knife.
"Sweet dove, child of my childhood, give voice to the lips, give voice,
Harken to weeping of sounds or else a dream will be drowned. . . "

Suddenly — a kiss on my lips. Who am I, where am I? The castles
Open up by themselves. The muteness — sliced by a knife.
Pearl and pearl and pearl, filled with mysterious sea rustlings,
Raining down from my lips, I am caught in a pearl terror.

. . . Crickets, like cobblers, hammer the grasses into my brow,
A meadow swims up in my attic and leaves a tear on my cheek.
Slaughtered roosters crow to honor one moment of mourning.
Melted snows pour ignited spirit in my ear.

Who intoxicated my fingers to write a verse like this:
All who ended their lives have sown in my heart their courage?
"Sweet dove, you gave me a mirror — a sheet of paper that sings,
My wandering words you took in, and spread over them your wings!"

III

Sheet of paper, you monument, the dove builds a nest in your body,
In you, not in marble, eternal is the face of the dreamer.
Here, between rough echoes, among sunken clay forms,
I gather silver syllables, to feed my childhood's dove.

Sunset sings in an oil lamp. And under the magic lantern
I build of bony sounds, coated with my blood — a temple.
He did not finish his word: rough and unhewn is the Word!
The volcano of poetry glows, sealed in bronze abysses.

Here, with my pen, I conduct my own silent orchestra:
Souls fly in with the rain, trickle down through my ceiling.
Cherries, immured in trees — I order them to change places:
They come on their purple feet to live as cherries in words.

Drawing by the poet.

A worm appears in the temple. He may not cherish such magic.
Real cherries in words scratch his palate like sand.
The dove coos like a sister: "Command the return of cherries:
You are the weight and the weigher, vanished visions inherit!"

IV

Girl dancer, my love, who are you? Were you born of a violin?
My throbbing garden body your dance has dug up with a spade.
Sick is the little dancer, somnambulent, in silver nightgown,
She swims away like a wave into cold, splashing worlds.

My head is filled with remedies to heal her heavenly figure —
Meanwhile a boy from the moon fell in love with my love.
Like Saul, I hurl at him spears — the boy hides among branches.
If I would bind him in poems — he gives me a silver finger.

Double windowpanes I order, to shelter my luck from men. . .
The panes are as whole as my love, and pure and double, but *he*
Swallows her out through the panes, lures with a beautiful gift:
Instead of dancing in the temple, she dances on the rim of the moon.

"Sweet dove, you tell the moon: it must not burn too hot,
Teach the dancer to fly, flying so high one must know!
I shall reward you with seeds, the rarest seeds and the best,
Let her not fall on thorns, if she must — let her fall on my breast."

V

To build and build the temple, with sunny thought to build it!
The devil comes in a fire, to set for my dove a temptation.
Gray is the sun in the sky. He spins gray mold on all colors,
The temple is burned out, its pillars flee like beasts.

Children like golden birds — he lays them out in skeletons,
Venom on lips of sounds, to poison the hearts of poets.
Faces are stuck on necks, like shadows of axes below.
Happy are all the dead when iron and flesh are brothers.

A mire, the earth and sky, and I am sunk to my neck.
Fire — and I in the dark. A stone with extinguished sparks.
Only the saved sheet of paper in my believing fingers,
The fires must kneel before it — here, they lose their dominion.

I know: my sheet is the dove who won't let my fingers freeze,
Words like grandchildren must remember the time of tyrants.
Days with no dove are moths. Hail to pure forms that I love!
I gather silver syllables to feed my childhood dove.

VI

"Yes, I am guilty, guilty, it was a sin to demand
That you bring back the dancer to me, to the earthly stalks.
An abysmal fire has devoured her young, unique blue,
Now my brow is searing with pearls in ash — with her gray."

"No, you're not guilty, not guilty, the dancer dances the same
Warm dance of your youth under smiling blue vaults.
You wander from land to land, cut off mother-earth from your navel,
Above you, the dance will help to hoist the world on a pitchfork."

"The dance above is a dream, where should I wander, my dove?
Eyes of the dead like nails all over my body, nailing
My soul to the Nothing. My bread and my salt — a ruin.
Under my steps is my homeland, moldy with grass is my country."

"I shall give you my wings to fly, pull out of the nails your body,
A white thought like a sail will swell up with a wind of freedom.
You are not indentured to death, the days will go around for a while,
Eternal is only the legend and it will appear with a smile."

VII

World. What is world? Just its tune — like a wave, like a woods, like a world.
Its celestial tune will wail in my veins and demand: prevail!
I extinguish the wailing with seas, unfamiliar cities greet me.
Stop! A rain of terzinas was played here by Master Dante.

"Master of Hell, would you like to exchange Hells with me for a moment?
I shall stroll easy in yours, and you — in the fires over there . . .
It will not diminish, master, your eternal, marble glory,
You are still Alighieri, your hell — still an allegory."

Men . . . Where are they, men?! How can we envy the dust?
Only the words of *one* bear their spirit, their faith.
Graveyards toll sounds—but unheard . . . For me they are a shelter.
Stop! Like a lion, Ha-Levi[59] sang my yearning from Spain.

Hey, you poets, without you, life is a fleeting dream,
Without poetry, life would have knelt before death like a camel.
Man and beast would have tortured themselves, alien and mute,
My faithful dove would not have accompanied me on her flute. . .

VIII

Oh dancer, tell me, where are you? My hair feels close your flutter. . .
The dove is unable to tell me: Where is your home, your stage?
A gazelle in sunny dew sometimes brings me your eyes,
Who is the garden tremor where bloom Chagallian blues?

Beyond the forest, in a rain, who inhales me, like a rainbow?
Who is the naked wave—no limbs and so supple, a bow!
Who is the snow avalanche, shining over rims of rock?
An eagle would kiss her breast, and she pours wreathes on his body.

Who is the mirror in tears? Who are the new faces?
Who is the woman in the coffin, the rose-covered funeral?
The wheels of the years, they turn, and devour and spin my shadow,
On this very day, a spade has covered itself in a grave.

Who is the white transformation, that cannot get out of a birch?
Who is the echo of silence and who is the silence in pink?
Will no one answer me now? Inside me, is madness in heat?
On this very day, the stones stoned themselves in the street!

IX

A stone meteor fell—far in the world, its tune
Drew me to travel through jungles, till once I saw it lying,
Full of the scents of stars. Nearby, on a boulder, a lion
Forged tolling bells with his roar, and a flame melted them all.

Who is the stone? I know it. Music under golden ribs.
The skychild calls me by name. Lips are drawn to lips.
"*I* am the dancer, don't ask . . . Hail to the lion's roar!
The king told me in advance your coming, your coming, your coming."

Limbs gel. Until my body, consumed in the flames of love,
Is altogether extinguished — "Oh, calm my lips, come close!
I shall leave you a sign: my last three drops of blood,
Before the moon becomes a tombstone white at my head.

I am the snow avalanche, the white birch, the mirror,
I am the echo of silence, encompassing you all around.
Gather the sounds, the images, in your region a hunger may swell. . .
Live them, enliven, describe!"
                                        And thus did we say farewell.

X

Under a tree at the Red Sea. The waves will finish my ode.
Hush. In its shadow — a millstone, nimbly turned by the sun.
I inhale the white locust dunes — the guardians of time and memory.
Here my people wandered for forty biblical years.

Under the sand, miles of footsteps, vast as the desert their number.
Let the locust dunes reveal more profoundly my visions!
Where are *my* four decades — in the desert, along with those?
Bones remained, only bones — the grace of a blind hyena?

And the dove coos on my shoulder: "Good morning! And may I ask:
Years, are they really bones? A puff — and they play vis-à-vis.
Stalks with children's eyes are moving under the dunes,
Resurrection of stalks, and above — a cloud with violin strings!

"Dear dove, are you the same, your wings not gray, could it be?
Shall I build my temple here, as I built it day after day?
Shall I take my magic lantern, make it grow green, bloom blue?"
"To build and build the temple—with sunny thought, build it anew!"

1954

Else Lasker-Schüler[60]

Stooped over, the donkeys are weeping in Jerusalem.
No more the holy old woman, the singer Else.
No one will come to feed them with sparkling sugar
And help them bear the wounded stones of the Kastel,
The stones that fall with a groan from the hearts
Of all who come to this land—a treasure of stones!—
To build a home for the homeless King Messiah.

Once upon a time, a donkey rolled down from a mountain,
Lost his front tooth. The old woman then melted
Her wedding ring at Nissim the Goldsmith's in the Old City
And the donkey was given a gold tooth as a present.

And who understood like her the weeping of the Creator?
He finished creating! Eternity, for Him already eternal—
A chain on His neck, and there is no other . . .
On her Blue Piano,[61] in a hotel, she plays His remembrance,
When He was the master of chirping birds and lions,
Wrote with trees His fresh Paradise poem,
Kneaded a feminine rhyme from a masculine rib.

The ashen fingers, playing, are tranquilly dying.
She must not yet die! A young ant, deep in love,
Bitten till blood flows, strayed into her room —
And plays with the old woman on old keys of the piano.

She must not yet die! A sunflower fell in the garden —
A world fell! The seeds — gold-skinned men and women.
They will be sold in the market, their skins flayed . . .
She must free the slaves — the gold-skinned men and women.

She must not yet die! In the sea, waves are born.
They cannot speak. They demand with infantile hands!
The prayer for the baby waves must be sung to the end,
The storm must not swallow today their pink souls.

Where is the beginning of heaven? — in Jerusalem.
The old woman, now a star hovering over the buildings.
A Blue Piano, the city. A veiled bride.
I walk on the carpet of stone with Else,
Drunk on the Blue Piano and spliced by her dazzling sight.

Jerusalem, February 27, 1957

My Father

My father is a floe on rivers of Siberia,
My mother is a bonfire on Viliya's mire,
But both are inside me,
The floe and the bonfire.

My child, they will stay inside me,
Behind the eyelids of my eyes —
The bonfire and the floe of ice.

Hours

You remember when your hours
Were born one by one:
Every hour — another hue and fate.

Now you stand before the hours, stooped:
All the poisons mixed together
By a mad apothecary.

In a mortar, in the dark,
He mixes blindly and in haste:
Iron, pearls, herbs, narcotics,

All the There's and all the Here's,
In one potion that overpowers —
He lets you drink your hours.

The Saw

A man transformed himself into a saw.
Except for me, no one could see him breathe.
And people, when they crossed his jagged path,
Could feel in their own flesh his sawing teeth.

He sawed apart his time, his home, his world.
He sawed the marble sun, the rain, the stone.
And only *words* he could not saw apart.
And no one saw him, only I alone.

Smoke of Jewish Children

Only smoke, smoke, hovering smoke,
Dead children — puffs of living smoke.

They call: Mama, mama! from the smoke,
The whole panorama is in smoke.

The dolls and their worlds are smoke.
And over them the birds are smoke.

The dead children wrap themselves in smoke.
The dead children trap their play in smoke.

1957

Hail

I

So many pomegranates in your clouds!
Lightning splits them,
Hail falls.
My lips, Creator, savor your taste.
And you yourself went wandering
Through my soul, as the sun through a thick forest
Where no one walked before.
A bird is born in your own image,
Translates your silence
Into silent sounds.

II

All the trunks come together.
All the branches shut the windows.
You get lost in green flames,
In the thick forest, the most beautiful.
You get lost in a net of dew,
In the shadows when they run wild . . .
You get lost behind my vision,
And I shall show your way in images.

From Myself to Myself

How long is the road from myself to myself?
Sometimes half a moment,
That's all. Here is wholeness. But a serpent
On the path between the two gates.
And sometimes seven worlds, seven frosts long
Is the short walk from yourself to yourself.

Trained Animals

Words, words! Trained animals behind bars,
I release you. Flee back to the jungle, sweet slaves!
Anonymous new hymns — veins of silence,
I am drawn to their sex not-unsealed.

I shall find among desert rocks
That alphabet with no words, understood by
Locust and rain. What an enormous discovery:
The dead will answer and a stone will smile!

My poems will be read by metals, minerals,
Fires, devouring one another, turn to ash.
— Hey, Rimbaud, you sorcerer, splitter of vowels,
Tell me, boy: what's all the fuss about you?

The Road to Paradise

Of all the precious paintings in the Louvre
(Centuries match up a wall with a wall),
I am haunted by a skinless face of fate:
The cow with her flesh-split breast — by Rembrandt.

It seems:
The tremendous Dutchman gulped down
His gilded goblets of colors,
His secret wines,
And suddenly saw in his drunken skull
A gallows.
A hanging cow.
And here, his dream immortalized. . .

A. SUTZKEVER   *285*

He put his dream on the butcherblock, skinned it —
To reveal the color of a cow's moo.
And prayed, and covered his canvas with wounds,
To bring into the Louvre paradise
The cow.

A Hundred-Year-Old Woman

Her body — clay. Freed of hate, of love.
Her crow's look, beyond all nay or yea.
Her body — clay. A formless blob
Covered with canvas, as in an atelier.

Facing her, the noisy swirl of
A carousel. The background flax is.
And like the carousel — the images in her,
But liberated from the groaning axis.

Take it easy. . . The carousel is outside
The old woman's bones. And years away:
A dream that no one will divine,
Free of hate, of love, of yea, of nay.

— A man will soon roll up his sleeves,
Pull the canvas off the clay
Which has no more a living hue,
Where all the creases blindly stray —

And masterly, re-knead the woman's body.
On the bench, a Venus will appear.
And he will leave her just two small
Fleshless silver earrings, as a souvenir.

Chosen Tree

When Stradivarius felt: he is about to carve
His last violin — on a stormy night, a gray old man,
He went off to the woods, stooped over with his stick.
Like burning violin bows, lightning attacked him.
He kneels at every tree, applies his breathing ear:
Oh, which chosen tree will now reveal
The one great tone? Which tree will give the wood
For Stradivarius to carve his last violin?
The smallest seed of sound — its pain
Weeps in him. The pain of raising
Violins. As if he himself had liberated from a prison
His own death
Along with the purest sounds.
He asks forgiveness of the shadows
For sawing off their heads — to capture
The nightingale inside his violin and to unravel
The grief of a tree after the first rain, a tree
That cannot flee assaulting saws . . .

With a cold iron glove, the storm fells him.
A cloud stands at his head with a spade.
And Stradivarius barely
Whispers: Chosen Tree,
Saw apart my body — the weeping form,
And carve from me, paint with my blood — the last violin.

Blind Milton

At forty-four
(My galloping age),
Perhaps at this very moment —
Milton went blind.
His words played
A trick on him:
Would he love blindly
A "tree," a "dog," a "rain"?

Half a body on the sofa,
Head down to the floor,
He lay
Drunk on his own blood.
He sought in blood the floating suns,
To ignite black marblewords
In a strophe.

Until the blind Milton
Solved the riddle:
In his blood he found
His lost paradise.

At forty-four
I am struck
By seeing. Like a geyser, gush in me
The bloods of a generation.
Drunk on my seeing,
I will always see it
In my veins, the blind generation.
Till I find my lost hell — —

_____

The Red Foot

Daybreak. A hut in the steppe under lanterns of snow.
My father is sick. His soul wanders off
Naked in the snow. I see its footsteps.
Days, waiting for a doctor. Suddenly — a neighing,
Like redhot stones rolled in ice-cold water.
Mother, in hairy felt boots, opens the door,
Father — his leaden eyes. Bending over the porch,
A horse — a bonfire in his mouth, smoke in his nostrils —
And someone above him pulls on his reins and stops
The horse from galloping in to my father.
Soon a head appears in a snowcovered, outlandishly high
Sheepskin hat — you could use it as a dovecote —
And Yiddish words melt the fear on the windowpanes:

"I saw on the doorframe glimmers a mezuzah —
So I don't need to ask if Jews live here.
In short: on my heels, a gang of Kirghizes,
They want to take me alive. My name is Lipa.
And she . . . (He points to a blond creature, lovely,
Cuddled in the foamy milk of his open fur) —
She's my girl, my woman, her name is Nina.
Allow me to leave her with you. A good soul
And doesn't eat much. Like a bird: peck, peck.
See you, friends! Hey, and let our enemies choke!"

And before Mother puts two and two together —
The horse strikes up his oars in the snowy waves,
As if each of his legs were a separate pony,
And Lipa — a wolf, nails sunk in the flesh, on his saddle.

A sleigh, seven bell-bedecked northern dogs in the lead.
He finally came, the only doctor around.
At first he refused. It's war. The money's no money.
Till we promised to give him a pouch of salt —
And it helped. A dark softness in the house.
The beams drip gummy tar like honey.
Such an otherworldly creature will heal my father?
One eye running over — a rotten eggyolk. . .
The other eye, twitching, drowns in swampy tears.
His face — a beggar's moldy loaf of bread.
And no one understands his strange, one-syllable language . . .

With hasty, straw fingers he feels the dying man.
And out of his doctor's breast, as out of his heart, he pulls
A handful of leeches. He licks them to see if they're alive —
They are! (In my eyes, they are enchanted rings
Around his straw fingers . . .) The leeches alive —
But lifeless, outside the whole scene, is my father — — —

Barefoot, I lie close to him. His legs grow cold.
I am a heap of silence older. A silkworm
Spins with his innards white stretches of cloth.
And the Creator creates the melody of life:
Facing the misty body, that just now was
My own father, from behind a skinny sheet,
Where the girl was quartered, the abandoned Nina —
A concert erupts. A chirping that pierces the ceiling.
Amazing: not at the head of the dead is
Our only wax candle — now mama, candle in hand,
Is with the stranger behind the sheet.

The candle — a golden owl. The sheet — a tempest.
Mother and doctor — two sunset shadows in a storm.
Both draw out a dark little man,
Tied to the homey bed with a string.

Drunk on the shadow-potion, I run to the sheet.
On the border, my foot is flooded with the blood of the storm.
Barefoot, I flee outside, to blue-covered snows,
I sear them with fear-hieroglyphs, breathing and dazzling.
And to this very day, behind me, a red little foot pursues:
— This is how you are born, my boy, always and ever.

1958

A Winter Night[62]

Separated from all nights, between cloud and star,
A winter night blares out a wolf orchestra:

Violet nettles — the searing snows bruise.
With the face of a gallows, my hangman pursues.

Under snow — a minefield. As soon as I row over —
The forest of firs is my armor and my cover.

Wolves with torn-off paws. Howling hollows.
Without a mouth, alone, a human voice follows.

"My steps," I say, "if you don't know how soon
Under snow a mine lies — I'll draw you a tune.

Step in its traces, sign for sign, carefully stroll,
So they won't say: because of feet, he lost his soul . . ."

Up to the forest the tune polished its traces,
And in them — my dancing footstep races.

— — — — — — — — — — — — — —

Under grass — a poemfield. To the same tune, I
Stroll among poems, for I know not where they lie.

A Pot from the Attic

A pot from the attic that sooted the sun in my childhood
Came back to me in the wire tangles of a dream.
Rusty voice of cracked cast iron,
He hurled spears:

—You see? No more attic, the cherry tree is gone.
No more dovecote, no ladder.
Just a pot from the attic — His Excellency Satan
Chained to you a concentrate of fear.

A fire spars with itself and is spent.
Art bursts like a light Parisian fashion.
But eternal is the fear — life's last element,
Except for fear, the rest is legend.

1961

Gather Me In

Gather me in from all the ends of time, from wood and stone,
Embrace me like letters of a burning prayerbook.
Gather me together — so I can be alone,
Alone with you, and you — in all my limbs.

Find me in a grave between the other world and here,
While weighing which of the worlds is better . . .
Find me as you avenge half a tear,
And when you see me cooling a hot knife in snow.

Remember, the cloud is sown through with my bones
And rains down with my lightning face.
Gather me together — so I can be alone,
Alone with you, and you — in all my limbs.

1961

Square Letters and Miracles[63]

(1964–1967)

Drawing by the poet.

What I Wanted to Say and Was Late

What I wanted to say and was late
Among so many different yous
Just to you,
What I terribly wanted to say and was late —
Would have been fewer than twin words,
Would have lasted less than three seconds.

What I wanted to say and was late —
I'm saying in book after book and am twisted,
Tormented,
By sundials, filled with sand and with sandy time.

What I wanted to say and was late —
I say in a prayer to a prayer of yours,
Till you return a signal
As if from a distant planet.
Even less: just a rhyme,
Just an *oy*:
The language of seed in the earth that creates its own heaven.
What I wanted to say —
I'll be silent for both.

1966

First Rain

What shall I do with so much memory?
Where shall I hide it,
Infuse it in veins —
For my grandchild to find it?
Perhaps, deep in the earth,
In its core?

Rain, rain,
Don't slice your veins with the sun,
Lest the grapes in the vineyard
Flee in fear.

Perhaps instill it in a mirror?
Perhaps, save it with birds?
Birds, soaring letters,
Take it!
My memory is yours.

Maybe a good-hearted bird
Will sing it into a hut —
And a man will make a blessing
Over singing fire.

1966

When the River Overflowed Its Bank

When the river overflowed its bank
I only came up to my knees.
But time stood before me on its knees,
When the river overflowed its bank.

Because of me, a thatch roof floated
With a rooster on his throne of hay:
His cock-a-doodle-doo, his haughty way —
Just like a gypsy, fine.

Years later, cut away by a stream,
I saw it, sharp as an axe in a dream:
The roof is mine, mine.

Because of me, a floating oak made his mark:
He tried to take off his copper bark,
Thrusting his molars, his roots, in the flow.

Years later — I saw in Africa his scion,
Floating in the grass in the guise of a lion
Stalking a trembling doe.

But one thing I envy above all:
A piano floating, legs shot off, almost sank —
On it, Chopin wailed like a rain,
When the river overflowed its bank.

Years later I grasped that the piano in the flow,
With its black bent wing followed by a floe,
Was just a coffin swimming toward my fate —

And I was lying in that coffin dank,
When the river overflowed its bank.

1966

The Ailing Poet to His Friend

Music of torments.
Who is the conductor?
For whom do they play a crescendo?
Later, will any hands applaud?
Who are they? And who the conductor?
I want to see him!

Even a murderer under lock and key
Is not denied his last wish.
I want to see the conductor!
His baton is a knife.

Just the knife is real.
The past — a splendid superstition.
Faces of clay in the black hall
Have gone to a different zone.
She's no longer she: a separate beam.
In my heart, I call her: my widow.

Day and night the conductor waves.
In his footprints,
My childhood arrives,
Dressed up in silver manuscripts.

Will any hands really
Applaud —
I do not know. If I could only
Give you a sign: tomorrow
You will know whose
Greeting or crippled hands.

Day and night the conductor waves.

1966

With the Hundredth Sense

Till I love you with my hundredth sense,
The black scorpion will stray with the kiss in the sands,
And I will not doff my gray cloak of skin.

Down with the counter of senses to five or to six,
The miser who counted them off like moldy sticks!
More beautiful things I would throw to stray dogs on the roads.

A fiddle is tree and is water and is ship and is tone,
When the fingers are dead and the bow rows homeward alone.
So I will come with my hundredth sense to my bliss.

A branch will tell his neighbor: there is a God . . .
A human ear is fated to hear where He trod
When over his bliss the solitary man will reign.

With its hundredth sense, my time, an invisible wind,
Will find its cosmic form in body's labyrinth.
And the helplessness of both I will throw to the dogs.

1965

Zeykher Le-Ghetto[64]

Close the Window

It's not for you to finish. Not a time for wholeness.
Tatters of texts more eternal than marble.
Close the window. Let shadows put on sackcloth
When ghosts play Carmen, Rigoletto.
Leave an empty line, a blot —
A memory of the ghetto.

1965

In Blue Gowns

In blue gowns — like bells down to their soles,
Bound to one another's hands with rope —
They march through Hell Street of my memory,
Past the Green Bridge,
Twisted, gall-splattered huts,
Between blond rifles and genuflecting Gentiles —
They march for years and years and years
From madhouse to ghetto — sick Jews, madmen.

A boot shoved me in among them. I become
A bone of their bone. A dream of their minds.
I feel good. Good morning. *Blessed are
You honest voyagers.*[65]
Dressed in the same blue gown, on my hands
A rope — it will lead us all together
To new gates, to new walls.

Such a huddling with Jews is a blessing.
Never felt such joy with Jews in my grief.
Late-summer blue. Messiah our Lord marches
With us all, in a gown blue as the Viliya.
Every head is shorn, naked,
But the face — a palette of a wild, dead painter:
Dried up, unused colors, still breathing,
A shadow of a brush dances on their skull.

Thus they march through Hell Street of my memory,
From madhouse to ghetto — madmen, in an alien
Otherworldliness, in long blue gowns,
They march for years and years and years.

And I thank today, as then, for the honor
To be chained with the lowest of the low,
Marching on the pavement to the ghetto and the bonfire,
Further away,
To be further away
From Germans.

1966

The Smile of Maidanek

I

No thicker than the membrane of an eye —
My neighbor's door.
No thicker than the spungold tavern
Where a weary dewdrop staggers in
For the night.
No thicker than a shadow
Flayed from the flesh —
Wherefore do I never succeed in opening the door
When, after all, the door was never locked?

And he, my bosom-friend,
My poison-friend,
Wherefore can he not go through the same door to his neighbor
And simply say to him good-morning?
The door is lucid as fear,
The door is not locked.

II

How far is a bygone second?
Just one second far
From any today and tomorrow.
My neighbor is himself a bygone second
Covered with a mask
To conceal
His wound.

III

My neighbor knocks on the door
As if to say:
A hollow attic vessel, the earth is cracked.
Just hit it a little harder
And it crumbles into ash and dust
And all the seas swing back into the sky

And put out the bonfires we call the stars.
So maybe you can lend me wings
To fly away to a safer planet?
Without a second thought, I'm moving out of here.

God's mercy on the earth-born.
Is it the apple's fault I carry such a hump?

IV

On a crematorium chimney in the Land of Poland,
Barefoot,
Feet dangling,
As in childhood
Fishing in *lulav*[66] reedy water —
My neighbor sits.
He's dreaming:
The hook of his own pole
Trapped him
With a glimmering worm.

He is his own catcher
On the long
Thin pole.
He is himself his own legend.

V

What do you think he's doing on the chimney,
When someone long ago dredged up from the red belly
My neighbor's parchment city of Jews?
He holds a little mirror in his hand
And casts,
As in childhood
Spots of sun on grandpa's face —
A green smile, raining panic on old and young:

It won't let you dream, be silent, talk —
He casts out, casts into you
The smile of Maidanek.

VI

The smile of Maidanek falls
On wedding and *bris*.[67]
In opera.
Theater.
In the wings.
In creases of your bread and salt,
Salty conscience.

The green smile falls
On your elegy, your ballad,
On every tremor
Of a sound.

The smile falls
With hissing fire
Into the best wine,
Burgundy
Or Tokay.
It falls on squat depots,
Barely mapped, like mushrooms.
On the tall building of the United
Nations,
And higher — on the silver wanderer
To the abysses.

VII

And nobody knows that on anointed,
High-domed
Summer nights,
In snowy or rainy spaces,
Barefoot,
Feet dangling, as in childhood —
My neighbor sits in Poland on a chimney,
Ponders the beautiful reality that is not real,
And what my neighbor does is ever the same:
He holds in his hand a little mirror. Nothing more.

1966

Emblem

I

And the three of us, on a narrow, one-oared
Sampan, swam out of the port of Aberdeen[68]
Into the sea. The waves — thin,
Transparent shells,
Lose their weight and turn into foamy amber
Between British Isles
And China.

The isles — kingdoms for dragons
And miniature runners. With rickshaws, temples, mottos,
With silkworms spinning banners from their innards,
And smiling little Buddhas in the heart of a blue lotus.

Ya-Tang was born here. The peak of that rock —
He points to it with a cherry branch. The rock — his bride.
She sings, a kitten
Meowing.

Patiently, on the smooth sea, swims the night —
A black coffin.

In the black coffin swim my years.
And the Chinese madonna
Keeps on meowing.

— Ya-Tang, where to? I see in him a dwarf,
The dwarf drinks a toast to the pearl bottom of the sea.

— My lord, this is the tavern of wine and love,
Where he jumped out to catch the moon,
The godly Li-Po.

II

The Morning Star lets his star inherit a wave,
The Morning Star lets his morning inherit the sea.
Godly Li-Po unravels the braid around his waist
And dozes off in the pearl tavern, along with him.

A conch is my ear and the conch weeps Chinese.
One-syllable needles fill my hearing.
And differently cries a wave, differently flies a stork —
Where are we, what vision approaches us?

A different sea: a rainbow between us and islands —
Is it after a rain, before a rain? Tell us the secret, Ya-Tang!
Red, split water-strings of his oar splatter gleams,
And go back to the sea, to its indifferent movement.

—Such a rainbow, says Ya-Tang, is not from the rain:
With children on their shoulders, with a spear and a sack of rice,
Chinese swim in the nights of the great land—across,
To dream-islands . . . and dolphins are fed.

Oh, rainbow, red as an open heart, emblem of Asia,
Did the godly Li-Po, the splendor of all sons,
See you in reality, as I do, or in a dream? —
You gave me a poem on the shores of Aberdeen.

1965

To Read, To Write

I

I want to be your reader and try to read the heavy
Sanskrit of your brows that lack so little,
One hair, no more, to become one, intertwined, unique.
I want to be the reader of your tears.

I want to read your silence, as the lining
Of trembling, silver leaves on a poplar,
When, below, an axe is lifted, glittering with treason.
I want to be the reader of your veins, your navel.

I want to be your reader, your only understander,
As a wolf who understands the dead howl
Of a she-wolf pierced by a bullet behind the evening
Veil of snow, amid warm pleasure.

Drawing by the poet.

II

Instead of paper — a leaf of thin, spring air. I want to write
Uninterrupted for a second, with teeth instead of pencil,
Like fire, fearing water more than fire.
I want to write one second, so an eternity remains.

I want to write for the beggar, the value of a coin.
I want to write for the sound, that should not work in vain.
I want to write for my childhood in a winged blizzard.
I want to write for the grass growing out of me, green.

I want to write for the silkworm, to spin out his silk.
I want to write for the suicide, to soothe his pain.
I want to write for the dying, run out of time to suffer.
I want to write for the mirror, like the hand of Leonardo.

1967

A Witness

Amazing: a tiny ant —
An atom,
Pulls the lead planet of an old elephant
Into the corner of its eye, the very abyss,
And still has a little
Time and space left for his grandfathers— —

And still has one empty pupil
To swallow up the witness.

1965

Morning After a Night in Jaffa

Believe the *Times* when I hardly
Believe in time, that *golem* facing me
Like an artist's painting
That ultra-abstracts?

And a voice replies: Abraham, Abraham,
Better not believe in yourself
Than not to believe in the facts!

And this is the fact:
In a frame, a black sore,
Sealed suddenly a name:
So-and-So is no more.

So-and-So, just yesterday in Jaffa
At the sea, read to me a sonnet.
And strode on like a young giraffe:
A Liliput, Lord, is Your planet.

So how can it be,
That he should suddenly not be?
The conch at the sea is the same
As yesterday.
The stiff-necked stone was and is
And goes on slaughtering
The foamy necks of the waves.
Even the glowworm amid deep green
Thickets —
On that teensy creature, the same *Shekhina*[69]
As yesterday —

So how can it be,
That he should suddenly not be?

What a lunatic game,
To create so many *isn'ts* all the same.

1966

The Shard Hunters

With Nostrils of Dogs

The shard-hunters — this is my company.
At midnight, we begin to advance
From the Red Sea, the coral inn,
In the rhythm of old caravans.

The shard-hunters lurk. In their
Primeval memory, emerges from the deep
The morning doe, as if a bride forgot
To remove her veil before a sleep.

And evoking in the same memory:
A sliver of a jar, a pot,
Where dead great-grandfathers grind rye
To leave for their grandchild — on this spot.

Thirstier for pebbles than for springs,
Nostrils of dogs with fine sense and measure,
Advancing through a wadi, they attack
The shards of its stolen treasure.

A. SUTZKEVER   *313*

Desert Sun

A thorn grass in the Desert Zin. Thinner
Than a needle. Sucked out blue.
Alone. In sand. With those who are envious,
Who would bring him to the Moloch. Dry hue.

A whole day, at his feet, at his head —
The sun. In his scorched mind engraved,
Burned out, his dream about a drop.
The savior strays. How can you be saved?

It seems: the sun determined just
To scorch the thorn grass, to burn.
Oh miracle: livelier, longer falls its shadow
At the sun's lonely return.

So are you, poet, scorched in dread,
Time essayed to lay you waste:
Time declines lower, closer to her end,
And a long shadow falls from your waist.

The Third Silence

I see two scales hanging in the air:
On one scale, silence of the sea. The other —
Silence of the desert. Someone must weigh them.
Their primeval weeping is my escort.

The needle pulls back and forth. So far,
Undecided which silence should weigh down.
Do not escape, my heart, stay a moment.
There is a third silence — eavesdrop:

It has borne life. It is immortal.
There is no sand not sown with its seed.
The shard-hunters kiss its shards, they call it
Death, but it has a different name.

At night, when the scales turn silver,
Glow blue with sea- and desert-silence, unheard,
The needle dozes off, no voice, no sound —
The third silence talks in her sleep. The third.

Eilat, June 1966

Covered with Half of Jerusalem

Covered with half of Jerusalem up to
Their breath,
Covered with walls, hanging balconies, up to
The spring of an eye, up to
The genesis of colors —
Covered with stars
Through thin olive branches
Etched on nightmetal
With a needle of silence —
Covered with springs where angels bathe
Before turning into peasants, blacksmiths —
My fingers stretch, strike roots,
For generations,
Stretch and touch, palpable as clay,
Grasp themselves
And all the nonexistent.

1966

A. SUTZKEVER   *315*

Ripe Faces

(1968–1970)

Drawing by the poet.

✷

The eye of my soul weeps images —
For itself as for another,
For another as for itself.
The eye of my soul weeps images
As sunset weeps clouds:
Where and to whom to confide?

I burned up my desk. It's a disgrace
To bow down to wood. I exchanged it for a wild night
Of struggle in the desert, where an eagle whirled,
Where the eye of my soul weeps images,
Pristine images imploring: Describe, describe —
For yourself as for another world.

1968

Land of My Children

Such a sleep I didn't have for half an eternity.
Such a sleep visits you only from inside copper.
Was I transformed into a beehive?
Someone, I feel,
Plunges into my body and extracts a bunch of honey.

Only when the Morning Star,
Blue as himself,
Called my by name and I sensed
A difference between my heartbeat and my dear shadow,
Did I grasp that in my sleep, I lost a rib.

A rib has vanished.
My lord has stuffed the gap with words,
Thrusting out of the seal on my lips.
And facing me, from my rib, my lord built
A land,
A Morning-Star Land,
For my children.

1968

Branch with Last Cherries

Where there is no more my home, no more my mother,
There is my blue home and there is my mother.

Perhaps someone lives who still recalls her face.
Among copper scorpions I will walk to seek him.

Elijah, I shall call him. Elijah.
Him, the Chosen One, who recalls my mother's face.

I will kiss his feet and beg: Elijah,
By virtue of my wounds — please, breathe out her face.

Just for a moment. If it's too long: half a moment.
With the rest of my years I am prepared to pay.

Oy, as to a branch of last cherries, through a mist,
I shall come close, and fear to come closer.

In that half moment, I shall ask: Tell me, mother,
Could the Creator look you in the eye?

1968

Barefoot

We took off our shoes
In the middle of the hot city.
And we looked so loose,
Like newborn and pretty.

With the same speed, if we could
Free our thoughts for a while
From their heavy boots —
It would be easier, mile after mile,
To leap barefoot into childhood.

1968

My Armor

As the desert porcupine darts
Its white and black arrows
Into the hollow circle
Drawing it like a Fata Morgana,
So, in wandering to your face, I dart
The days and nights of my body,
Spread them over miles,
To defend myself
From death:
From myself.

1968

Falling Water

"Falling water has no depth" —
Thus I heard a sheikh in Dimona.

But when it falls? When it falls, I add,
Its depth
Can drown a river and the moon in the river.

Fall from the mountains,
My borrowed time,
Like a rain,
Fall from the mountains with your childhood music
Toward me,
Before you give yourself back
To your borrower.

Fall like water
Before I rise like fire.

Fall from the mountains
Like a melted mirror,
That already saw
To the depths of its vision.
Before your lord drops his eyelash
And you are no more.

Fall like water
Before I rise like fire.

1968

Signs

Show me a sign that I am your sign,
I will become a hymn, soaring like a pine.

A sign that I am chosen in your field
And all my falling leaves are healed.

Show me a sign in a buzzing bee
Seeking red honey for the grief in me.

A sign that you ache with my gray hair
And cuddle my feet in grass so fair.

I seek your voice from first dawn blue,
That the last breath has meaning too.

A woodpecker pecks at a tree. Send a beak
To peck into me the essence oblique.

That I belong with the lightning and with the worm
And with the sea, pulled out of your arm.

The sea lands on the shore and won't swim back.
Show me a sign. Like of foam a speck.

Show me a sign that in your memory borne
Is a red rose of me the thorn.

Just one image left to see
Of all the visions you revealed to me.

1968

Report of a Journey

A ship slid me off and
Off.
Slid me off a fat butcher table and
Off.
Slid me on a strange island
With Indonesians, Burmese, Malayans.
I run up to my neck in water. Want to catch up with the sinful,
Catch her by her braid
Of smoke and fire —
In vain. No ship. Her braid has turned
Into a tongue. It seems: the tongue sticks out a tongue
To the cheated, stranded islander who will nevermore see
A beloved. Not a familiar face. Not a Yiddish book.
I felt like Napoleon on St. Helena.
A chill ran down my back.

No one here understands my language. It's mutual. Man, where to?
I see a sign: a painted bread. I ask in sign language for a loaf.
A dwarf with the face as large as a lemon
Serves me instead of bread a snake with hissing sulfur.

I show the address of the poet Machayo,
The world-famous, the papers sing his praise —
And the driver bows sadly and takes me around
An hour, and two, and three, and leaves me over an abyss
Where lepers, with little hammers on metal plates
Ever beat and ring so no one should approach.

Back in the city —
And there is no more city, but a blend
Of pieces of night and sea and stone and smell of hashish.
But where the night leaves a trace there is a woman.
"She will understand my non-language on the horror island."

I ask her where Buddha lives,
Sakya-Muni,
Buddha.
She points at her diamond hump: a child,
And dancing out of her, the *she* in the mirror of a knife.

But when I lie down to sleep on a mattress of the ground,
I hear a familiar language: a cat's meow.
I answer her in the same tongue. She — back. I — again.
Such intimate talk you will not hear
Between two sisters. Bride and groom. Brothers.
Where else can you find such universal chatter?
Two lonelinesses never understood each other better.

1968

The Sculptor

The sculptor says: once upon a time, I had an atelier
In the ear of a needle. But it was roomier
To blow out of the clay faces and muscles
Than here in the old palace — a gift from the king.
On top of that, in that sweet ear,
With no regret,
I settled with a model — Lili or Lilith,
I don't quite remember her name. Just her shining body
Remained stiff in my memory. Just her body.

I swear,
When from the veinous marble
I hewed out, called up her hot breasts —
They spurted buzzing milk.
A sign that a man too is a partner to a birth.

"Music, you breath of statues" — Rilke wrote.
For my sake, I would have turned it around:
Sculptures are the breath of music.
Basalt, granite, and marble are classical music.
The sculptor is the conductor:
He just makes them play.

His chisel and hammer is the baton.
A cut,
A chisel with a cosmic challenge,
And musically, the breath of granite is molded
In the marble orchestra.

But now I am old.
I have a face of basalt.
I need no more raw stone
To pinch out limbs.
It's enough for me to open the shutters at dawn
And white marble of the day fills
My atelier, my quaking ground.

I throw myself upon him and chip off
Pieces of the day.
I want to expose his muscles. Leave just the essence.
The cut-off hours lie mute in a corner.
Till nightfall. Till both fall drunk from the struggle.
And drunk, I hear the tick-tock of drunk atoms.

And again my atelier is in the ear of a needle
With Lili or Lilith — I don't quite remember her name.

1968

From Old and Young Manuscripts

(1935–1981)

Reuven Rubin, portrait of the poet.

✡

And it will be at the end of days,
And thus it will happen: the son of man
Will bring to his hungry mouth
Neither bread nor meat,
Neither fig nor honey;
He will savor only a word or two
And be sated.

1978

Fragment

Oh, Lithuania, homeland mine,[70] serpent's bite in my heart,
Storks, vaulted in my memory over your black forests,
Like Kabbalistic signs, gild the rims
Where your fir trees rustle on Viliya's banks.
The body-burners are your fire witnesses.[71]

The body-burners. Day and night, in my bones, ring
Their swinging chains, pleading: Give us meaning.
With the clatter of the chains, my words are
Welded in the copper labyrinths of a dream,
Have no reality — to dream, to rise.
I am an incarnation of the body-burners of Ponar.
My bread is baked of ash. Every loaf — a face.
The sun their memorial candle, and no one knows it.
And when I walk the streets of Jerusalem in the rain,
In its diamond mirror, I see their souls
In wound-colors: Living brother, give us meaning.

And I pray to the sheet of paper: Be cold as rock.
Reveal a miracle. Let my searing syllables
Straying over you, not turn you to ash.

1950

Recognition

I thank and I praise the scorpion
For giving me drunken pain.
Before poppies light up and go on
And the mist is blooming again.

In his sting to my very quick,
In the drug of his pinpoint needle —
The eternal secret, the trick
That only pain can unriddle.

In the beginning was the scorpion.
He sought for life a word.
Before poppies light up and go on
Over all the atoms he is lord.

1978

Subforest Laughter

I know a forest: a madhouse for trees,
Locked in the forest. The watchman keeps the key.
The trees rip the birds off their heads. Rustle to the silence.
In a storm, they drink the wine of its lightning.

Through the corridors, green as copper-eve,
Stroll the days. One by one, they come, in white
Robes. Through the same green aisles
They flee with searing stains on the white.

Every tree a prison in a prison. Only roots
Streaming out with mossy, subforest laughter,
Groping and clutching bones and skulls,
Drilling into them the madness of life.

1978

A Bunch of Grapes

I

In love,
I drowned in grass.

At thirty,
I drowned in tears.

Now I drown in the desert
And am ever thirsty.

II

I saw in the desert a bunch of grapes,
A bunch of grapes with a drunken gaze.

And I must rush,
Run for miles,
To come back
To yesteryear's day.

III

You are too near for me to go away.
Unless I doff the linen dream,
Unless I go far from myself
Till the last abyss.

The sages say:
Not just the earth is of sea and of rock and is round
As a tear.
I shall come to the gray-haired mirror
And smite it so uneternally long
With the bone of my skull,
Till a Voice-of-Thin-Silence rises
In the void behind the glass:

You are too near for me to go away.

1978

Yosl Bergner, illustration to "Winedrops."

Winedrops

I

A string of birds seeks in the sun strewn seeds of sound
To sing silence to a dreamer in the grass.

II
Fewer words.
Fewer, fewer drops.
Soon, the goblet will run out
Along with the wine.

1978

Elegy

The dead live in another domain.
I am their time. I say: It rains. And comes the rain.
I say: Snow. And violin strings of snow fall.
They love to hear my poems and I read them all.

I say: There is no death. I hear a roar:
Death is our life, is life no more?
I say: We are one, let us not split in two.
They love to hear me read my poems, and I do.

1978

Yosl Bergner, illustration to "Divine Comedy."

Divine Comedy

When in another incarnation
You seat me in your garden spheres,
Do not create me young again
And fervent, but replete with years.

And later, do not drive me out
Full of God's mockery and wrath.
I want to taste both from the tree
Of life and from the tree of death.

I want to taste the real tree
Of poisoned pain in your dark shade —
In vise of silence I endure,
For in your image am I made.

A serpent then may flick its tongue —
One snake, a second and a third —
Just so that night with its gray hair
Should not impose its rule, unheard.

Just so that to the gushing spring
The mouths of my thin fingers flung —
Till every drop inside my body,
Instead of growing old, grows young.

If I live long enough to see
My childhood, in my youth advance —
My cat will wash her gentle paws
And in his joy my dog will dance.

1979

Wooden Steps

For Freydke

I don't remember faces. People erased. Of many stairs,
Only the creak of wooden steps without a bannister.

The wooden steps up to my garret, six by six,
Where under the roof sparrows come to parties
And drink and cry and laugh till daybreak.
I don't remember faces. Their heirs are ruins.

The creak of wooden steps up to my garret winces:
Ah, the poet Leyzer Volf,[72] not the creak of my princes . . .
Who taught a shadow to play in the nights?
A flash inscribing in the clouds sky-notes.

Fiddle cases of wooden steps. Inside — the musicians,
Their music drew us off to different regions.
Up to our neck in silences: catastrophe —
But I caught Sirius in a single strophe.

The garret went off to Ponar. The faces too. Of many stares,
I remember the creak of wooden steps without a bannister.

1979

Legend

When Rokhl Sutzkever,[73] the gentle painter of our
Young Vilna and young life,
From wounded ghetto alleys
Walked barefoot
To the whirlpool — the gate,
From the knapsack on her girlish back,
The twins — two brushes — poking out.
Earlier, she dipped them in her own two eyes.

I saw: the brushes see,
Swimming to the gate, they say farewell
To falling leaves, balconies, steps, dolls,
To their models in the sinking city.

In a moment, the brush-gold of our painter
Will be a legend.

I whispered: Rokhl, Rokhl, did you take
In your knapsack
Canvas too and tubes of paint?
Or will you paint with a single color: red?
No matter what, I will
Come breathless to your exhibit
Personally
And see for myself,
Admire a horrible still life — —

1979

Needleshine[74]

And thus it was: When I returned
After the Liberation
To my hiding place
Between God and Satan —
Through the thin tin vaulting
I once pierced with a nail,
Fell the same oblique shine,
The same heavenly needle of light,
In whose grace I needled letters
Into the silver parchment of my body
For all eternity.

Let me unravel the secret:
Liberated, when I returned
To my hiding place —
In the same needleshine I saw,
Quivering in the ray of dust,
A familiar figure. I could swear:
I it was. And am. And shall remain,
Strung on a string of dust
With the same needle.

1978

A Prayer

For years, a prayer sails in my veins,
And its waves my strophes bend:
Dear God, let us exchange our memories —
I will recall the beginning, you will remember the end.

1978

Small Elegy on the Extinction and Resurrection of a Single Word

Of two lips, a he and a she, you were born, Wonder.
Springtime entered to rise in you.
Separated from the two, you conducted
My blood symphony.

Oh, word of mine, unique
As a one with burnt out zeroes,
Sensitive as a magnet's needle
To the North Star.
Of two lips, a he and a she, seeing and invisible.

I do not know whose dream embodied you, whose
Tearburst ardently extinguished you.
Without you, I was a cinder, I was
Without body-or-tongue.

And you, unique, my I, you heard
Under dust and shards
My breath.
You came to life, immortal as death.

1979

The Great Silence

In the Sinai Desert, on a cloud of granite
Sculpted by the Genesis-night,
Hewn of black flame facing the Red Sea,
I saw the Great Silence.

The Great Silence
Sifts the secrets of the night.
Unmoving, its thin flour falls on my brows.
Silently, whispering,
I ask the Great Silence,
If I could I would ask more silently:
How many stars did you count
Since your beginning, since your hovering steady
Over the Genesis-night facing the Red Sea?

And the Great Silence replies:
When I shall count it all —
From nothing to the very first thing,
Then, son of man, I shall tell you first.

1979

To Be Able to Say: I

You must possess the courage of an other,
From another time,
To be able to say: I.

To say: I
You must place on your lips
A black coal, whitehot,
And burn out all other words.

To say: I
You must bow
As when uttering the Unspeakable Name.

1978

New Poems

(1987–1990)

Yosl Bergner, illustration.

Remembrances of Others

I

I shall write only remembrances,
Other people's remembrances,
My own, my innermost,
I leave behind
For another,
In whatever distant future.

I want to write the remembrances of Adam
When Eve
Was the only woman in Eden
And he — the only man for both of them.
Did she, even then, know jealousy?
Was anybody there who cherished her envy?

I want to write the remembrances of Job
And reveal
The dreadful curse
He never cursed;

And all the way to the remembrances of Leyvik[75]
Who saw in his first dream,
As he told in Tel Aviv:
The earth — a fireball
And he himself — born of fire.

Alas, the hammer dropped from his hand
When he forged his dream — —

II

I say to the remembrances of others:
Be mine,
Spun of time as silk of silkworms.
I put my ear to a stone,
An ear to an ear:
Outside of what is, the nothing too
Does not exist.

Emerge from the past,
Emerge from once-upon-a-time,
I want to paint you,
Describe
As no one before,
As long as my fingers
Are soldiers on the battlefield.

And let the mute raise hell
And winds throw stones:
I want to paint you,
Describe
As no one before.

III

Bunches of grapes in an arbor are the remembrances
Of others, laden with wine only for me.

I had only one pair of lips. Now I am laden with lips.
Lips on my hands, my veins, my thoughts.

Bunches of grapes in an arbor. Lips of fire
Drink the remembrances, long forgotten.
I am the heir of the bunches of grapes in an arbor,
Saturated, laden with wine only for me.

IV

With rolled-up sleeves and iron muscles
You hoisted up your life to know its weight.
Never mind. The iron waves, your muscles,
Would have lifted with the same force
Ten more lives. But the iron waves
Hoisted your life along with your enemy.
And amazing:
Chained to your feet in the air
The ball of the globe remained hanging, it couldn't
Rip the rope you once used to hang your shirts
Out to dry.

And I thought:
Out of the blue, in my cell,
Appeared a painter — Where did he come from? —
And with his blue, never seen in museums,
Painted the taut canvas of your face
And left his smile too, a legacy
For the mirror.

V

Atoms lie under white sheets
With heart attacks.
I tuned my hearing from here to over there
And running lightyears beyond.
A miracle may happen:
The last string of my hearing
Will soon not burst.
So far, the last string is divinely taut
And hears sun-systems tremble under white sheets.

Atoms struggle with heart attacks
And no one knows who will vanquish.

You curious one, do not lift up a sheet,
Atoms write hasty wills on screens
Spread above, over their heads.
And you must know how to read the script. A lightning in a forest,
Shot through by the roots of night, is not easier
To read, to grasp.
A teacher with a pointer hovers in white space.

And when no difference remains between death and life,
As no difference will be between dogs and princes,
Calm and peace will rise on our good earth
And on its better
Planet provinces.

VI

Axes in the air undercut the sunset eagle,
But axes cannot undercut my word.
My kingdom rises alive because of a garden,
Because of its fruit, even my creator
Once made a blessing on that fruit.
My kingdom rises alive. And I —
Among my remembrances
Of others.
Among slaughtered sounds and their family.

I myself am my people and I bear myself on the shoulders.
We shall both start a newborn silence
In honor of a language giving up the ghost.
Among my remembrances
Of others,
Among slaughtered sounds and their family.

1987

Paris 1988

Topsy-turvy city. I am your river. Bridges and buildings
Topsy-turvy into me a circus upside-down.
I see what only the waves in my memory see:
I am still drinking a glass of wine while writing in cafés.

From flayed walls — fresh wallpaper flowers,
A couple like a cat and a tomcat in a green niche.
A cloud with a blue beard. And at the bookstalls
Someone seeks a book which refuses to exist.

A man leaps into me from a bridge. What does his leaping mean?
His thin coat sails but remains in my circles.
Topsy-turvy policemen whistle like a train.
So far, no one knows that that man is Paul Celan.

Inside Me

For Barbara and Benjamin Harshav

I

Inside me, a twig of sounds sways toward me, as before.
Inside me, rivers of blood are not a metaphor.

Inside me, they gather,
Those who blessed me, those who rose
Against me:
My great friends and my little enemies.
Inside me, it feels so warm with them, and more.
Inside me, rivers of blood are not a metaphor.

Inside me, my friends the wonder people
Gave me their breath, a moment before
I lost my own between the whip and the gore.
Inside me, rivers of blood are not a metaphor.

Star-shards on the eyes. A lash quivers.
I thank the wonder people, the wonder givers
Of silence alighting on my head. As of yore.
Inside me, rivers of blood are not a metaphor.

II

In — side, in — sight:
I rolled
Mountains into an abyss —
Still not enough.
A volcano looming
Closer,
Its lava barely breathing,
Stone.

In — side, in — sight:
A blind Samson praying,
For strength to bring down
The pillars of sun.

Then he will lose
His blindness.
Big pupils will see on the bottom of the sea
The treasures sought in the dark,
By the last dark,
Couldn't find in the dark.
The treasures, without them might
Life and death be unbearably
Light.

In — side, in — sight:
Both life and death are truly light.

III

I must not drain it altogether. I must not.
Even if the well may not well up forever
With new riddles, even
When lips kneel from above — to kiss them.

I must not drain the black honey,
The sweet lunacy of my bones,
Even when lips kneel from above:
Pity us,
Let us quench our thirst with fire.

Oh, lips, lips, I love you more
Than all the fruits of the world, but I must not.
On the bottom, I must leave the sight:
My Lord and Guardian.

Two slender feet of sunset quiver
In rainweb.
The deep sight
Becomes pupils of light.

IV

Two-legged grasses, familiar faces,
Come to my home, my four-walled places.
They kiss the mezuzah and sneak pretty
Fast into my bed where I mumble: Take pity,
Winged woe, reveal your expertise
Of stinging poison into my mind, into my memories,
Of blowing every bitter spark in hiding.

Two-legged grasses, do you bring good tiding?

A. SUTZKEVER   *353*

Two-legged grasses, solve the riddle for me:
What creature would rejoice in iron combs sweeping
Body and soul?
Who would rejoice in such a reaping?
One moment, please,
One more question:
Shall I leave to you my legacy, my vow?

The two-legged grasses piously bow.

1988

Green Aquarium

(1953–1974)

Drawing by the poet.

Green Aquarium

I

"Your teeth are bars of bone. Behind them, in a crystal cell, your chained words. Remember the advice of your elder: the *guilty ones*, words that dropped poisoned pearls in your goblet — let them go free. Grateful for your mercy, they will immortalize you. But the *innocent ones* who will trill falsely like nightingales over your grave — don't spare them. Hang them! For, as soon as you let them out of your mouth or your pen, they turn into demons. May the stars fall out of the sky if I'm not telling the truth!"

This was the legacy left me many years ago, in my living hometown, by an old bachelor, a cracked poet with a long braid hanging down his back like a young birch twig. Nobody knew his name or where he came from. I knew only that he composed rhymed missives to God in Aramaic Targum language, deposited them in the red mailbox on the green bridge, and strolled, contemplative and patient, on the banks of the River Viliya, waiting for the postman from heaven to deliver an answer.

II

"Walk through words as through a minefield: *one* false step, *one* false move and all the words you strung in a lifetime on your veins will be blown apart with you."

This my own shadow whispered to me when both of us, blinded by searchlight windmills, plodded at night through a bloody minefield and every step I took for life or death screeched on my heart like a nail on a violin.

III

But nobody warned me to beware of words groggy from otherworldly poppies. I became their slave. And I cannot understand what they want. Or whether they love me or hate me. They make wars in my brain like termites in a desert. Their battlefield reflects in my eyes like the glow of rubies. And children turn gray with fear when I tell them: "Good-dreams . . ."

The other day, out of the blue, as I lay in the garden and, above me — a branch of oranges or children blowing golden bubbles — I felt my soul move. Oho, my words are getting ready for a journey . . . Having won a victory over one person, they apparently decided to conquer fortresses so far impervious to words. Victory over men, over angels, why not over stars? Drunk on otherworldly poppies, their fantasy soars.

> Trumpets blare.
> Torches like burning birds.
> Accompanied by lines. Frames of music.

To such a word, wearing a crown glimmering with my tears, riding in front, the leader perhaps — to such a word, I fell on my knees.

"That's how you leave me, with no 'good-bye,' no 'see-you-soon,' no nothing? For years we wandered together, you gnawed at my time; now, before we part, before you conquer worlds — one request! But promise you won't refuse . . . "

"OK. I give you my word. But make it short. Because the sun is bending over the blue branch and, in a moment, it will fall into the abyss."

"I want to see the dead!"

"What a request . . . Well, I've got to keep my word. . . *See!*"

> A green knife split the earth.
> And it was green.
> Green.
> Green.
> The green of dark fir trees through a mist;
> The green of a cloud with a burst gall bladder;
> The green of mossy stones in a rain;
> The green revealed through a hoop, rolled by a seven-year-old;
> The green of cabbage leaves in splinters of dew, that can bloody your fingers;
> The fresh green under melting snow, in a ring around a blue flower;

The green of the crescent moon seen by green eyes under a wave;
And the solemn green of grass making seams on a grave.
Green streaming into green. Body into body. The earth transformed into a green aquarium.
Closer, closer, to the green eddy.

I look inside: Humans swim around like fish. Myriads of phosphorous faces. Young. Old. And young-old in one. Those I saw throughout my life, death has crowned them with a green existence; all swimming about in the green aquarium, in a silky, airy music.
Here, the dead live!
Beneath them, rivers, forests, cities — one enormous, palpable map; above, the sun swims in the guise of a man of fire.
I recognize acquaintances, friends, neighbors, I tip my straw hat to them. "Good morning."
They reply with green smiles like a well answering a stone with broken rings.
My eyes strike with silver oars, rush, swimming among all the faces. My eyes roam, searching for *one* face.
Found, found! Here's the dream of my dream — —
"It's me, my dear, me, me. The creases are just nests of longing."
My lips inundated with blood are drawn to hers. Alas, they remain on the pane of the aquarium.
Her lips too swim to mine. I feel the breath of burning punch.
The glass is a cold knife between us.
"I want to read you a poem about you . . . You must listen!"
"My dear, I know the words by heart, I gave you the words myself."
"Then I want to feel your body one more time!"
"We can't get any closer, the glass, the glass . . ."
"No, the boundary will soon disappear, I'll smash the green glass with my head — —"

After the twelfth bang, the aquarium shattered.
Where are the lips, where is the voice?
And the dead, the dead — did they die?

No one. In my face — grass. And above — a branch of oranges or children blowing golden bubbles.

The Woman in the Panama Hat

One day, in the Age of Slaughter, I sat in a dark nook and wrote. As if the Angel of Poetry told me: "Your choice is in your own hand. If your song inspires me, I will protect you with a fiery sword. If not — don't complain . . . My conscience will remain clean."

In the little room, I felt like the clapper of a bell. A movement, a tremor, and the bell starts ringing.

In the silence, words hatched.

Then, knuckles rapping on the door.

The silence ran off over the floor like quicksilver out of a broken thermometer.

"Danger, a friend is warning me." I pulled the bolt.

A woman appears. At first glance — a beggar. Nothing unusual. In the pause between life and death, when hunger reigns in all its skeleton glory, hosts of beggars swell like a swarm of locusts. But *this* beggar surprised me with her clothes: a straw summer hat, a kind of panama hat, trimmed with dried wild strawberries; a long old-fashioned crinoline — a rainbow of rags; at her side, a bag; on her neck hung a thin jade necklace with an ivory lorgnette; and the points of her polished shoes — two shining crows with blood-red beaks, gaping open.

I didn't ask anything, just offered her a piece of bread with moldy crusts.

She advances a step, takes the bread, puts it on the table and then — cackling like a cookoo, she says:

"If I'm not mistaken, you are the person I'm looking for; so I won't take this bread."

"Sit down, auntie, you'll feel better. The bread? Yes, indeed, mold. But, on my word of honor, I don't have any other bread. We shall live to eat challah again."

I indicate to the woman the only stool and I myself sit on the table facing her.

"Oh, that's not what I mean, believe me." She lifts her crinoline so as not to wrinkle it, like a dancer, and sits down on the stool.

"Might I ask about a small matter?"

"A small thing is a small thing, auntie. You don't have to wear gloves with me."

"There are sheets of paper there. The ink is still fresh on them. Who wrote them?"

"Me . . ."

"Are you a writer?"

"Yes, a writer."

Not only from the corners of her eyes but from all her wrinkles did tears drip. A rosy smiling freshness, like a mist after a spring rain, bloomed from her soul.

"That's good. Now let me pour out my heart. For these few minutes, the Almighty will repay you with years."

She pulls out of her sleeve a pink handkerchief with a silver border and wipes her lips. From the handkerchief comes the dying trace of an old perfume. And she tells:

"My name is Felicia Poznanski. The writer I. Y. Singer has immortalized me in a novel. Once I looked different. But that's not important."

Out of the other sleeve, she pulls another handkerchief in a medley of peacock colors, with another perfume, wipes away the moisture under her eyes, and goes on:

"As for Felicia — let's say it's another person, not the beggar sitting here in front of you — she was once a rich woman. That is, her husband, Ignatz, was a millionaire. Nine factories, hundreds of spinning machines. In one of his palaces lived the president of the city. In addition, he was Honorary Consul of Portugal — —"

The sunset lit up her wrinkles with the green light of glowworms. She became thinner, more shriveled, looked like the mummy of an ancient Egyptian princess.

"Nobody liked Ignatz, not even his own family. He was considered a misanthrope. Well, maybe he was. We mustn't judge too easily. There was a reason for his hatred of men. As a child, his nose had been broken like a clay pot and the greatest professors in the world couldn't put it together again. He had to wear a false nose, a rubber one. Because of that, his voice lost its virility and he spoke so thinly, too thinly, like a newborn kitten."

But Felicia loved him. Not for his wealth or for his manners. She loved him for his writing. He was writing a poem about Job in Polish . . . At night, in his study, he would take off his rubber nose so he could breathe more freely and would write until daybreak. And Felicia was the happiest woman in the world. No, this wasn't Poznanski the industrialist, this was Heine,

A. SUTZKEVER   *361*

Byron! Byron lacked a piece of foot — but wasn't he the greatest poet of his century? Just like Poznanski, who lacked a piece of nose . . .

The sunset heats up the copper bell of my garret. The tears of a hidden child wander to his creator. And the woman in the straw panama hat goes on:

"On the first day of the war, the wheel of fortune turned. Splinters of a bomb struck Ignatz in the head. Before he passed away, he made me swear: Felicia, my dear, take care to save my work, my whole life is in it. My world here and my world to come . . ."

With a little valise in hand, Felicia fled the city. Inside — the poem about Job, a packet of diamonds, and the costume she wore to the masked ball where she had met her husband. When she tried to sneak across the Lithuanian border[76] by the river, her boat capsized and the valise sank in the water. Miraculously, Felicia swam to the bank and told the ferryman about her diamonds. He dived in a few times and fished out the valise. He was an honest peasant and they divided it as agreed: he took the diamonds and she took her husband's share of eternity, his work, and the costume she had worn to the masked ball . . . You can see it, Felicia is wearing it now . . . She wants to wear it to the masked ball of death.

The woman in the panama hat suddenly stands up and curtsies, as once upon a time in that celestial masked ball. But what happens? She can't get up again. Her face grows dark, changes color like paper as it burns, and, on the brim of her panama hat, the strawberries are bleeding.

"No need for water, no need. A twinge of the heart, nothing. Where were we? Oh, yes, I'll make it short — "

Standing, she examines me with her lorgnette and her voice takes on another tone, as if one of her veins had burst:

"Now I am a beggar. Almost a year now. For a while, I taught Portuguese to two girls and, for each lesson, I got two potatoes. But since the girls disappeared, I don't have anybody to teach Portuguese to. I go begging from house to house. Not just for a piece of bread. I wanted to find someone like you, a writer, and give him the masterpiece of my dear husband. For I, dear sir, don't have much longer. I'm going to join the two girls . . . Give me your hand that you will keep the poem about Job just like your own papers and after the war—you understand, don't you? Give me your hand! . . ."

As her bony right hand with the delicate pianist's fingers was closed in mine, her left hand pulled a pocketsize notebook out of her sack and put it on the table, next to the moldy bread.

When the woman was gone—the bell started ringing. It could no longer bear the silence. The silence of old people snatched up in the street.

Children's Hands

The single pane of glass in a cellar, covered with frost. On the pine forest of the window pane, the print of two children's hands, open as if in a priest's blessing. Through the forest and the handprints, the sun falls into the cellar like a corpse into a tomb.

The walls are lined with downy snow and glimmer like a salt mine.

On the ground, in a corner—the scattered rags of a pallet and, among them, like gold teeth, gleam scraps of hidden straw.

On the rags, a thick *Korbn Minkhe*, a woman's prayerbook, covered with candle drippings, printed by the Rom Widow and Brothers . . .

Next to it, in a pot of sand—a stiffened wax candle like a bird piercing its own heart with a dead beak.

And in the middle of the cellar, between the children's handprint on the window and the *Korbn Minkhe* on the rags of the pallet—a bronze horse's head with a silver spot like a stab wound on the brow and cold, eternal eyes of black marble.

And the children's handprints on the window pane speak:

Dear head, forgive us. It is not we who cut you off your living neck. When the last ones, the very last ones crumbled into ashes—we found you in a butcher shop and dragged you, slowly, hidden under a stranger's long coat, to the cellar. With you—we wanted to feed an old woman. Lonely like you now, the old woman was lying here in the corner. At her head—a burning candle. But all of a sudden—dogs. Dogs. Dogs. They attack the old woman, attack your frozen flesh. Attack the boy we belong to . . . Oh, how we wanted to help him . . . We ran to the window pane, to the snowy forest, and where are we, where are we? . . .

While the children's handprints on the window pane speak — the icicles melt on the bronze head. His skin starts glowing, becomes alive. His left ear drops like a lock of hair. And tears appear in the black marble eyes.

Lady Job

From pulverized clay nests, from the grids of cellar apertures and broken doors, burning pages of Holy Books rise to the sunset — children with outstretched hands as if the sun had given birth to them in the Synagogue Yard[77] and now they fly back to their mother.

When the sun hides her children behind a cloud, they leave black tears — burned-out soot — on the gallery of the synagogue.

The two-storied gallery, rising to a pyramid over the rickety ruins of narrow streets and alleys, is not the same as before.

The gallery has metamorphosed into an eagle on top of another eagle!

The eagle on top, with the head of an animal and a blue breast between purple wings, like a brook amid rosebushes, plants his four claws of bronze into the eagle below.

And the eagle below, with the head of an angel, a gleaming serpent around his neck, and his wings — two rocks facing each other over an abyss — bows over the synagogue. His ten claws — columns carved of salt — falter under the heavy wings.

Above, between the bronze feet of the eagle on top, leaning on his blue breast, I see a hidden little man.

"Little man, who are you?"

"I am the painter Yankel Sher, the painter of the narrow streets . . ."

In his green velvet vest, he stands in front of a canvas. It was a vest he once got in Paris. In our town, it was unique. People used to stop in the street, admiring its beauty. He fastened it at the neck with a big copper clip. Its folds shimmered like a peacock's feathers. It had ten different pockets stuffed with brushes, pencils, and notebooks.

Now the vest hangs on him, puffed out, covered with mold, not a garment for a man but for a hen. And the brush he holds in his teeth looks like a ritual slaughter knife.

The squinting, watery eyes bulge out over his nose and two twin tears enclose it.

The painter looks at the twisted narrow streets, then looks at the canvas and doesn't believe his eyes. Ever since he hid in this gallery, today is the first time he has seen how his world had changed.

What wind blew him up a church opposite? And how did the medieval city hall get here where the butcher shop was?

Who lit the lights in the dead Synagogue Yard?

Why, dear God, does the Gaon's Prayerhouse[78] deserve stoning? And why was the tree over the gate condemned to fire?

Only the sewers haven't changed.

They too! Shimmering with blood . . .

Yankel Sher wants to smear the canvas with paint. Where is the truth — inside him or outside?

Maybe it was his palette that was guilty?

He once saw a violin in the hands of a virtuoso. Right in the middle of the concert — alas, the sound was gone. The audience was bewildered. The violinist turned pale as the rosin on the strings. But soon, he bent his ear and said: Honored audience, this violin has just given up the ghost. I beg you to stand up and pay him a final homage.

He brings his ear to the palette. It lives, it lives.

Bunches of soot of the burning pages of Holy Books fall on his hair, fall on the canvas.

Now he pulls the brush out of his mouth. The brush, with the hunger of an artist, devours colors. The spots of snow vanish from the canvas. From the young, fresh, springtime earth, *an old woman* emerges.

That's just how she looked, the eighty-year-old woman. Now she lives again, lives again! A black Sabbath dress with little crystal buttons. Her hair white, dazzling white, like frozen milk. Her face — a ball of silver creases where springtime rivulets shimmer. Plop, plop. In the rivulets, the sun dances. Casts little beams in cold bayonets. And the old woman, just a bit bent, carries a blond girl on her shoulders — —

Behind the old woman — faces. Faces. A chimney with a slaughtered neck.

On one knee, a window bends in the air. And the gate over the narrow street, where the old woman makes her way, has a black slit.

Yankel Sher recoils a step. Yes, that's just how she looked, the eighty-year-old woman. It just lacks . . . Oh, what is missing?

His watery eyes bulge even more. Spill over onto the palette. A damp flush covers his face.

The old woman walked . . . with a tefillin box on her forehead . . . she picked up the tefillin box from the ground, from the sewer . . .

"Yankel, you're a painter, paint the tefillin box!"

He dips his brush in the fallen tears, in a spurt of red; and the old woman, with the blond girl on her shoulders, now passes under the split gate, between bayonets, with a little box on her brow, where God lives.

"*Lady Job*, that's what the picture will be titled . . ."

A shudder came over the gallery. Both eagles rose. Two pairs of stormy wings. Along with the painter Yankel Sher, along with Lady Job, along with the kneeling window, along with the whole alley — the eagles vanish in a lightning cloud.

The Last of the Blind

Her eyes did not dwell in flesh like everybody else's. They lived inside, in a separate face — two small magnetic needles.

The needles attracted flowering branches, sun and shade, colors like throbbing veins, faces and, most important, the face of her blind lover.

The two of them met like two nights and their stone blindness gushed out sparks.

And when he, with a face like a windowpane in the rain, clambers over the walls at night, so the moon would throw him a silver herring, he plays on the long flute he inherited, plays a melancholy tune, a kind of funeral march for a bird; and she, in her garret, sees her lover in a mirror of his tones.

Once, he didn't come back. A deaf veil darkened the mirror. And she — as if another blindness had seized the blind woman!

She gropes for his shadow. The pompadour of his shadow. The magnetic needles do not attract him anymore. . .

Someone stuck a knife in a corpse!

Her fingers — ten droning bees — dance around the hollow garret, where the air is consumed like white ash.

"Come, sister!"

Her little sister who can see, half naked, a book under her arm, two little braids like open scissors, looms up out of a glimmering corner, with a lantern in her hand.

"Teach me to dance, I have never danced, never, never in my life."

The lantern — a one-eyed owl — remains hanging on a beam. Underneath, in the light of that bloody eye, the two sisters dance. Accompanied by the vanished flute, the bird funeral march. . .

"Thank you, my dear. Now leave me alone. I want to see if God is blind."

A shudder went through the garret, like a nest at the touch of a saw.

The blind girl slowly approached the lamp, her buzzing fingers unwound the cylinder, moistened her braids, her dress with kerosene, and the owl-eye cast a jet of fire.

Over streets — caverns of ghosts — sun. Sun. Sun.

Sun in bandaged windowpanes. Sun in faces. Sun in corpses who haven't found death . . .

Men, sundered into two separate profiles, become skeletons again in the rosy glow of her dance.

And she herself, the blind girl, all of her in her fiery eyes, inflames the streets with her dance, inflames the city, inflames the clouds:

"If you are blind, my God, take away my fire! . . ."

Honey of a Wild Bee

This is how the night will remain forever: An old maid sitting till her braid turns gray.

The moon, who left all her dear ones on earth and can see no one, prays a confession on her marble deathbed for the only creature left in the city, the gravedigger Leyme[79] huddling down below, on Rudnicka Street, in a heap of sighing leaves.

Leyme, a gravedigger ever since he can remember his own face, who sowed half the graveyard with the sons of man, will bury no one anymore.

Children, old people, all those born here, all entered the kingdom of the stars. At first — they became flaming branches. Bony winds, in tatters of shirts with Magen-Dovids, have scattered their sparks in a bloody crown over the skull of the earth.

They shamed his graveyard.

Shamed the tombstones.

So they sink with downcast heads, like offended in-laws when the bride disappeared from the *Chupa*.

Shamed is Leyme.

"Spade, where are you, I must bury the moon . . ."

Now he sees the moon with his glass eye. On the other eye hangs a padlock. The silver key is no longer in *This* World.

Once, half a century ago, a wild bee stung out his left eye.

The story of the wild bee is written in a chronicle:

One nice summer day, when Leyme lowered a corpse into a grave, the dead man's soul, disguised as a wild bee, flew with him into the grave. It had to whisper a secret into his ear before they parted forever.

Leyme, a simple man, did not understand the machinations of ghosts. He didn't like any of this hanky-panky and he swatted the bee with his clay-caked shovel.

The bee uttered a childish cry. Its polished, sunny face assumed the countenance of the dead man. A minute later, a screech was heard. Leyme grabbed his left eye where the wild bee entered as into a beehive; and the eye soon ran out in a red, buzzing wax under the gravedigger's hairy paw.

The whole city was up in arms about it. His gravedigging was menaced. They wouldn't let him near a distinguished corpse. But Leyme didn't give in and the "arms" subsided: Dr. Tsirulnik put a glass eye in his socket, an eye as blue and almost as big as a hen's bellybutton. And along with the clods of earth on the Zaretshe Cemetery, Leyme buried the story of the bee.

Winds, coupling like cats, meow at his head.

No savior. The dead are far away. No one to bring him a cup of water . . .

"Hey, spade, where are you? I must bury the moon!"

But his spade, his graveyard wife, is out of reach.

Hush. His spade is wandering above him. Wandering alone among hanging sparks. His spade is digging the ringing eternity.

Leyme stretches out a long hand to the moon, puts a star to her nostrils. The silver feather does not flutter. . .

Then — I saw it with my own eyes — the wild bee flew out of his glass eye and stung into my heart her last fiery honey.

1953–1954

Where the Stars Spend the Night

(1975–1989)

Yonia Fain, illustration to "Lupus."

Lupus

I

Seven turns of the key to bolt the door of beaten copper. I hide the clever key, notched with serpentine teeth, like a treasure on my heartbeat: in the lining of my red velvet waistcoat.

Such a trick deserves a medal: Who am I guarding that key from? If the thief is outside, he can't come pull it out from the inside and, if he's inside, what good is it to keep it hidden in that tiny pocket?

I live on the top floor of the highest tower in town and my only visitors are gangs of drunken clouds, like Rubens's lusty bodies, entering through my only window, and in the whole town, there isn't a ladder that can reach my window, not even with our ardent firemen — nevertheless, for the sake of supersecurity and for fear of a cosmic evil eye, I have barricaded all the inside shutters and have mercilessly hung brocade draperies over them.

All that so nothing and no one will come disturb my chemical and alchemical experiments designed to transform an orphan shadow into its former living owner.

II

The battered and polished lamp I bought for a farthing in the bustling fleamarket of old Jaffa drinks only good old kerosene, odorous greetings from the bowels of the earth. It suits my taste and temperament better than insipid electricity. Electricity means electrified barbed wire, the electric chair; since such a chair exists, it may well be that someday soon, an electric bed, too, may become popular, with brides and grooms giving birth (or death) to electric children.

My family wonder why I keep from turning on an electric switch. When I do, my nostrils revolt: they smell an odor of burning human flesh.

But I feel as much affection for that obsolete lamp as for a living soul. The kerosene lamp is my first critic. At night, I read to her my poems, just extracted with tongs from the forge and, by her mien, by the flickering of her flame, I understand clearly what is good for nothing and what merits heaven. Sometimes I ask her for advice or for help in solving a riddle and, peeping through the black lips of the hood, her little tongue of fire — a poppy petal in the wind — gives me signs of yes or no; she is more useful than a colleague for unraveling a psychoanalytic tangle. Sometimes the lamp hiccups with unclear, cracked sounds like the confession of a dying philosopher and then I see that the lamp is talking to me in a language of other worlds.

Who knows where this lamp hung before and whose wisdom she inherited? I would give up many faces to see the face of her former lord. Now the lamp, with its bulging glass belly, hangs on a chain of copper tears over my desk and draws a gentle halo on the parchment of the ceiling. She is the magic sun of my nights in my fortified, book-lined retreat between heaven and earth.

III

Between heaven and earth, it is so silent you could hear the dead breathe.

It must happen tonight. Every wave, even if only once in its life, must reach a shore. The orphan shadow is chemically ripe for me to transform it into its former living owner. Fortunately for the shadow, I took pity on it; otherwise, wild beasts would have hacked it to pieces and I would have barely found its black bones. With mouth-to-mouth resuscitation, I breathe a warm dream into it. Its limbs begin to move. In the convulsed darkness, its phosphorescent ribs emerge. I recognize the rib whose clay was used by a sculptor to mold Eve. The waiting shadow invades my thoughts. A smile flutters and plays on its almost-face. This is how a drowsing wave in the river comes alive in circles when a swallow swoops onto it, splitting the water with his chest. And see, see: from the mirror in ferment opposite me emerges a tottering creature and I hear a living voice:

"Why sacrifice a dream? Why create a being out of nothingness? Is the shadow willing to be harnessed to veins? And is its former owner so important? White shrouds don't have pockets but black ones don't either: the resurrected corpse is going to pay you back in ringing curses!"

"Who are you? How did you slip into my four walls?"

I jump out of my chair and prepare to stab my visitor with the stiletto I use to open envelopes.

"With a stroke of genius, you guessed my intentions," gurgles the apparition with obvious pleasure. "That's just why I loomed up here. Be so kind as to take your dagger and return me to non-life. You wanted to transform a shadow into a man and you have a man in front of you: transform him into a shadow! It will be easier and it will be worth it. I myself cannot do it. I have burned already but tears put out the fire; I leaped into the water but the river ran out. So, may I sit down and smoke a pipe?"

Go ahead, burn and smoke, I'm tempted to grumble. But all the same, I'm curious to see what that encounter will cook up for me and I begin to play the gracious host:

"Invited or not, a guest is a guest. Of course, you may sit down and smoke your pipe."

I raise the wick of the lamp hanging above the desk, better to examine the figure.

"These are things you never heard, but I am not so rare a bird," my visitor rhymes tongue-in-cheek.

He's already settled in, his legs crossed, not on the other side of the desk but on this side, so close that, stretching out my arm, I can touch his face, a clump of dried moss with two glowworms in the middle.

He draws on his pipe. A smoke dancer escapes from it. And as her feet tap out their beat on my skull, it occurs to me that there is only one stool here in my room and I ride on its saddle into worlds beyond. So it is clear, and obscure, that my guest is sitting on air.

IV

OK, I think, let him sit, let him hang, as long as the shadow forgives me for making him wait for his resurrection. Meanwhile, the uninvited guest says to me:

"To tell you the truth, I would have thought you'd recognize me right away, I who am privileged to be the object of your hatred. You still don't recognize me? Oh dear, man remembers neither the moment of his birth nor the moment of his death. What does he remember? All right, enough innuendos. My name is Lupus. My parents named me Velvl and that's what they called me. But later on, in the university, among my non-Jewish classmates, I was baptized with the name Lupus."

"Not just Lupus, Lupus the Cyanide Merchant," I added, confirming his title of nobility. "No need to gurgle out to me how you managed to slip into my house: instead of bolting the door of beaten copper and hiding the key in my waistcoat, it's quite another door I should have barricaded and with another key. So here I am at your mercy."

"And I at yours." The two glowworms winked in the middle of the clump of dried moss. "Now that you know I'm Lupus the Cyanide Merchant and through which door I slipped into your four walls, I can put my cards on the table."

Aside from the stool I'm riding on, as far as I remember, there never was another stool in my study. But nothing is as illogical as logic: I see and hear Lupus moving closer to me and tapping his pipe against the foot of the nonexistent chair to knock out the ashes. A spark leaps out of his pipe and, with a pungent nip, dies on the tip of my tongue. Lupus stuffs his pipe and puffs out a new smoke dancer:

"The secret of my strength and my weakness is that I have spent my life not agreeing with myself. But the present hour is different from all my other hours stitched together: you have my full agreement to give me back non-life. I am going to put it in black and white and sign it. I will add a codicil: you will be my only heir."

Although my tongue was nipped, the words don't succumb, they rebel:

"Lupus, my guest, before I accept or reject your request, we must unfurl an old scroll. If your hands tremble, don't be ashamed, admit it. I will unfurl the scroll myself. I have a good memory because I don't have the strength to forget. I see you nod your mossy hair. You yield the honor to me. Thank you. I unfurl the old scroll:

Of all the nights past and to come, we have one winter night left. Together with us, the winter night is fenced with electric shovels. But the winter night, loyal as it were, will disappear with the dawn, while the shovels will fling us as fodder to the ravenous maws of the earth.

Wrapped in our snow shirts, we lie in an icy lime kiln. No one is cold. And the child, frozen to its mother's breast, is certainly not cold. The stars are smiling. Delighted to escape the firing squad.

Suddenly, a shudder among the marble skeletons: a savior appears, bearing a pouch of cyanide! He too is wrapped in a snow shirt and his breath — a honed knife.

The stars are smiling. Delighted to escape the firing squad. But we, the chosen stars of the earth, don't envy those of heaven. We envy only the fortunate among us, those born in silk shirts who hid a ring or a jewel and can still use their power to trade or beg a portion of death from the Cyanide Merchant.

Ice chandeliers stretch their ten branches:

"For pity's sake, a thin slice, a crumb . . ."

"So dawn will not shame me . . ."

"Good man, just for my little birdie . . ."

"I played chess with your father . . ."

"Lupus, save me from life, I'll marry you in the other world . . ."

But Lupus doesn't distribute his merchandise for nothing. There is a price and the price grows higher and higher. And the less cyanide is left, the more precious stones you need for it. And he has a certain manner, Lupus, the manner of a billygoat who has just torn a wolf to pieces!

V

The third dancer escapes in coils from his pipe. She is dreadfully black, a sparkling necklace around her waist. She taps castanets. Or perhaps it's my temples tapping like this?

Lupus catches the thread of my thoughts and cuts it:

"You unfurled a genuine scroll. All we've just seen is as real as your charred tongue. The soul would have left me long ago but it is fastened to me with long nails. Nevertheless, you didn't notice everything: *who* took cyanide first that winter night? Me — Lupus! But in my veins there flowed an even more violent poison that mocked the cyanide. It was then, only then, that I became the Cyanide Merchant: let others too be persuaded that death had become as meek as a lamb, that the poison flowing in their own veins was stronger. That was the last consolation. Poor creature, are you seeking a reason for all that? As soon as you find a reason, you lose your reason."

"But why didn't you offer poison to the poor, those bereft of everything? Why did you trade it only for precious stones?"

"I didn't want those holy rings, those jewels, to end up in the executioners' pockets. Later, I threw them over the hedge of shovels into the abyss."

"Where, Lupus, in that icy lime kiln, where did you get cyanide?"

"I pinched it from my father's pharmacy and hid it on my body through all the tribulations. The poison delivered my father right at the start. The cyanide was then still stronger than the red poison in our veins."

"And who was that woman who begged you to save her life?"

"Amalia. A student. My beloved. My god. But God is too far away to betray."

"Lupus, I believe your commentary on the scroll. I had seen a lot, I hadn't seen it all. Both of us are incredible errors of that winter night. The meaning of my survival, however, is not to take life; and if you were the object of my hatred, my hatred has now evaporated like the cyanide of that winter night. Let's drink *l'chaim*, to life. Taking life isn't in my power as creator . . ."

A. SUTZKEVER   377

VI

I went to get some slivovitz and two glasses. When I returned, Lupus was no longer there. In the margin of one of my manuscripts still rose the mist of his curlicues: "I thought you were wiser. That you would understand me better and hasten my meeting with Amalia. Only there will I really be able to drink to life."

The wick of the lamp had drunk the kerosene to the last drops and the nocturnal sun on the parchment of the ceiling had consumed itself entirely, leaving only a halo of ash. But another wick which had just been lit, bathing up to its neck in an ocean of kerosene, pierced the diamond sparkle of a mild goodmorning through the cracks of the shutters between heaven and earth.

1975

Where the Stars Spend the Night

In the little park forsaken by summer, we were both silent, I and the setting sun. In truth, hardly had our silence on the rickety bench begun when the setting sun was ready to set out on his way. Linger a bit, my friend; why this haste? Do you prefer to sink in the sea? The sharks will rip your flesh and, on your gilded skeleton, the coral will build a metropolis.

My teeth pierce his cosmic flesh. I want to hold onto him. At least let our silence finish its first chapter. But instead of holding onto him, preventing him from drowning himself in the sea, I slice my own tongue, and keeping silent becomes harder for me.

Sparks rain down from the almond trees. A bird crowned with mourning, in dark peacock feathers, returns from a funeral. And here I am again in a twosome: instead of the setting sun, a woman, emerged from the purple alley, settles down next to me on the bench. "A young-old-woman-from-birth," my sliced tongue prattles in me. "A young-old-woman-from-birth."

"Volodia, how did you turn up here?"

I am no more Volodia than I am the king of Portugal. But how do I know who I am? "I — it's somebody else," a poet's line comes into my head. And I nod like the bird returning from a funeral who is now perched on a branch opposite me:

"Yes, dear heart, you guessed . . ."

"You're alive? Marvel of marvels! But how can you live when your soul — your one and only — is no longer in your head?" her silence rustles in my left ear with the tickling of a velvety stem.

"This is how I've lived since my birth and maybe even longer and, up to now, no one has ever thrown that up to me. To tell you the truth, I've never seen my soul and yet I can swear to you that it is buried deep inside me and no cunning soul thief has yet succeeded in lifting it from me."

"Don't! Don't!" She seals my lips with her strange fingers wafting the perfume of cinnamon. "Don't dare swear. A false and perverse oath — that sin the Almighty won't forgive. *You*, you've never seen it, *I* have."

"When and where did you see it?" I ask her, breathing between her cinnamon fingers as I breathed into a harmonica in my childhood.

"Soon you'll ask me my name," she said condescendingly, liberating my lips.

"Don't blame me, I'm asking you *now*. My memory has started to limp lately, like a horse that's lost a shoe."

"Lili, Lili the Blond. That woman and that name — you didn't have the right to forget them."

All of a sudden, she puts her head on my lap, her pert little face turned toward me so I will remember better.

And I would swear again: I'm seeing that face for the first time. The name is also strange to me: Lili the Blond. Even in the twilight of the extinguished park, I easily convince myself that the woman is blond as a crow. Isn't it enough that I need all my strength for the truth, do I need it for the lie as well? Yet I silence what I want to say. Curiosity is twinkling — a beacon for wandering thoughts. Again I nod, consenting.

"I remember, Lili, I remember."

"God be praised. At least memory isn't a horse. Now, Volodia, you're going to hear when and where I saw your soul and what happened to both of us, you and me."

Call me Volodia, call me Tom, Dick, or Harry, Lili is clearly confusing me with somebody else. OK, let her enjoy it. Yet, something is bothering me: that my face — so totally mine, a mysterious manuscript on old parchment — can be confused for another. Would an art forger have reproduced my flesh portrait? Or perhaps, I think, Lili the Blond doesn't have all her wits? If she doesn't have all her wits — the wits have her. The shadow of a bird sings better than the bird himself.

"Begin, dear Lili, with the *when:* when was my soul revealed to you? Then the *where* will be clear. . ."

Her ruffled little head suddenly jumps off my lap and rises like a released spring. Lili snuggles up to my shoulder and hugs me. Her little feet dangle under the bench like a dwarf's:

"I didn't string time on a thread. Its pearls — forgive the expression — I can't count them. I only remember that it happened when the city was transformed into a black clock, with human figures spread out in a gigantic circle. And, in the circle, a fiery hand spun around the human figures, slicing, slicing."

Death in the city wasn't kind to us. Both of us escaped to the forest, into its icy depths. There too the hands of the black clock were slicing, slicing. We escaped into its subconscious — into its shaggy swamps where the hands were only reflected.

"Lili, stop pouring your silence into me. I remember as if it were today, as if it were tomorrow. We both foundered in two separated tomb-swamps where a body can't touch another body. Only our hands — red desires — reached out to each other, day after day."

"Volodia, let me finish: hunger sucked the marrow of our skeletons and yet we were not sated. We ate poison herbs and frog roe. And one night, a wedding gown rustled lightly over the swamps and they started freezing — then I saw your soul swimming out of your mouth and approaching mine. It gleamed with a luminous blue like a sapphire and, in shape and form, looked like a dove's egg. You know, my dear, hunger croaked, a mouth is greedy and I devoured it."

"Thank you, Lili, you did well; otherwise it would have foundered forever. I would like to go on a pilgrimage to those swamps. Where are they? In what latitudes can I find them?"

"I shall give you a sign: there, where the stars spend the night . . ."

1975

Faithful Needles

I

For the *yortsayt* of their father, known to the world as Moneske the Tailor, the two younger sisters, Tzertl and Tzirele, rushed to their older sister Tilye in her solitary and weatherbeaten turret on the seashore.

Yonia Fain, illustration to "Where the Stars Spend the Night."

Tilye, the oldest of the three sisters — you might say the oldest, you might say the liveliest — had lived in that turret at the seashore ever since her happiness had drowned.

That happened when her girlhood flickered out and, in the cracked mirror, the first white hair — an uninvited relative — appeared.

That happened in ancient times when, coming from her home in Lithuania, she wound up here. Times people now call before the Flood.

Tilye had wound up in this place along with the cracked mirror.

How Tilye had found out about the day, or the night, of her father's end remains a mystery for the author or witness of this story. For, in those regions of Lithuania, not a single stone remains intact, nor a human being.

And even if somebody did survive, she would have been afraid to meet him. As for her two younger sisters, Tzertl and Tzirele, who had wound up with their father in a Slaughter City, they couldn't or, perhaps, wouldn't give her any more details.

The author or witness of this story is even inclined to think it was Moneske the Tailor himself who had whispered to his oldest daughter the day or the night of his *yortsayt*.

II

The two sisters, Tzertl and Tzirele, appeared under the vault of the turret. They looked like two scared gray seagulls. Tilye kissed them and, by her expression, you could see that her sisters' lips and cheeks tasted of salt.

In a niche of bricks grown into one another, shot through with veins of straw, sputtered a tall, waxen *yortsayt* candle, legacy of the sunset.

"Remember, children, you're at home here," she smiled maternally at her guests. And she remembered that there, too, in the tailor's house, she had liked to call her younger sisters "children." A smile was peeled off her aged face like the skin of an onion.

Behind the iron bars of a little window, the sea polished its waves and, far far away, on the horizon of the horizon, a fiery hand drowned, not finding anything or anyone to grasp.

"Children, you must be hungry, we're going to eat supper," said Tilye, helping her sisters fit into old rickety chairs on either side of the table, facing one another. "I've made a nice little meal for you like you haven't tasted in a long time: honest-to-God potatoes in their skins."

But Tzertl and Tzirele exchanged a mischievous wink and, for some reason, preferred to sit on the same side of the table, next to each other.

When their skins were taken off, a wolf's breath came from the potatoes. Tzertl devoured them as if she had come from the Land of Hunger.

"Tilinke, you always were an artist. It's been ages since I've savored such a delicious dish."

As for Tzirele, she barely touched her plate.

"I've been full ever since I've been hungry."

Tilye hardly ate either. While preparing the meal, her appetite had disappeared. She poured wine into three goblets and, bowing to her sisters, drained her glass to the last drop.

III

Either they were drunk with wine or from the *yortsayt* candle. Tilye awoke, fearing her sisters had stolen her dream. Her frantic eyes groped for them:

"Children, today is our father's *yortsayt*. I have sent for you, my dears, from far away, to honor him and to tell one another our memories. It's true we're three sisters but we didn't have three fathers. Let us show him our love."

Tzertl shuddered, a shudder of rustling silk:
"He was a gay blade, our father. He loved to play tricks. I was still a little girl at the time but I remember one day a carriage stopped at our door and the mixed-up son of Lord Guintillo, the baron of Kalvaria, came into our house. He looked like a pale white plant that had grown in a cellar. Lord Guintillo had sent his treasure of a son for papa to make him a suit. Papa squinted, took his measurements, and ordered him to lie down on the floor and stretch out his hands and paws. And when he did, papa drew his shape with a piece of chalk: that's how he measured for a suit."

Tzirele uttered a half-laugh, broken by regret:
"But when the suit emerged from papa's needle, it fit that fop like a glove. The Lord and Master of Kalvaria, old Guintillo himself, came to our house later on to pay papa and to thank him."
Another smile peeled off Tilye's face:
"You were only babies then both of you, you don't know why the old baron took the trouble to come in person to thank papa. In fact, Guintillo suspected his lady of having a lover behind his back. Papa gave him a recipe. Take the tongue of a toad and put it under the lady's left breast as she slept. She would spill everything. And that's just what happened."

The three sisters grew closer. Tzertl and Tzirele remembered their goblets of wine and raised them to their salty lips. They wanted to say "l'chaim, to life," but were ashamed.
Tzertl flushed from the first sip. Her goblet was spinning in Tilye's eyes in a whirlwind of silence. A melted flash shimmered in it:
"Which of you remembers how Moneske the Tailor, our father, became a matchmaker, sewing for and dressing orphans for nothing and leading them to the *khupa*?"
"I do!" Tzirele called out in a mischievous voice. "I even remember that, at one of those celebrations, papa was wearing a top hat and he fed the in-laws and the newlyweds on rhymes. Yes, he was the life of the party. But us, how come he didn't lead us to the *khupa*? Weren't we also orphans?"

Tilye rapped on the table with the bony fork of her fingers.
"Tzirele, you who ran off with a student in a pointed white hat, what do

Yonia Fain, illustration to "Faithful Needles."

you have against papa? And you, Tzertl, you too believed in the bluebird of happiness but the bird soon stopped singing. And am I any better? I had to disappear overnight so as not to rot in prison. His needles were more faithful to him than his own daughters."

All three of them burst into tears, as if the needles Tilye had just recalled were pricking their hearts. The tears of the oldest were real human tears; the tears of the two younger ones, a salty echo of the music of the sea incessantly going away from the tower and incessantly coming close to it. Going away and coming close.

Tzertl was the first to calm down and shake the foam off her eyelashes:

"But later on, when we found each other in the Slaughter City, Tzirele and I were as faithful to him as his beloved needles. Maybe more. For a whole winter, we hid our papa in an attic, we warmed his feet with our breath. But that didn't do any good: they grew numb."

"Let's add," Tzirele hissed, "that even in the attic hiding place, our numb papa was still the life of the party. Who did he want to cheer up? The people hiding with him in the same attic. Papa was only sorry he couldn't laugh at the top of his voice so his laugh would reach the ears of the One he prayed to."

Tzertl leaned over the narrow table and, with her wings spread, encircled Tilye's shoulders:

"With his good humor, he gave courage to his faithful needles so they wouldn't rust, God forbid, in the hiding place. But I must tell the truth: the last time I saw our papa, he had become so pale I thought I saw the shroud shining through his skin."

IV

The flicker of the *yortsayt* candle leaped up twice as high. It seems that the flicker which had been drowning a moment before, struggling with waves of wax, had triumphed over them and darted up.

A whistle was suddenly heard. Tilye also rose up twice as high: Who is whistling? A ship coming close? Oh no, it was only the blue teakettle whistling in the kitchen. She had forgotten it and now it reminds her in its whistle language: Finished, you can drink tea.

Glasses of tea — full of water-gold. Sails of lemon floating in it.

Again, a burned smile peels off Tilye's face:

"Drink, children. I've put aside for you a few crumbs of sugar from before the war, the kind you don't find anymore today. They're hard as a rock, you must have healthy teeth, like the teeth of mice. And all that because our papa loved to drink tea with a lump of sugar."

"Hot!" shouted Tzertl, as if she had burned her palate.

"Cold!" shouted Tzirele, looking as if she had been falsely accused of something shameful.

Tilye swims up in their eyes, searching:

"The farther you flee from one cemetery, the closer you get to another. Just now, one of you started telling about a last Time. And afterward? What happened to papa *afterward*?"

They heard a wave break on the shore. Tzertl's lips were covered with foam:

"Papa begged me to leave him in the attic, in the hiding place; his faithful needles, he said, would protect him."

A. SUTZKEVER   385

"It's true, it's true," Tzirele echoed in the same tone. "Papa also begged me to leave him in the attic and save myself. It's true, it's true. But that his faithful needles would protect him, that I didn't hear. I know, Tilye, what you're hiding in your thoughts. You want to ask us if we always obeyed papa's requests. No, Tilye! In fact, I escaped through the sewers. I was swallowed up by a forest, but I did *not* obey papa and I went back, I returned to the Slaughter City, to our numb papa. You see this little red hole in my forehead? On the way back, I got a kiss from a bullet there. Tzertl wanted to go back to the attic too but the tears of a little baby, her baby, prevented her."

V

The two sisters started up. Began packing to go. Time to go home.

Tilye embraced them like a mother. Tzertl and Tzirele now looked like her two burned wings, grown back on her:

"Children, don't rush. I have good news for you. Our papa is alive. He is with us. There he is, sitting in his old chair, at the head of the table. . ."

The two sisters, with Tilye between them, all three entwined, saw with their own eyes: on a chair at the head of the table, lighted by the *yortsayt* candle, a little bush of thorns: Moneske the Tailor.

His face among the thorns began sprouting leaves.

A swarm of flaming needles stuck on the buds of his vest.

There's papa's finger crowned with a thimble.

And there, the green ribbon of the measuring tape wound around his neck.

And their papa, known to the world as Moneske the Tailor, laughed at the top of his voice out of the thorn bush.

And when he finished laughing, he spoke thus:

"It's all true, daughters, I swear by my life."

1977

The Hunchback

It happened and then happened again when the starry sieve of the autumn night kept sifting over and over in the narrow ghetto streets *who is to live and who is to die: to live* — twenty-four hours, maybe less: *to die* — an eternity, maybe less.

The starry sieve is pulled over the narrow streets. An unseen hand shakes it. Sons of man tumbled by scoops, innocent, falling in sighing silence — sifted into an empty, overturned sky.

Here and there, prayers drill. The shimmer of their words, emptied of crying and congealed.

A split voice, like a stone talking in its sleep, seeks refuge in the cranny of my ear:

"Old fellow, how can you go crazy?"

It is the Hunchback Kheme. The only hunchback left in our kingdom.

When did we meet? Ah, I remember: when both of us swam among thousands into the stone veins of the narrow streets.

It was his majestic hump that drew me to him then. You might have thought that, still alive, he was carrying his tombstone on his own shoulders.

The hump was only the form. I soon realized that here, form and content are not twins but a perfect unity.

I was drawn by his name: Kheme. Where did they cook up such a curious name?

At our first verbal pingpong in the stone veins of the narrow streets, when I asked if he was born in this city, Kheme hissed without blinking his tongue:

"I'm transplanted from another planet."

And though I was used to his demonic paradoxes and his trenchant dicta, cutting to the bone (I wrote them down on relics of scrolls, locked my treasure between earth and sky, but later lost the key), caught in the starry sieve of that autumn night, I was stunned by the revelation of his question: How can you go crazy?

I stroked his hump for luck:

"Why, all of a sudden?"

Kheme turned around and butted me with the point of his hump like a billy goat with his horn:

"Till now, I believed that everything my eyes see is a delusion, a dream. When I saw a pair of children's shoes in the mouth of a dog, running to find a barefoot child, or when I saw a cherry tree hanging on the gallows, or a shadow waking with a start and not finding its owner — to all this I had a chant of denial: a dream, a dream, a dream. Now, at this late hour, I've lost the power of denial, I see that the dream is bleeding."

A blue old man, over his head a Torah scroll in a mantle of sparks, cut his way through the hordes of people. Some believed the old man would save the

Yonia Fain, illustration to "The Hunchback."

Torah scroll. Some — that the Torah would save the old man. Both the former and the latter were sifted more and more through the starry sieve of the night.

Kheme shrank. His tombstone started sinking. In his tattered rags, he looked like a thousand-year-old feathered owl. The pupils of his eyes turned into incandescent rings:

"Every end is a beginning. Now is my great beginning. But it all depends on you: You must anoint me a madman. With the power of madness I will drive the enemy crazy and we will all be saved. No serpent was ever poisoned by its own venom."

A thought somersaulted in my head: only the impossible can still make sense. I lay my hands on his mop of hair and anointed him a madman.

Incandescent, anointed, Kheme pulled a Shofar from under his jacket and blew into it such a howl as if he were joined by all the breaths left over from the annihilated ones.

Suddenly, the starry sieve of the autumn night collapsed. The conquerors of the city went out of their minds and bit through each other's throats.

The Boot and the Crown

I

Trofim Kopelko can't stand tears. Tears, he says, are ladies' buttons, a real man has no use for them. He would have hanged all tears if there were such a gallows.

Only once in a while, his own left leg, the wooden one, the one he himself carved out of a young, juicy fir tree, weeps a few tears of honey tar. It happens when the low sun warms the bones of his festive wooden leg.

Trofim Kopelko can't stand such tears either. He pours the embers of his pipe on them. But from the embers, the tar tears catch fire and Trofim Kopelko can't stand burning tears, even less than tears that died out.

Nevertheless, Trofim Kopelko found a way to deal with his tears. It happened like this: Kim, commander of the partisan brigade, remembered Trofim and appointed him executioner of the forest court. He, Trofim Kopelko, had the honor of dunking his victims in the swamp with his wooden left leg. And then, among the serpents frozen in the swamp, the tar-tears of Trofim's wooden leg froze too.

In the Narocz Forests, people say that, just yesterday, Trofim Kopelko's guys, wearing the uniform of the enemy, were ambushing partisans. Forest men who fell into their clutches were sawn to pieces by his band.

But Trofim Kopelko is shrewder than time. When the Germans lost their iron britches, Kopelko shed his skin: he stretched out his left leg to his adjutant, the little Tartar, who pulled off his boot. Trofim Kopelko groped for a long time inside as if he were looking for his luck and plucked out from the lining the sweaty medal for heroism he won in the Finnish war.

With the scoured Soviet medal on his Berlin-made uniform, he jolted his blond advisers.

Ever since, armored by their weapons and experienced in action, Trofim Kopelko became famous throughout the region.

One autumn dawn, while cutting deeper into the Narocz Forests, a mine blew up under him, and his left leg, along with the boot, hung like a dead crow on the crown of a birch tree.

His loyal gang, who went on serving their beloved leader, would later swear that Trofim Kopelko almost bit through his pipe in pain, but his wolf's eyes remained dry as gunpowder; and when his adjutant, the little Tartar, begged him: "Sweetheart, saw off my left leg and put it on, it's yours . . . ." he sank his teeth into his pipe and spat sideways to his Tartar: "No need . . ."

To this day, the little Tartar in his lamb's wool hat is still Trofim Kopelko's sublime subordinate. They ride together, they clink their glasses together, and he always leaps up with fire to light his boss's wrathful pipe.

The little Tartar built a bath in the forest for the two of them: a kind of underground bunker over a spring with bubbling water, colder than ice. Pour a bucket of spring water over glowing stones and you get steam as good as at home. The little Tartar sweeps all his limbs and parts, including the wooden leg that Trofim Kopelko won't give up for a moment.

From his hairy cloud-body, lightning flashes.

The big Kopelko is red as a lobster.

Then the little Tartar takes him naked on his shoulder, hurls him outside, and rolls him in the snow.

The points of his copper moustache hanging down under his chin are Trofim Kopelko's scales of justice. The sins of spies and traitors are weighed in their pans. True — the eye over the balance is the vigilant eye of the commander, but Kim is generous, very generous. And Trofim Kopelko's moustache swings back and forth, back and forth — —

The frozen sun warmed itself. In its own red ashes, it puffed up the sparks and sprayed them over the snow.

Through the needles of the evergreens, a green hand, growing out of the earth, threaded a green thread.

A single stork, a bow without a violin, arched over the forests.

Yonia Fain, illustration to "The Boot and the Crown."

And then he thawed, Trofim Kopelko, and shone in all his glory.

He galloped through panic-stricken forest and behind him — his faithful bloodhound with a drooping scarlet tongue, the little Tartar.

They rode back leisurely. Behind them, hands tied, the ropes pulled by the riders, limped teeteringly, barely recognizable, the most beautiful gals of the forests: Katya, Lyubochka, Halinka — the lovers of company commanders, commissars, and brave officers. Trofim Kopelko was a Caesar and the little Tartar — a little Tartar.

IV

In one of those early spring nights, two young horses whinnied over the dugout of my company hidden in a nest of branches near Lake Myastra.

The silence freshly frozen in space was splashed by the supple steel of the horse laugh.

I woke up under a face crucified by three burning dark eyes. The third eye was the fire of a pipe.

"My name is Trofim Kopelko," the nocturnal messenger introduced himself. "Commander Kim ordered me to bring you to headquarters."

Why this game, since we know each other? Why does he play a cat when he usually plays the dog? That's what I think, but I don't ask any questions. I grab my fur coat, insert a bullet in my rifle, stride out of my dugout into the disturbed silence, following the traces of a boot and a wooden leg.

The suspicion of my comrades accompanies me from the dugout. The breath of their looks puffs the sparks in my spine.

When we are both sitting in the saddle, I behind him, Trofim Kopelko orders his little Tartar:

"Get the horses drunk so they'll gallop faster, but don't forget to leave some for the three of us."

The little Tartar unties a flask of homebrew from his saddlebag and pours it in the gaping maws of the horses, first ours and then his.

Feeling a burning springtime in their guts, the horses lash themselves with the whip of their tails and their joyous gallop swallows the forest miles. The little Tartar bounds ahead of our panting horse and feeds fire to the demanding pipe.

Single shots, like overtones of nearby wolves, crease the space.

The last hairy snows, like frightened rabbits, slide down fir branches.

Our drunk stallion stands on his hind legs and we metamorphose into a marble monument.

Trofim Kopelko gropes in the forest with his nostrils:

"Enemy shots. I know them by their echo. A defeated army is closing in on our bases. Before the sun slices the ice, we must gallop over the Myastra!"

The little Tartar zigzags deeper into the forest. I imagine: he wants to gather the shots . . . and he catches up with us in the middle of the lake on the splitting ice.

Dawn swings on a branch on the horizon: a purple ghost.

V

Trofim Kopelko leads me to the commander's dugout. The silence in the earthen hut—a secret map. And springtime is not just overhead, a partner of the sun, springtime is down here too, in the veins of the earth, its rain smell wafts from inside, in the branch-covered dugout.

A warm, trusty hand clutches mine. I notice that the brigade commander has changed: the creases on his young face are older now than the face itself. And his beard, blond as a newly plucked chick, is too mild for his deep creases:

"You want to know why I called you in a hurry. Here's why: I received a radiogram from partisan headquarters in Moscow to send you there. Get ready. Tomorrow, three armed partisans will escort you to our airstrip. There, a small plane will land and fly you over the front. I must warn you the roads are full of danger, but, if you're lucky, you've got your wits in your feet."

"And a little bit in your head too," I play the role of a cold fish.

"No, the main thing is: keep your wits in your feet," the commander persists. "When you walk through a minefield, what does your head know about the mines lurking? A true partisan puts his soul down in his feet."

As Kim goes on talking, I feel a glow in my feet: my life hangs on them.

Trofim Kopelko teeters in. His wooden leg, it occurs to me, is cleaner than his conscience. He whispers something in the commander's ear.

"Only the girls!" Kim rages and signs a crumpled piece of paper. "And don't let nobody in, nobody."

Kim comes close. His voice sounds closer and more trusting:

"You heard: girls. The branches whisper the secrets of the roots. Let me solve the riddle for you: the Germans, convinced that we're stronger than their armies, that the forests are graveyards for their generals, came up with a clever trick to subdue the partisans without a single shot. They caught girls, every one prettier than the next, infected them with syphilis, trained them thoroughly and unleashed them like foxes into the forests to spread syphilis among our best, heartiest boys. I won't deny it, the devil's game worked pretty good. But most of the girls are caught in our net. I just signed their sentence."

Kim leaps up from his stool and paces back and forth in the traces of his shadow:

"I don't care about the girls, let the swamp choke on them. I care about the diseased comrades, company commanders, heroes. I'm keeping them in a dugout under guard but I can't drag it on for long. And I can't let them go either. We're about to meet a defeated enemy army. The horns of a gored ox are stronger than his own body. Trofim Kopelko advises giving the same sentence to the gentlemen as to the ladies. Don't stand on ceremony. But now, things are changed: I'm sending you over the front. When you fly to the other side and get to partisan central headquarters, tell them about the diseased boys and let them decide *there* what to do — —"

They will not see their last sunset.

One by one, eyes blindfolded with their own stockings, the little Tartar leads them out of their prison.

Katya, Lyubochka, Halinka . . . — each one clasps a branch and the little Tartar pulls them.

He leads them out of their prison to the dry, flayed, huge trees, hollow trees.

There, only a single person reigns: Trofim Kopelko.

Brief shots ring out, like titters of laughter.

With the horseshoe of his wooden leg, Trofim Kopelko smashes a pane in the green-and-thinly-frozen swamp windows and, with the same leg, he swings the girls one by one into the swampy, splintered sky.

VI

Krasnogur, Maligin, and Leybele Blatt — my escorts and guards of the next day.

Krasnogur bustles about the horse and sleigh, Maligin bends over a map, Leybele Blatt cleans a machine gun.

Trofim Kopelko is hospitable: my escorts and I will spend the night in his dugout. The little Tartar prepared supper for us.

I am the last one at the bonfire.

The bonfire struggles with a wet fir.

The fir defends itself with its acrid smoke, but fire teeth rip up its veins and muscles.

In the dugout, the partisans are sleeping. Someone is playing on a harmonica and falls asleep in the middle.

I lie down on a bed of straw and pull the fur coat over my head.

My last night in Narocz Forests.

Tomorrow at this time, I will be-or-not-be over a minefield, trying to muddle my way through to the partisan airstrip. Kim is right: if you're lucky, you've got your wits in your feet.

Suddenly: can a dream explode? Is a dream a minefield? A thunderclap inside me, near me, in front of my awakened dream: a white lime kiln swirling in a ring.

No. It's not in me. It's in my neighbor Trofim Kopelko. Standing over him, the little Tartar, with a gun sticking out a smoking tongue to the lord of the swamps. Enthralled in the sweet joy of vengeance, his erstwhile comrades and subordinates dance around the shot Trofim and dismember him as ants dismember a dead beetle:

One runs with Kopelko's wooden leg and throws it into the hungry bonfire;

Another one — with Kopelko's shirt. Against the freshly painted moon, he looks through the shirt to see if it's worth it; and the moon is strangely red and warm drops drip from it on an island of snow;

And again I see a face crucified by three burning dark eyes. The third eye — the fire of a pipe;

Cursing, the little Tartar pulls off Trofim Kopelko's only boot and doesn't know what to do with it. Let it fly to the devil: to its brother boot on the crown of a birch tree!

And he pins on his heart his commander's medal for heroism.

1977

Glikele

I

First I got her letter: not handwriting but heartwriting, the signs you see on the paper accordion of an electrocardiogram: violet scratches, short flashes which, without warning, announce an impending, crashing thunder-clap.

Barely did I have time to plumb the secrets of her letter when here she is in person, in flesh and blood, chatty, the same violet scratches as in her letter etched on her silvery face.

Is this really Glikele, my first love? Glikele, the redhead, nine years old? Her tresses are webs of old ash and the pins in her hair are rusty.

But her voice brings back the savor of childhood years, the savor of that voice is not changed.

"I don't know how to begin," she began. "You think I'm somebody else but that's not true. Every person is like somebody else, much more than himself, but I am only like myself, like two drops of gall. Yes, I really don't know how to begin, just as I don't know my age before my birth. So I'm going to shut up, ruthlessly, and let my tongue run free: Tongue-tongue, play out my lost world, or else I'll kill somebody."

When Glikele let her tongue run free, her familiar little voice crept into my ear with the same fiddle tone as before. Her eyes too, I thought, are the same as before, the eyes of a girl: two little green watches with a phosphorescent glow in the dark. Surely the woman is right: she is only like herself, like two drops of gall. But why, hammers my skull, is the same another?

"Your best friend is the one you meet in a dream, he's always warning you and never betrays you," Glikele or her tongue said to me, nourishing me with her thoughts. "And that dream friend ordered me confidentially, as soon as the war against me began, to take my father's sacrificial slaughtering knife with me wherever I went. I already carried a warm, living slaughtering knife next to my heart. But I obeyed and, with a cold slaughtering knife, I protected my warm one."

"Do you remember, Glikele, when the two of us were children, I whittled a little stick for you in the forest, with your father's slaughtering knife?"

"My memory is my treasure. Listen to what happened: the three of us, I and my two slaughtering knives, ran away from Ponar, from under a heavy blanket of corpses. It was a winter night but I didn't feel I was naked as the day I was born.

"Where to go? Where? No Luckytown anywhere. But go, run away from here, till you're out of breath. Under my feet, the snow didn't make the slightest peep, for I was barefoot. When I turned around, the traces of my footsteps had become steps of light rising to I don't know who. What do you think? Can Elijah the Prophet disguise himself as a peasant woman?"

"If he can disguise himself as a beggar, a magician, he can also disguise himself as a peasant woman."

"As true as I wish both of us long life, so I believe in it. The ninety-year-old Papousha was Elijah the Prophet. She hid me in her hut, in a chicken coop under the oven so the cackling and squawking of the chickens would smother the crying of the child I gave birth to there.

"Do you know what is a day in black shrouds? I do. In the chicken coop, typhus consumed me and to stay there any longer was dangerous for the child. What do you think? Can Elijah the Prophet catch typhus?"

"I don't know . . ."

Glikele took me by the arm:

"Let's take a stroll in the other region."

When the two of us went toward the door and our two heads swam through the hanging mirror, I saw, I realized that my real existence was there, inside the hanging mirror.

Her arm in mine, like a squirrel curled around a branch, we let ourselves be carried off to the other region.

Yonia Fain, illustration to "Glikele."

When Glikele had come to me, the ripening summer was bursting with colors and odors and the sun cooled its muscles in the stream. Now the stream, as in a coffin, lies under a heavy cover of ice and a pale gray snow falls from the unextinguished fire in the sky.

In that pale gray snow, a single hut stands out with a chimney in the shape of a boot. A stooped old woman, loaded down with an armful of branches, hobbles over to us; at her side a dog barking shrilly leaps and scratches the earth under his paws.

"Glikele, that's where you gave birth," and I point to the hut. "I see your thoughts as clearly as I see the willows next to us. I can feel them as I can feel the willows."

"Cut them down or saw them up, can you do that too?"

"No, that I can't do. Maybe it's better to say: I don't want to."

"Then the tongue is superfluous since you know my thoughts anyway."

"Glikele, what you wanted to say just a moment ago is that there, you also abandoned the child."

"True."

"Suffering from typhus and burning like a torch, you ran away beyond the green pond. In the forest, you crept up to a fir tree and the merciful fir tree warmed you like a mother with her bark; later you had a guest, a she-wolf. You sucked her warm milk and that milk cured you."

"Instead of my child, I was the one who sucked. Do you think the she-wolf is still alive?"

"No, Glikele, the she-wolf has been in the other world for a long time now. The one who brought her down is the one who aimed his bullets at you. But you leaped down from the fir tree and your slaughtering knife sliced his breath."

"If that's how it was, I shall light a memorial candle for the soul of the she-wolf."

III

The closer we got to the hut, the farther it receded. The dog's barking also, strung on a silver thread, scattered its yelps in the snow. A wall of marble grew opposite us: Forbidden to Approach.

On the way back, through pale gray snow, the region grew summery again.

When the stars came out, we entered the living city. Young couples, like eagles with wings spread, were lying in wait for their prey — their own flesh.

Glikele stopped at a fountain where a water-dancer was ripping off her clothes:

"Now do you see my thoughts?"

"You want me to show you which of the lovers is your son?"

"I've been searching for him ever since I lost him. Every time I find him, it's as if a flow of melted lead were poured over me: it's always somebody else."

At that moment, Glikele tore herself away from me, fell on her knees before a disheveled young man who was kissing a girl right in the middle of the street.

"Papousha, Papousha," Glikele stammered from the ground, to stir some memory in her son.

The young man, freeing the girl from his embrace, picked Glikele up from the ground and stroked her hair spun of old ash.

Now it was I who took Glikele by the arm. She was light, as if the ground underneath her had lost the force of gravity. Her little green watches began to gleam with a phosphorescent glow:

"Again somebody else . . . How long will he be somebody else?"

1977

The Beggar with Blue Eyeglasses

I

You see a beggar, a bundle of walking rags. Or a beggar's hand, a shell cast out by the sea onto the shore: no ear to listen to its weeping. Or a beggar-invalid, his legs have betrayed him, gone to someone else — and you pass by him with antimagnetic thoughts.

The idea of getting to know him doesn't occur to you. You're not curious to ask him his name or if a mother gave birth to him. Or if that mother had ever been a maiden.

But sometimes it happens: passing by a beggar, an idea pursues you, as a lightning colt pursues a cloud: You want to get rid of your past sins. So you stop and let a metal drop fall onto the beggar. Your conscience is eased — that's all. You're not there. Without a word. Without a smile.

Why deny it? I too seldom smile at a beggar. Seldom even smile back, although I answer a skeleton's greeting. Things went on like that for a while, a long while, a short while, until . . . until whoever is in charge of my pen decided I must write this tale.

And for my sake, he created a beggar in blue eyeglasses.

The man with blue eyeglasses made his appearance at the corner of my narrow street, next to the sunset-red mailbox I stuffed for years, like a living creature, with my friends and enemies. Quite possibly he had stood there before and begged and it could be that I had already seen him but, all of a sudden, I *noticed* him. It's a long way from seeing to noticing.

It happened like this:

One fine morning, I dashed out of my house into the street, carrying a still warm letter for the red mailbox. The city was still empty, without a human breath. Two birds sang to each other in their sleep.

Yonia Fain, illustration to "The Beggar with Blue Eyeglasses."

I was already holding the envelope at the rusty gullet of the mailbox when, behind it, a voice came to me speaking my mother tongue:

"A golem you give alms and a beggar not?"

And then, for the first time, I noticed him. As you notice a tree surfacing out of a fog.

Aside from his blue eyeglasses, a goatee, like a radish just pulled up from the ground, is etched on my memory.

And the blue of his eyeglasses — what did they remind me of? Splinters of blue glass, found in childhood, that give you more joy than the discovery of a treasure.

Let the mailbox go hungry today, I decided. Anyway, I was content to have the beggar's reproach as an excuse: I had written that letter to my beloved in a state of agitation, stimulated by irrepressible, juvenile jealousy. And if, God forbid, the iron golem had swallowed it, I would have had to go search for matches and set fire to its innards.

I ripped letter and envelope into minuscule pieces and the jealousy in me crumbled into pieces too. But instead of thanking the man with blue eyeglasses, a needle jumped off my tongue and pricked him:

"Working so early?"

A bony smile twinkled on his face:

"Only the dead have an easy life. If the living knew who I am, they would even come from Honolulu to see me."

"Let's say I'm from Honolulu. But first, let's get acquainted." I held out my hand to him. "My name is . . ."

"To a beggar and a hangman you don't hold out your hand and, if you do, it's with a coin." A bony smile twinkled again.

To my misfortune, my pockets were empty. The man with blue eyeglasses took pity on me:

"An honest man settles his debts at home. Here is my card."

Meanwhile, the city started moving. A cascade of bricks fell off the buildings and became hurrying people. Cars were shuffled like cards. The sun had risen to the seventh heaven.

The next day and the day after, I did not see the beggar in the blue eyeglasses next to the mailbox. I was already beginning to think: a dream figure. A nightmare. But in my pocket, my fingers found his card:

> Horace Adelkind
> Philosopher and Sage

And the street. And the number of the house. And that very evening I went off to pay him a visit.

III

No, it's not a false address, my suspicion was in vain. He himself, the philosopher and sage, bowing courteously, led me into his room. Here, at home, he looked slightly different: he was dressed in a cape and a silver-embroidered *yarmulke* was perched on his skull. His blue glasses were lying atop a pile of papers on a little table illuminated by a hanging lamp.

"Now I'm not a beggar and I can give you my hand," he hissed. "And let's address each other familiarly. I don't like to be so formal. Yiddish is so juicy but praised be our Holy Tongue: a familiar language. Talking familiarly to the beggar and to the prince."

He pushed up a rickety chair for me:

"Cognac or a glass of wisdom?"

"A glass of wisdom, but a strong one!" My chair started to teeter underneath me. "However, before this glass goes to my head. I have a question: Why this comedy? Why the disguise of a beggar?"

"One glass of wisdom isn't enough for you," he said coiling himself into a rickety chair facing me. "Every human being is born with a mask: his own skin is the mask. Nevertheless, he puts on other masks to hide the previous one. If I didn't disguise myself as a beggar, I really would be a beggar."

"Where's the logic?"

"Logic plus logic equals demagogic! How can you ask such a question? It's all a matter of habit. Get used to it and you can be an eagle. If man was born with seven legs, the two of us would look like pitiful creatures in comparison. Man is not a cosmic animal, as my colleague Schopenhauer teaches; but man is a Cosmic Man, as Horace Adelkind teaches. And Cosmic Man, of which I am the classical example, is not content to change only the mask on his face. He must change so that death will not find him. If this is what you call comedy, that's a personal tragedy. Let's shuffle the cards again: if I hadn't been begging, your eyes would have wiped me out of the scene and you would have really put your letter in the box. Do you know what would have happened then?"

"I would have eaten myself alive."

"On that diet, the two of you — her and you — would have starved to death."

IV

Both rickety chairs and us inside — two ends of a ship — pitched on sighing waves. The former beggar with blue eyeglasses, currently philosopher and sage, Horace Adelkind, struck his oar:

"Since you already know the secret of my disguise, I am going to reveal to you why I revealed it to you: you owe me a debt. But your debt is more than all the coins I have collected. This is what you owe me: be my heir! I, the Cosmic Man, no longer have anyone on this planet. My friends and relatives have gone to the galaxies. My only friend is a strange creature. I am so alone that I have recently asked a psychiatrist to make me schizophrenic, to split my personality so I won't be so alone."

"Did it help?"

"Yes, I became twice as alone."

"Is *that* my inheritance?"

"Not at all. I want to leave you my wisdom, my aphorisms. I have written seventy thousand pages of them."

"And when you die, what should I do with them?"

"Publish them in seven hundred volumes, bound in leather, gilt-edged."

"Before I take on this sweet burden, I ask the privilege of hearing a few aphorisms."

"Here's one:

> We understood each other perfectly,
> The gorilla and I.
> First peel off me these bars,
> She said,
> Then I'll talk with you.

"Another:

> A single moment is as old as time.

"A third:

> You are too close for us to get close,
> You are too far away for us to be far.

"A fourth:

> "One of you will not betray me,
> Said Jesus to his disciples.
> And *he* himself was the one.

"A fifth:

> Tears are the sparkling words of the eyes.

"A sixth:

> Men were created in plural
> Women — in singular.

"A seventh:

> Stupid painter,
> Do not reproach the tree
> For growing and blossoming
> Realistically.

"An eighth:

> I am the tenant
> Of my own body.
> With my tears
> I pay the rent.
> If I had nothing more to pay with —
> The landlord would throw me out
> In the cold and rain.

"A ninth:

> Too soon has become too late.

"A tenth:

> I am no less than anyone here

Except myself.
Only to myself am I a babe
Who has barely cut his teeth."

V

Nimble as a cat, Horace Adelkind leaped up, unhooked the lamp hung on a chain, and aimed it at the heavily loaded shelves:

"Dear heir! All around us, on every one of these walls, huddle my writings. Congratulations, they're yours now. My past is my future."

A barely heard knock on the door.

His voice grew hoarse:

"It is my only friend. It's his time to come. I hinted earlier that my only friend is a very strange creature. He's a worm! A white-headed worm, who comes to share his thoughts with me and I write them down. The poet Slowacki was the secretary of an angel, so he says, and I, Horace Adelkind, am the secretary of a worm. Would you like me to introduce you?"

I blocked his way:

"Some other time. That's enough for today. Is there a back door here?"

Horace Adelkind raised the lamp above me and pulled me by the sleeve:

"Of course, of course . . . and you are going to take a gift from me: my blue eyeglasses. So you can disguise yourself as a beggar and become a Cosmic Man."

Slashed Lips

Youth is a tree. And the tree of youth, my radiant woman, shakes off its summer garb to rustle younger again, even younger than last year.

These are the words murmured by an elderly man with his slashed lips to a very young woman barely emerged from a summer mist.

The elderly man, wise and foolish, his curls dusted with the ash of a lime kiln, murmured these words not to the whole female figure but only to her smiling hand, as he brought his slashed lips to her gracious fingers to savor anew the taste of his youth.

And then, not only in his slashed lips, in his frozen mouth, but also in the dried up roots of his bushy hair, the elderly man sensed, fireclear, the young,

Yonia Fain, illustration to "Slashed Lips."

sweet taste of sharp raspberries and the gushing odor of sap in the forest underbrush where the raspberries hide.

And then he experienced something strange: where his soul ends, another soul begins and where that one ends — death is dying in him.

A moment later, when the young woman withdrew her smiling hand from his lips, death itself stopped dying in him.

And, through the magnifying glass of his tears, the elderly man plunged into the mystery of a single one of her fingers, a bit higher than the others, and began again to mumble with his slashed lips:

"The tree of youth is farther than your shadow of yesteryear. You may not taste its Paradise wine. I would swear: your real face is the small, damp face of this finger. Its little face inscribed in circles of wrinkle after wrinkle: and the teensy half-sun on the horizon of your fingernail will never shine higher, to warm my bones.

"You are a wave that has swallowed a man.

"Your wrinkles are older than my fear. Older than both of us.

"You are older than the four-legged old woman, who sits at the museum all stitched up in black silk, throwing peas to the gracious and merciful pigeons."

The Coin from Heaven

I

Why do they need money in heaven? And who mints silver coins in the firmament? Anyway, what can you buy with those coins? Stars, clouds on the moon? —

Such questions buzzed in my curious brain when Shloyme-Leyb, my teacher, in the snowed-in hut in Siberia first taught me the *alef-beys* and a good angel had just dropped a silver coin for me on the first page of my *Siddur*, where the letters of the *alef-beys* glowed like black stars.

I could utter them freely with my mouth but not with my eyes.

With all the questions I asked myself, there was not the slightest question that the silver coin was really meant for me and that a genuine angel had tossed it to me. Shloyme-Leyb wouldn't dare lie. The proof was the little wings about the coin, glimmering with a mysterious sparkle — the sure sign of its origin.

I protect the coin in the warm nest of my fingers, in my left hand. A sweet thrill spreads through my limbs. The heavenly wings flutter and curl up in their new home. For nothing in the world will I let them go today to the beet-red sunset.

Shloyme-Leyb is my neighbor in the next hut on the frozen bank of the Irtysh. How did the two of us get to the snows of Siberia — I don't waste any time thinking about that. To tell the truth, I did hear something from papa and mama, I recall a few fragments of words: war, wandering . . . But if the sun had followed me in this wandering, then it wasn't so terrible.

In our hut, I also learned that life or time had long ago been cut into parts

Yonia Fain, illustration to "The Coin from Heaven."

they called years. According to this accounting, I was sliced into five equal parts. And when I am cut into a hundred parts, I will be exactly a hundred years old.

Shloyme-Leyb is tall, his face is dark. His glowing eyes are the color of the skin on his face. And his hairy growth is the same color too. Shloyme-Leyb walks with wide strides, his stiff, high felt boots come up over his knees and creak, no — he plays a tune with them on the frozen snowtwinkles, a living path between the huts. I could crawl into one of his felt boots and be nice and warm there.

A. SUTZKEVER   *407*

Why is it I learn the *alef-beys* from dark Shloyme-Leyb and not from my papa, known throughout the area as a God-fearing scholar and a wise man? I finally learned the reason: my papa is sick with typhus and a sleigh stole him from our hut.

The heavenly coin in my fingernest beat along with my heart under my fur coat the next day when I run back to my teacher Shloyme-Leyb so he would etch in me the marvelous letters of the *alef-beys*. This time, I think, not just one by one, but letter after letter, strung into words.

For a whole day and night, I was terrified to open my fingers and delight in my heavenly coin. I didn't allow my sinful looks to take pleasure from an angel's gift. Who knows when the evil eye might appear. An angel won't give me another coin so soon. Nevertheless, I lift my head from my *Siddur* every now and then and look at the ceiling.

"My boy, the book is down here," Shloyme-Leyb nudges me.

"But I think it's up there," I tell him innocently.

"How is it up there? What's on the ceiling?"

"I'm looking for the crack. There must be a crack in the ceiling."

"What crack? There's no crack up there. What's going on in your head?"

"If there's no crack, then there's a question: How did the coin fall down to me from the ceiling?"

My question confuses Shloyme-Leyb. His dark face gets all wrinkled up like the water in our deep well when the chain lets the bucket down into it and shakes up its mirror.

Having put Shloyme-Leyb to a hard test, I take pity on him and come to his rescue:

"I know! On the silver coin I saw a bird, it must have flown in through the chimney."

IV

How long will I keep my silvery secret a prisoner? Of course, I have to protect it from ordinary glances. But from my own eyes? I myself won't give me any evil eye.

The day is chiseled in snow and piercing sun but the cold is king. If you spit in his kingdom, a sliver of ice falls down. But I don't because, on the snowy plains behind the huts, a glowing *alef-beys* is scattered and a tall, windy Shloyme-Leyb is shuffling it back and forth with his diamond teacher's pointer.

Pale, nude, not the lightest shirt on their backs, the birch trees shiver in the wind along the frozen Irtysh. One day, the Kirghizes made a bonfire there and the birch trees revived, then breathed a warm breath. Now even the bonfire is frozen and the birch trees barely breathe inside themselves, like the waves of the Irtysh under the ice. But I, in my fur coat and with my silvery secret in my fingernest, am not afraid of the cold and its whip.

Along the birch trees at the frozen Irtysh, far from the huts and the people, I awaken the coin from its heavenly sleep and expose it to God's world. Its little wings flutter with joy. They wave and sparkle in the chiseled, translucent splendor.

Now a weird question sneaks into me, followed immediately by another: What is the difference between heavenly money and earthly money? And what can I buy in the market with this coin, I'd like to know.

To the second question, I have an answer right away: I wouldn't give the coin even for the whole market.

I will give it only for medicine to make my papa healthy.

And I give my heavenly money a kiss and hide it in my pocket.

V

Ever since I kissed the silver coin, I am disturbed and frightened by its sharp, twitching smell. My God, where have I smelled such an odor? Was I ever in heaven?

Someone is weeping in me and the tears are mine. They melt the frost birch trees off the window panes. But the clouds of the moon know nothing about it.

Whom shall I ask? Whom shall I confide in? Papa is far away, a sleigh took him away from me. Mama isn't here either, she followed him in the sharp ruts in the snow. Should I ask my Kirghiz friend, Tchangouri? He'll laugh at me with his yellow laughter, yellow as salted butter. No choice, I won't be shy, I'll ask Shloyme-Leyb.

Today's lesson isn't like the one yesterday or the day before. I don't lift my head up to the ceiling anymore, don't look for any crack. Let my teacher think the coin flew in through the chimney. I lean closer to him and his pointer. But I no longer hear his deep voice and I no longer see the letters. Now I learn only with my nose, only with my nostrils.

"What are you sniffing?" Shloyme-Leyb sweeps me with his shadow.

"My silver coin . . . the smell . . ."

"Little fool. Don't you know I deliver kerosene to the huts all around? Come on, let's study some more."

To this very day, whether we study or not, a glowing *alef-beys* is scattered over the snowy plains behind the huts and a tall, windy Shloyme-Leyb is shuffling back and forth with his diamond teacher's pointer.

The Artist

The Artist even enjoyed Death. And what about Death? Oh, he envied the Artist.

There is a silkworm and there is a silkman. And since the silkman never stopped weaving his art, so the One-With-A-Thousand-Eyes never stopped competing with him: let's see who can do better!

In a snowy violet fire, he froze a scared birch forest which clasped a lake. He didn't yet want to freeze the lake. He just forged the shores all around with glimmering silver.

Among shattered mirrors of birch trees, condemned people built his fortresses.

A marble hunchback, the earth. Axes and picks thrust into him and fingers snap like icicles. And if a prisoner falls, either the hungry ones assault him or — this "or" is not that simple: the sons of man have no strength to cut graves in the frozen earth. With every thrust in the stubborn marble hunchback, wolves' eyes leap up as if the One-With-A-Thousand-Eyes were huddled under the axes and picks.

What do the sons of man do then? They hack out pieces of ice on the edges of the lake, they cut out a pallet in the ice, they put on it the dead body, cover it with a piece of ice, to seal the eternity. And they let the crystal sarcophagus float away in the waters of the lake.

The sarcophagi float and the sun, the frozen sun, cannot melt them. The frozen sun itself is a burning man in ice. Its bony rays cut through the crystal graves, and the living discern their friends from afar.

Sometimes, the dead meet each other. Two sarcophagi, of a man and a woman, collide and melt the ice with the force of their lips.

And at night, in the glow of a single star, the beacon for the floating sarcophagi, the Artist paints with a black coal on snow. He paints and his

Drawing by the poet.

heart floats into his fingers. In glowing ecstasy he paints the vision over the lake.

1953

Hanukkah Candles

A few hundred of us, born once-upon-a-time, all with one face, we lay in a tangle of limbs, like one multi-eyed creature, on the icy cobblestones of Lukiszki Prison.

The yard — a horrifying square mirror framed in barred walls. And where the walls meet at sharply joined corners, watchmen in steel helmets rise and, from rubber hoses like long, demonic throats, aim lightning streams of water at us, over us, the once-upon-a-time born as men.

Are they firemen? Who's burning? No one is burning. Everyone is freezing. And the ringing swords of the waterstreams dance on our naked bodies.

Now the prisoners understand that the firemen want to freeze them. Thus, once upon a time, a volcano played with the people of Pompeii. In the morning, when invited guests come to the exhibit, they will enjoy the ice sculptures.

A woman with a child at her breast is almost frozen. Her breath above the breath of her child — a smoke-diamond dove hanging in the air over a broken egg.

And here is a *klezmer* with a fiddle under his chin. The strings are drawn from his fiery beard. Sounds — snow and ice — cover him. Slowly his fiddle ceases: a ship among floes.

I hear fragmented voices:

"Why is the snow not cyanide?"

"I tell you, brothers, the creator envies *us*."

"Today is Hanukkah, the fifth candle!"

A voice or an echo?

Half-frozen black pupils, where tears laugh at tears, saw up their bars and float in the marble air. They seek the echo and find it:

Five burning fingers lit by a Jew with his own hand, five Hanukkah candles rise with golden tongues over the ice sculptures. And they melt their own iciness, and they burn the firemen and the barred walls.

1953

A Black Angel with a Pin in His Hand

I

All his life, he was nicknamed Moyshe-Itske. The few in whose memory he is still gasping call him by this boyish nickname to this very day.

Moyshe-Itske was born because he wanted to be born, as he told me. And added mysteriously that a pack of dark forces did not want to let him light up but his will was stronger and the anointed writer Moyshe-Itske was born — to live forever:

"Just as I am I shall remain," he looked me over from head to toe with a face that looked as if it had just now surfaced from a cracked mirror. "Death has nothing to do with me. We belong to two separate worlds. Too bad that, a thousand years from now, you won't stroll in the streets. You would have recognized me in a crowd. I shall not change, as a stone doesn't change."

He burst into a moldy laugh and, as if possessed, he went on:

"You mean a stone gets covered with moss? Well, so a beard will grow on my big soul. According to you, sparks lie dormant in a stone? In my veins, they sing! And the torrent has not yet been born which could put out my sparks."

II

I had the privilege of hearing the songs of his sparks. In most lines, the sparks have burned the song. But poem-sparks and poem-fires gushed out of him and indeed the torrent has not yet been born that could put them out.

During our strolls and chats on the Castle Mountain, I learned from him that he was a mighty heretic: of all world history and world literature, he recognized the greatness of only three humans: Moses, Napoleon, and Dostoevsky. All the rest are just *books*, not great people:

"There are zillions of books, show me one that is alive!"

I tried to bargain. To add to the chosen three at least one poet:

"And what about Byron, how can you reject him?"

Moyshe-Itske brushed it off with his hairy paw:

"He limped in his poetry too."

One summer evening of great transparent amber, as we walked down the Castle Mountain and turned to the Viliya, I was bold enough to bargain off a bit of Moyshe-Itske's eternity:

"All three of them, the greatest — Moses, Napoleon, and Dostoevsky — they all died. So how can you imagine that you, Moyshe-Itske, will live forever?"

A crease cut into his rusty forehead: a flash on a cloud at night. A glowing spiderweb broke out from the skin of his face. And with the voice of a strayed echo, he roared:

"*One* can break through!"

III

He lived on Gitke Toybe's Alley, in Meirke's yard, where the Vilna jester, Motke Habad, had once resided.

His father had two professions: butchering and stitching shoe tops. He cut meat in the winter and stitched shoe tops in the summer. What he did at other times, I don't know. For his son, the father thought one profession should suffice, the nobler of the two, stitching shoes; and Father himself taught him.

But Moyshe-Itske's hot blood drew him to the slaughter house. Where the condemned calves and oxen low and roar; where the ritual slaughterer plays the violin or cello on their hot throats; where his father afterward cuts off their double crowns, pulls off their purple boots.

As his bar-mitzvah approached, the boy grew more restless than ever. He decided to buy his manhood by saving at least a few oxen from the slaughterer's knife.

It was murderously cold. Dawn. Over the slaughter house hung a single star. Moyshe-Itske snuck into the slaughter house through a narrow aperture.

A single ox, like the single star overhead, stood tied to a pole, kicking his hind leg. Moyshe-Itske warmed his frostbitten ears in the ox vapor.

In the slaughter house, two lads like oaks appeared with ropes and flaying knives. Soon, wrapped in a huge fur coat, and with a case under his arm, the ritual slaughterer entered. That morning, Father had *yortsayt* for his father and was late. And when the ritual slaughterer began to peel off his fur, Moyshe-Itske peeled out of a slaughtered shadow; nimble as a bastard, he leaped to the block where the ritual slaughterer had left his case, snatched the slaughtering knife, and slipped it under a heap of sawdust.

The ritual slaughterer was sure he had forgotten to put the slaughtering knife into the case. The butcher boys stormed off, cursing. The single star, too, bloodily reflected in an icicle, absorbed the mysteries of the earth in the memory of its eye and then vanished.

Inside, two remained: Moyshe-Itske and the rescued ox.

Meanwhile, the sun appeared in the slaughter house: the slaughtering knife meandered out of hiding and slit the space.

Now Moyshe-Itske approached the ox, entered his pen to get acquainted. A virtuous sweetness melted in the boy's limbs.

But who can understand the justice of an ox? Instead of rewarding his savior with a smile, with warm gratitude, he first bowed to Moyshe-Itske and then unfairly speared him on a horn — —

IV

All those details, images, nuances concerning the ox, Moyshe-Itske confided to me many years later when his poems roared on the hospitable pages of the Vilna newspaper *Tog* and the poet himself was admitted to the Young Vilna coterie.

From his hoarse, possessed voice I gathered then that the ox plowed his horn into Moyshe-Itske's brain.

The horn vanquished *someone*.

When Moyshe-Itske boasted grandly that he would live forever and that *one* could break through, I was ready to believe for a while that the someone pierced by the horn in the slaughterhouse was Moyshe-Itske's Angel of Death, who had occupied a bridgehead in his brain.

Like a soldier in muddy trenches, in a war with no end, Moyshe-Itske wallowed in madhouses and only during the cease-fires in his cracked soul was he awarded a furlough.

V

During one of those cease-fires, on the eve of Passover, returning home to Gitke Toybe's Alley, to the crumbling hovel, where he lived on the ground floor in a single room with a corridor, Moyshe-Itske saw a dogcatcher in leather pants chase a little dog in the street, catch it in the hoop at the end of a long pole, and pull it trembling in a half-circle through the mild, blue springtime air to his weeping wagon.

Moyshe-Itske's calmed blood flared up and flourished like the liberated springtime streams under thin cracked ice. It jolted him out of his vein bridle. And now his hands gallop toward the dogcatcher in leather pants:

"First, give me back my dear little dog or else I'll measure the city with your guts."

The dogcatcher in leather pants had already dropped the roped dog into the crying wagon:

"Don't give me any crap that the dog is yours."

Moyshe-Itske uttered a loud bray:

"Hamlet, tell him I'm your master . . ." (Moyshe-Itske called him Hamlet because the dog's fate was suspended between to be or not to be.)

Between the iron bars of the wagon, where an orchestra of street dogs barked and bayed and howled, the newly imprisoned little dog pushed through with the cute red glove over his face and wept like a child:

"Oy, oy, oy."

"Now, do you believe?" Moyshe-Itske, his mouth filled with hot coals, fired at the dogcatcher.

The dog executioner gave a beaming smile like a sliver of glass in a dungheap:

"You're both liars. But I'll give you a chance. You can redeem this pest for only ten zlotys."

Ten zlotys. Where could he get hold of such a sum? On the way home, Moyshe-Itske had bought some coarse-cut tobacco, a yellow pencil, and a few sheets of paper to compete with Byron and Dostoevsky, with the few zlotys his father jingled into the pocket of his blue smock on his last visit. All that was left was a farthing. Bargaining with a dogcatcher is an offense to your lips. This is the time and place for action. Hamlet's fate hung on a hair. If the wagon moved, there would be no more appeal. There was only one way: force! Beat up the hoop man and free the doggie.

But what happened was a double miracle: from the circle of people around both of them, a girl wearing a man's double-breasted jacket over a blue-flowered blouse like the newly hatched spring approached them and, sacrificing her ten zlotys, ransomed the imprisoned dog.

Her name was Yettl Gonkrey. And the second miracle was that, along with the dog, Yettl ransomed Moyshe-Itske from his solitude.

VI

He had left for the institution alone and now returned as a threesome, and the mildewed room on Gitke Toybe's Alley was filled with life.

The father with two professions saw at once he was superfluous. He went to stay with a relative and learned a third profession: to play and lose at cards with his butcher friends.

Yettl was short, with yellow hair — call it blond if you like. With a string of freckles on her neck, even in winter. One smile on her face teased another and both teased a third — Moyshe-Itske. He loved to tell and tell again that, at first, Yettle went into his head, later — into his heart. And that her skin was foggy; and that, if her man's jacket at their first meeting had been buttoned up over the blue-flowered blouse — nothing would have happened.

Yettl was a kindergarten teacher. She worked hard. Hard but easy: now she had someone to work for. Along with her own mouth, she had two more mouths to feed. Hamlet sat at the table like a person.

As soon as she came home from work (Yettl moved in with Moyshe-Itske on the seventh day after they met), she rolled up her sleeves. She cooked, scoured, kept house. She brought a huge copper pan for making preserves and soon every corner of the room lit up like the copper pan.

And Prince Hamlet became their faithful guardian.

VII

Not just head over heels: the teacher fell in love with Moyshe-Itske way over her head. She believed he would live forever, that *one* could break through.

Her only regret was that it was only *one*, not both of them. Moyshe-Itske instructed Yettl, explained to her why he of all people was the chosen one:

"When a man dies, Yettele, it is because the number of words God allotted him runs out; but the number of words allotted me has no end."

On another occasion, he added:

"You must know, Yettele, that when a man kicks the bucket, he has nobody to talk to."

She also heard him say such words of consolation:

"You mustn't be ashamed that you were born a girl. Someday, they'll write about you in the newspapers."

When Moyshe-Itske read one of his poems to Yettl or roared a story of one sentence a mile long, her cheeks flushed with the colors of passion. She lovingly accepted his philosophy of life. But one thing Yettl could not get used to: his sudden bursts of laughter. When Moyshe-Itske roared out such a sudden, unslaughtered laughter, she accompanied him on the keys of her tears.

VIII

One nice day, the room on Gitke Alley was enriched with a Singer sewing machine: Yettl's gift for her intended. Let him knead the air below with his feet for a few hours a day, she thought, and it will be easier to breathe above.

On another nice day, Yettl returned home from the kindergarten and walked into a cherry garden. What happened? Was she lost? No: Moyshe-Itske had flayed dozens-of-years-old wallpaper from their walls and, instead of writing with a pencil, he sewed on them with a black thread from the Singer machine, line after line, his latest work.

Behind the old faded wallpaper sprouted the earlier one, fresh and young and fiery.

Since then, the walls in their room and in the corridor took on the colors of the four seasons.

IX

"You are my living medicine," Moyshe-Itske soothed Yettl in a calm moment. "Since *you* are already *me*, I will break through together with you and it will count as if I alone broke through, for this is the only way it can be."

Yettl believed him.

"We shall not sneak into eternity by the back door, oh no," he pictured for Yettl their own personal afterlife. "I met him yesterday on Yatkeve Street, I stopped him and told him in so many words: 'We shall not sneak into eternity by the back door.'"

"Who did you meet?" Yettl stroked his bristly hair off his rusty forehead and pricked her finger.

"Silly people call him Death. But what he really is is a black angel with a pin in his hand!" And Moyshe-Itske burst into his sudden laughter.

This episode was told me by Yettl herself when I came to visit them in a very tall, late summer day.

On that visit, my memory was enriched with the following three events:

1. During the few months I hadn't seen her, Yettl's waist had shrunk, for Moyshe-Itske demanded her waist be as thin as the waist of the Singer machine.

2. Moyshe-Itske dreamed that a dentist pulled out one of his molars. At dawn, when he awoke — Yettl is a witness — the molar was missing from his mouth. Now Moyshe-Itske was waiting for the dentist to come and demand payment from his patient.

3. Hamlet became a lunatic. On a moonlit night, you could see a silver hand lead him by a silver chain over the cornices and sloping roofs of the city. Later on, Hamlet crept back into his doghouse and, in the morning, he didn't remember a *thing*.

On that visit the walls of the room were blue: the blue of the sky after a rain with the golden tail of a rainbow.

Yettl put a full bowl of hot limabeans on the table and Moyshe-Itske unfurled a stitched-out scroll and read me a prophecy, foretelling that hunger would soon end in the world: one man would eat another.

When Moyshe-Itske read his stitched-out lines, I felt the needle of the Singer machine dancing on my spine.

X

Our last meeting was on the first night of the ghetto.

Barefoot, in the tatters of a shirt, a scroll under his arm, he hovered like an eagle dying in mid-flight over the numb human waves barely breathing in the alleys.

A black angel with a pin in his hand, a single angel in many guises, flickered through the square pane-less skies and cracked attics.

The night rolled out of time and time vanished.

Moyshe-Itske descended on me, illuminated by his own blood.

"You still think one can break through?"

He unfurled his scroll and pointed to a verse:

"Son of man, I broke through already, I am already eternal."

And he burst into his sudden laughter.
The only laughter on the first night of the ghetto.

1980

The Gunpowder Brigade

I

It happened in the topsy-turvy time, when a plague of locusts covered my city. The locusts did not devour stalks and herbs but young and old, babies and graybeards. And along with flesh and bone, for the death of them, they had to saw up with their sawing teeth that part in man called the soul.

For them this was the tastiest part.

Then, on an early autumn dawn, I was caught in my garret by a messenger of the locusts — just yesterday a student in a white cap, my neighbor — and he and his cronies lined me up in a column of people caught all over throughout the night, and they drove us up street, up street to the mountains that start where the street ends.

On both sides, the maples had already shaken off their yellow patches.

Where the street ends, the column was driven further, chased between two mountains, one staring dumbly at the other.

The belly of the first mountain was circled by barbed wire and crossed irons. Its innards were soon revealed: trenches around caves, fortresses and redoubts, prepared by the former power to defend the city.

The column entered the trenches.

Another messenger of the countless locusts, in mouse-gray pegged pants, climbed out of a cave and made a brief speech to the prisoners: Since we had ignited a war to subjugate the world, we had to pay dearly. The first payment: to carry on our backs and shoulders the gas bombs and stink bombs lying in the belly of this mountain — to the other mountain, opposite.

II

The space between the two mountains, at arm's length when they started, now — under the weight of the bombs — lengthened bizarrely, as if the earth were turned into dough and rolled out to the horizon.

His Excellency My Fate fixed it for me to march in the gunpowder brigade (as someone in the column called it) under a load of gas bombs. I was in the middle of the gunpowder brigade, stretching out in pairs.

My partner was stooped under stink bombs. I measured him from the side under the first autumn rain of sweat: a face overgrown with silver nettles, shadowed under a straw hat — in memory of summer. A pince-nez with a string around his left ear on my right side. With each step, the pince-nez jumped up like two lovers on a carousel. (This grotesque simile has stuck in my memory ever since!) For a moment, I released my right hand from the load and attached the pince-nez on my partner's nose.

The gunpowder brigade marched and didn't even begin to march. With each step forward, the mountain opposite recoiled. Under the demonic music of groaning bones, I got acquainted with my partner. A staccato-panting dialogue began leaping between the two of us to make us forget our miserable role and the distance we were destined to swim through the wasteland to the desired shore.

Dr. Horatio Dick, his name and title. A psychiatrist in the lunatic asylum.

III

We are both afraid to look ahead. Dr. Horatio Dick was luckier than me: his pince-nez was coated with a glue of dust-and-sweat and he couldn't see what he didn't want to see. And I was drawn even more to lift my leaden eyelids. My eyes became alcoholics, yearning to drink the pure and strong spirits of the air.

An explosion was heard. One of the first men in the gunpowder brigade fell under his burden. A fountain of red smoke spurted over the blue sheet of the horizon. In the brief commotion, my partner cleverly peeled off his gray coat. The explosion gave him strength to continue trudging on.

Dr. Horatio Dick told me his pedigree: he was a grandson of Isaac-Meyer Dick,[80] author of hundreds of popular stories and novels.

It seemed unbelievable. I happened to know the biography of Isaac-Meyer Dick and was familiar with many of his stories. I tried to calculate when Isaac-Meyer was born, married, had children and died; and something did not tally.

Scholars of the novelist, if I'm not mistaken, never mentioned that a grandson of his still resided in the city.

"Perhaps a relative, a great-grandson?" — I tried to bargain off some of the distinguished doctor's pedigree.

My partner did not yield: a grandson. He even remembered Grandpa's jokes and proverbs. When Horatio was a child in *heder* and still called

Hirshke, he heard the old man say: The time has come to chew the earth but I have no teeth.

A transparent smile remained hanging on his face like a spider web in the sun.

Somebody else in the gunpowder brigade fell under his burden but there was no explosion.

The opposite mountain grew weary of plodding backward and remained like a dummy in the same place as yesterday.

The messenger of the locusts in his pegged pants roared by the gunpowder brigade on a motorcycle. He shot above our heads and between one pair and another.

When the oven of the sun above us descended lower to bake our bodies into Challah for Shabbos, the same messenger of the locusts was waiting for us on the other mountain. He stood there like a scarecrow at a clay pit which for years had fed the surrounding brickyards with wagons of clay.

In the clay pit silence snored. With purple sealing wax on their foreheads, some of the gunpowder brigade were dozing off. The clay pit seemed to give birth to the dead. And at the clay pit where we unloaded our bombs, the creature in the pegged pants granted us an hour of rest.

IV

Now I could observe my friend better. I decided to put off researching his relation to Isaac-Meyer Dick to another time. (I believed in time.) Meantime, I tore strips off my shirt and applied them to his wounds.

But Dr. Horatio Dick was a little sore at me for doubting his status of grandson.

I pricked up my ears to hear his language: it had a German twist like Isaac-Meyer's, as if I were reading Dick's story "Chaytsikl Alone" or "The People of Duratshishok."

Out of curiosity, I asked him if he was a native here and, if so, why his Yiddish was so old-fashioned.

He answered obliquely: "Ja, ja, in dieser Stadt, colleague, even a bath-house goy spoke Yiddish to the steam."

My partner in marching and in fate already spoke of this city in the past tense.

At the clay pit, he groped for a sweet flower and was revived.

I decided again to stop my pedigree searching. At the clay pit, everybody's pedigree is the same.

Dr. Horatio Dick became more intimate with me. He changed the subject. He leaned on his elbow and told me about an experience he'd had in the lunatic asylum: Dr. Dick ordered that the service staff was not to be drawn from outside the hospital but from inside, from the crumbled souls. Furthermore, there was a schizophrenic, a doctor, who healed himself through healing the lunatics. The head chef was also a patient in the hospital.

One fine day, as we say, Dr. Horatio Dick went into the kitchen for no good reason. Suddenly the door was shut behind him. The head chef and his aides tied him up and the head chef approached him with two long knives:

"I'll cut you up and cook you. At least once for old time's sake, we shall have a tasty dinner."

His life hung on a second. But in that second, Dr. Dick remembered that the craziness of the head chef was that a thief had stolen all the salt of the city and without salt, food had no taste. Isaac-Meyer's grandson called out: "Mr. Handeles"—the chef's name—"what are you talking about? The dinner will be entirely without salt, without taste, let me go and I'll bring a handful of salt."

This is how Dr. Horatio Dick was saved on that occasion.

His conclusion: only if you accept a lunatic's reason do you have a chance to escape his knives.

V

The messenger of the locusts reappeared at the clay pit: recess is over. Now, in the same order, we must carry the bombs back to where we got them, behind the barbed wire fences on the opposite mountain.

Then, suddenly, light as a bird, Dr. Horatio Dick arose and I saw and heard his fiery sermon to the messenger of the locusts: Since we prisoners ignited a war to subjugate the world, as he himself had said, and it is not yet clear who will win the war, it may cost him dearly if he torments us — —

The doctor was not little David and the messenger of the locusts was no armored Goliath, but the members of the gunpowder brigade went along with this life-and-death spectacle.

Even those who were dozing in the clay pit with purple sealing wax on their foreheads pricked up their dead ears.

Even the gas bombs and stink bombs seemed to choose sides in this unequal duel.

When Dr. Horatio Dick ended his sermon, the messenger of the locusts turned black and thin like a burned-out match.

"You are free," he brushed us aside with his arm. And he disappeared, leaving no trace.

But as a matter of fact and as a matter of history, we couldn't be free then because the clean, early autumn air was hanging on a gallows.

1985

Postscript (1990)

The Bottom Line

I shall leave behind nothing, nothing.
His Excellency Nothing I shall not leave
For others: over there, what has happened may recur,
With Adam-Eve like old acquaintances.

I shall leave behind nothing, nothing.
I must confirm a line in *From the Forest*:
Wherever my word can reach, there I am.
My every word an open eye. A Milky Way of eyes
Shone through me in the dark, illuminating
The visions of unseen atoms.

I shall take with me from the would-be nonexistence
My cradle, my broom I once wanted to compare
To a dried rain, my first dove
That learned humming up to her Creator.

And I swear I shall
Take with me the breath of my extinguished friends:
When I gnawed on wood, they fed me
With the honey of friendship.

I shall take with me a pebble
Inscribed with letters by no human hand.

February 12, 1990

On My Father's Yortsayt

Snowlight, field-in and field-out — up to my father,
Suntears drip in the snow — up to my father.
Seventy years I walk among snowlight
To reach my father on time.

Is it the silence that cries in the snow, or is it
His red violin accompanying me among snowlight?
What a destiny in snow to feel:
The distance gets close, ever closer.

Shall I tell my father from what place
I bear my breaths in my arms? Can I find
Words to awaken his silence,
To open up his frozen eyes?

Snowlight, field-in and field-out. Mustn't neglect
To tell him: Your son is the same.
For it may be: my father is no more,
Arose long ago for his resurrection . . .

October 17, 1990

Notes

1. **Lamed-Vovniks** — originally the Thirty-Six Just Men who live incognito in the guise of simple people and perform good deeds, thus saving the world.

2. **Tate-mame** — Yiddish for "Daddy and Mommy."

3. **Yortsayt** — yearly commemoration of a death, particularly of parents.

4. **L'Chaim** — a toast, "to life."

5. **Ghetto** — the poem was written *before* the War and the establishment of the ghetto in Vilna. The concept is used here as a metaphor for confined Jewish existence, based on the Medieval ghettos.

6. **Shul-yard** — the complex of courtyards in Vilna containing dozens of synagogues and prayer houses, including the "Gaon Shul." The Gaon of Vilna, Rabbi Eliahu, lived in the eighteenth century.

7. **Irtysh** — major Siberian river.

8. **Taiga** — evergreen forests of sub-Arctic Siberia.

9. **Kirghizes** — a Mongolian people, speaking a Turkic language, dwelling chiefly in West Central Asia.

10. **Yehoash** — Solomon Bloomgarden (1872–1927), major Yiddish-American poet, master of impressionist nature poetry. Sutzkever taught his poetry and organized a Yehoash exhibition in the Vilna Ghetto.

11. **Tallis** — a white prayer shawl with black stripes worn by Jewish men.

12. The poem refers to the outbreak of World War II in Europe. Vilna was spared until June 1941.

13. **Yesterday** — reference to the Soviet period in Vilna (May 1940–June 1941).

14. **Sheygets** — Gentile boy or young man.

15. **Sh'ma** (or **Shema**) — Jewish profession of faith, always recited before death.

16. **Stormtroopers** — The poet was taken to an SS outfit where teenage Germans specialized in abusing and torturing Jews.

17. This cycle includes parts of a long poem, unfinished and partly lost. We have decided to keep the sub-cycles as they were published. The sub-cycle, "My Mother," was published in the book *The Fortress* (New York, 1945) and in the collected works. The sub-cycle, "From the Poem Three Roses," was published from old manuscripts only in 1979. In the larger framework, the poet also planned to include the poems "A Wagon of Shoes," "My Every Breath Is a Curse," and "Black Thorns."

18. **Mogen Dovid** — the Star of David, the Jewish symbol used by the Nazis as a mark of humiliation, to be worn by every Jew. The poem refers to Jews identifying other Jews in the service of the Nazis.

19. **Siddur** — prayer book.

20. **Challah** — braided egg bread, especially for the sabbath.

21. **Khupa** — wedding canopy.

22. **Amsterdam, Worms, Livorno** — places famous for Jewish books that were written or published there. **Madrid** — symbol for the Jewish cultural center in Medieval Spain. **YIVO** — Jewish Scientific Institute, founded in Vilna in 1925. Under the Nazis, Sutzkever worked at the YIVO, which was turned into a Nazi research center for Judaic studies under the direction of the Rosenberg Staff. He was instrumental in stealing important manuscripts from the collection and hiding them in ghetto cellars.

23. **Teacher Mira** — Mira Bernstein, well-known teacher in Vilna, organized the school in the ghetto.

24. **Sholem Aleichem** — (1859–1916) classical Yiddish fiction writer, famous for his humor and popular style.

25. **Hirsh Lekert** — (1879–1902) a shoemaker and Bund activist in Vilna who organized an armed attack to liberate political prisoners. He assassinated the Russian governor of Vilna for flogging Socialists after a May Day demonstration and was hanged. Lekert became a hero of the Jewish labor movement and self-defense.

26. **Gershteyn** — well-known music teacher and leader of the "Gershteyn Choir," organized a choir in the ghetto as well.

27. **Peretz, Y. L.** — (1851–1915) classical Yiddish writer. The poem refers to Peretz's story, "Three Gifts," celebrating Jewish martyrdom.

28. **Snatchers** — Lithuanians employed by the Nazis to catch given numbers of Jews for forced labor.

29. **Levi Yitzhok's melody** — Levi Yitzhak of Berdichev (1740–1810), famous Hassidic Rebbe, or dynastic leader, argued with God in Yiddish and composed the one-syllable tune: *du-du-du-du* . . . ("Thou — thou — thou . . . ").

30. **Siberia** — The poet spent his childhood in Siberia where his father died (see the poem. "Siberia").

31. **Rom Printers** — publishing house and printing press famous for its classical editions of the Babylonian Talmud, distributed all over the Jewish Diaspora.

32. **Yerushalayim** — Jerusalem.

33. **Malinas** — hiding places in the ghetto.

34. **HGRA** — acronym for the Gaon Rabbi Eliahu. The letter H by itself represents God.

35. **Synagogue Yard** — a complex of courtyards containing dozens of synagogues. The Great Synagogue was a Medieval fortress built several stories below ground (see note 6).

36. **Last barricade** — the barricade on Straszun Street 6 where resistance to the Germans was staged. The Germans retreated from the ghetto and the partisans were able to escape through the canals to the forest.

37. **Mishkan** — tabernacle, a sanctuary tent erected by the Children of Israel in the Sinai Desert.

38. **Mama-loshn** — mother tongue, an affectionate name for Yiddish.

39. **Maharal** — Rabbi Judah Loew of Prague (1525–1609) who, according to legend, created the Golem, an artificial man of clay who was supposed to defend the Jews from their enemies.

40. **Shekhina** — the feminine, maternal aspect of God, Divine Presence protecting men.

41. **Elul** — Hebrew month of mourning before the High Holidays; here September 1943.

42. **Resurrection** — the poem refers to Sutzkever's return to Vilna immediately after its "liberation."

43. **Tekiya, Shevorim** — the blowing of the Shofar on the Jewish High Holidays, especially after Yom Kippur.

44. Allusion to Ezekiel 16:6 — "In your blood shall you live."

45. **In the Chariot of Fire** — the first book of poems written by Sutzkever upon his arrival in Israel in 1947.

46. **Shabazi** — prolific Yemenite poet (17th century), wrote Jewish liturgical poetry in Hebrew and Arabic.

47. See note 29.

48. See note 10.

49. **Kulbak** — Moyshe Kulbak (1896–1940), beloved Vilna Yiddish poet, perished in the Soviet Union.

50. **Yehudah Ha-Levi** — Hebrew poet and philosopher in Spain (1075–1141), who wrote the "Zionide," expressing Jewish longing for Zion, eventually sailed to the Holy Land, which he never reached. On this journey, he wrote "poems of the sea."

51. **Eilat** — Israeli port on the Red Sea.

52. **The Ascent of Scorpions** — rock above a deep crater in the Negev with a road winding down.

53. **Wadi** — a dry riverbed filled only in the rainy season.

54. **Let us all, all together** — Yiddish song of welcome in which the name of a guest, or bride and bridegroom at a wedding, is inserted.

55. **Gediminas** — founder of the Lithuanian grand duchy and its capital Vilnius. According to legend, builder of the fortress on Castle Mountain.

56. **Eternal Garments** — euphemism for shrouds.

57. **Shchara** — a river in Byelorussia.

58. **Blind Milton** — This section includes poems from several books: *Ode to the Dove, In the Sinai Desert, Oasis* and the "Closed Cycle" from the second volume of Sutzkever's collected poems.

59. **Ha-Levi** — Reference to Yehuda Ha-Levi's "Zionide." See note 50.

60. **Else Lasker-Schüler** — (1876–1945) German Expressionist poetess who spent her last years in Jerusalem.

61. **Blue Piano** — *Mein Blaues Klavier* (1943), the only book of poems published by Else Lasker-Schüler in Jerusalem.

62. **Winter Night** — reference to Sutzkever's journey through German territory, involving the miraculous crossing of a minefield, on the way to the partisan airstrip where he was taken to Moscow.

63. **Square Letters** — the holy Hebrew letters, the typeface brought back to the Holy Land from the Babylonian exile. The "square letters" are also used in Yiddish literature, endowing it with a sense of holiness.

64. **Zeykher Le-Ghetto** — Hebrew: "In memory of the ghetto," an allusion to *Zeykher le-khurban*, "In memory of the destruction."

65. **Blessed are . . .** — *Ashrey t'mimey derekh*, blessing to be recited before a voyage.

66. **Lulav** — a palm tree leaf used in the Sukkot service.

67. **Bris** — (or: *Brith*), circumcision ceremony on the eighth day after the birth of a boy.

68. **Aberdeen** — in Hong Kong.

69. **Shekhina** — See note 40.

70. **Lithuania, homeland mine** — the opening words of the famous epic, *Pan Tadeusz*, by the Polish Romantic poet Adam Mickiewicz, a native of the Vilna area.

71. **Body-burners** — Jewish prisoners forced by the Germans to burn in the pits of Ponar the bodies of about 100,000 Jews shot there.

72. **Leyzer Volf** — original Yiddish poet (1910–1943), neighbor and friend of Sutzkever (died in exile in Soviet Central Asia).

73. **Rokhl Sutzkever** — (1905–1942) a talented painter and the poet's relative, was a member of the group of painters and Yiddish poets known as "Young Vilna."

74. **Needleshine** — In the first days of the German occupation of Vilna in July 1941, Sutzkever hid in a narrow crawlspace under a thin roof where he pierced a hole for light and wrote poetry. He returned after the liberation of Vilna in July 1944.

75. **Leyvik** — (1888–1962) major American Yiddish poet.

76. In September 1939, Poland was defeated and divided between Nazi Germany and the Soviet Union. Vilna was returned to Lithuania (independent until May 1940, then occupied by the Soviets and, in June 1941, by the Germans). In the interim period, many refugees fled illegally to Vilna.

77. See note 6.

78. Gaon's Prayerhouse in the Vilna Synagogue Yard, established by Eliahu (1720–1797), famous Vilna Gaon (genius in Talmudic learning).

79. "Leym" means clay, as was much of the soil around Vilna.

80. Isaac-Meyer Dick (1814–1893), prolific Yiddish story writer of the Haskalah period who lived and published in Vilna. In his Yiddish, Dick used many "Germanisms" for loftiness of style.

אברהם
סוקלובר

Abraham Sutzkever,

one of the great Yiddish poets, was born near Vilna in 1913, and spent his early childhood in Siberia. He returned to Vilna, the "Jerusalem of Lithuania," and lived there between the two World Wars, where he became a poet, lived through the Holocaust, saw the humiliation and destruction of his people and city, was active in the cultural life of the ghetto (1941/43), saved cultural treasures from the Germans, fought as a partisan in the forests, and was flown out of German occupied territory to Moscow in the middle of the war.

In 1947, Sutzkever emigrated to Israel, where he still resides, and has since become the country's foremost Yiddish poet, never forgetting "Jerusalem of Lithuania" and the annihilation of his people in Europe. In Tel Aviv, he founded the Yiddish literary quarterly *Di goldene keyt* (The Golden Chain) in 1948, which he still edits today (130 issues have been published). The quarterly has given renewed life to worldwide Yiddish literature for nearly half a century, publishing the surviving Yiddish writers from Europe, the Americas, the Soviet Union, and Israel. Sutzkever has received many awards, including the literary prize of the Vilna Ghetto Writers' Union and the prestigious Israel Prize. His poetry and fiction have been translated into many languages, including Hebrew, French, English, German, Russian, Polish, and Japanese.

CPSIA information can be obtained
at www.ICGtesting.com
Printed in the USA
BVHW080938140119
537773BV00008B/161/P